THE
ENGLISH GARDEN
TOUR

THE ENGLISH

John Murray

GARDEN TOUR

A VIEW INTO THE PAST

Mavis Batey & David Lambert

Copyright © 1990 Mavis Batey and David Lambert

This edition first published 1990 by John Murray (Publishers) Ltd, 50 Albemarle Street, London W1X 4BD

A John Calmann and King book in association with Jane Crawley of Barn Elms Books

British Library Cataloguing in Publication Data
Batey, Mavis
    The English garden tour: a view into the past.
    1. Great Britain. Gardens, history
    I. Title   II. Lambert, David
    712'.6'0941

    ISBN 0-7195-4775-X

This book was designed and produced by
JOHN CALMANN AND KING LTD, LONDON

Designed by Richard Foenander
Map by Andrew Betteridge
Picture research by Sara Waterson
Typeset by Rowland Phototypesetting Ltd,
Bury St Edmunds, Suffolk
Printed in Singapore

Endpapers: Plan by Stephen Switzer from *Ichnographia rustica*

Frontispiece. Garden tourists have a long and distinguished pedigree. Visitors arriving at Studley Royal. One of a series of paintings, c.1762, attributed to Balthazar Nebot. (Private Collection)

Photographic sources

John Calmann and King and the authors are grateful to the following for supplying photographs and giving permission for them to be reproduced. If an illustration is not listed below then the photograph was kindly supplied by the owner of the item as given in the caption.

Frontispiece: Eileen Tweedy; 1. National Trust Photographic Library; 2. and detail on front cover. Fotomas Index; 4. Buckinghamshire County Museum; 5. E.T. Archive; 6. Leeds Castle Trust; 8,9. Sylvia Landsberg; 10,11. Mavis Batey; 13. British Library; 15. British Library/Fotomas Index; 17. Bodleian Library, Oxford; 18. British Library/Fotomas Index; 19. Courtauld Institute of Art; 20. British Library/Fotomas Index; 21,22,23. English Heritage; 24,25. Sylvia Landsberg; 26. Shakespeare Birthplace Trust; 27. Angelo Hornak; 29. Hugh Palmer; 31. Tradescant Trust; 32. Tania Midgley; 35. Mavis Batey; 36. British Library; 37. Victoria and Albert Museum (Crown Copyright); 38. David Lambert; 41. Yale Center for British Art; 42. David Lambert; 44. Courtesy of Mavis Batey; 45. E.T. Archive; 46. National Maritime Museum, London; 47. National Maritime Museum, London; 48. Angelo Hornak; 49. Christopher Wood Gallery; 50. Victoria and Albert Museum (Crown Copyright); 51. Fotomas Index; 52. Patrick Taylor; 53. Christopher Gallagher; 54. Bodleian Library, Oxford; 55. Hugh Palmer; 56. Courtesy of Mavis Batey; 57. English Heritage; 58. English Heritage; 59. Courtesy of Teresa Sladen; 60. Department of the Environment (Crown Copyright); 61. Fotomas Index; 62,63. Department of the Environment (Crown Copyright); 64. Victoria and Albert Museum (Crown Copyright); 65. Hugh Palmer; 66. Christopher Wood Gallery; 67. Gloucestershire County Library; 68,69. Hugh Palmer; 70. *Country Life*; 71. Courtesy of Dr Keith Goodway; 72. Keele University Library; 73. Courtesy of Castle Bromwich Gardens Trust; 74. *Country Life*; 75. Eileen Tweedy; 76. Heather Angel; 77. Christopher Wood Gallery; 78. Courtauld Institute of Art; 79. Michael Holford; 80. Mavis Batey; 81. Land Use Consultants/Historic Buildings and Monuments Commission; 82. National Trust Photographic Library/Sir G. Shakerley; 83. British Museum/Fotomas Index; 85. John Irving (Courtesy of the Trustees of the Bowood Estate); 87. John Calmann and King Ltd.; 88,89. Angelo Hornak (Courtesy of the Trustees of Blenheim Palace); 90. Fotomas Index; 91. David Lambert; 94. David Lambert; 95. Fotomas Index; 96. Victoria and Albert Museum (Crown Copyright); 98. Barnaby's Picture Library; 100. Fotomas Index; 101. Christopher Gallagher; 103. National Trust Photographic Library; 104. Alun Jones (Courtesy of Magdalen College Library); 105. Alun Jones (Courtesy of Trinity College Library); 106. Alun Jones (Courtesy of Magdalen College Library); 107. Hugh Palmer; 108. Bodleian Library, Oxford; 109,110. Fotomas Index; 111. Tania Midgley; 112. Huntley Hedworth; 113. British Library; 114. Peter Harding; 115. *Country Life*; 116. Mavis Batey; 117. Heather Angel; 118. N. Meyjes (Courtesy of C. Cottrell-Dormer, Esq.); 119. Tania Midgley; 120. Alun Jones; 121. Eileen Tweedy; 122. Courtesy of the Trustees of Henry Vyner, Esq.; 124. National Trust Photographic Library/M. Waite; 127. Clive Boursnell; 129. Eileen Tweedy (Courtesy Lindley Library, Royal Horticultural Society); 130. National Trust Photographic Library/John Bethell; 131. Angelo Hornak; 132. David Lambert; 133. Staffordshire Borough Council (Courtesy of the Earl of Lichfield); 134. British Library; 135. National Trust Photographic Library/M. Williams; 136. Courtesy of David Lambert; 138. Wellesley College Library, Massachusetts; 140. David Lambert; 141. Bridgeman Art Library/Roy Miles Fine Painting; 142. Painshill Park Trust; 143. Christopher Sumner; 144. Christopher Gallagher; 145. Painshill Park Trust; 148. Harry Smith Horticultural Collection; 149. National Trust Photographic Library/John Bethell; 151. Huntley Hedworth; 152. *Country Life*; 153. *Country Life*; 154. Courtesy of David Lambert; 156. Peter Harding; 157. David Lambert; 158. Avon Gardens Trust; 160. Heather Angel; 163. British Library; 164,165. *Country Life*; 166,167. Waverley Photographic; 168. Cambridge University Aerial Photographic Collection (Crown Copyright); 170. Courtauld Institute of Art; 171. Photos Horticultural; 172. *Country Life*; 173. National Trust Photographic Library/A.C. Cooper (Courtesy Tate Gallery); 174. National Trust Photographic Library/Tim Stephens; 175. Tania Midgley; 176. *Country Life*; 177,178,179. John Irving; 180. Eileen Tweedy (Courtesy Lindley Library, Royal Horticultural Society); 181. Bodleian Library, Oxford; 183. Edinburgh University Library; 184. Mavis Batey; 186. Courtesy of Mavis Batey; 187. Christopher Wood Gallery; 189. Mavis Batey; 190. Bridgeman Art Library; 191. Courtesy Mavis Batey; 192. William Salt Library, Stafford; 193. Eileen Tweedy (Courtesy Lindley Library, Royal Horticultural Society); 194–8. Mavis Batey (Courtesy of Lord Leigh); 199. Eileen Tweedy (Courtesy Lindley Library, Royal Horticultural Society); 200. E.T. Archive; 201. Mansell Collection; 202. Tania Midgley; 203. E.T. Archive; 204. A.C. Cooper; 205. Courtauld Institute of Art; 206. Hugh Palmer; 207. Photos Horticultural; 208. Harry Smith Horticultural Collection; 209. Courtesy Mavis Batey; 210,211. Mavis Batey; 212,213. National Trust Photographic Library; 214. National Trust Photographic Library/Mike Howarth; 215. Tania Midgley; 216. Harry Smith Horticultural Collection; 217–19. E.T. Archive (Courtesy Lindley Library, Royal Horticultural Society); 220,221. Trustees of the Chatsworth Settlement; 222. Clive Boursnell; 223,224. Trustees of the Chatsworth Settlement; 225,226. Mary Evans Picture Library; 227. David Lambert; 228. Francis Frith Collection; 229. Peter Hayden; 230. E.T. Archive (Courtesy Lindley Library, Royal Horticultural Society); 231. Peter Hayden; 232. and back jacket. Hugh Palmer; 233. E.T. Archive (Courtesy Lindley Library, Royal Horticultural Society); 234. *Country Life*; 235,236. Christopher Gallagher; 237. Christopher Wood Gallery; 238. *Country Life*; 239. Tania Midgley; 240. Michael Holford.

CONTENTS

ACKNOWLEDGEMENTS

It is a pleasure to record our gratitude to the friends and colleagues who have contributed to the preparation of this book. Jane Crawley has nursed it through all its stages and shared the burden with unfailing good humour and patience. Others have helped with various invaluable comments and information; in particular George Clarke, Dominic Cole, James Collett-White, Mavis Collier, Reginald Cooke, Maggie Culver, Brian Dix, Ruth Duthie, Dorothy Eagles, Paul Everson, Robin Faussett, Sally Festing, Peter Goodchild, Keith Goodway, Robin Harcourt Williams, Stewart Harding, Peter Hayden, David Jacques, Alun Jones, Harriet Jordan, Sylvia Landsberg, Professor Karin Lindegren, Julian Munby, Stella Palmer, John Phibbs, Jan Piggott, Margaret Richards, James Russell, Bob Savage, Lord Saye and Sele, Colin Shrimpton, Teresa Sladen, Eileen Stamers-Smith, Peggy Stembridge, Nick Stockton, Andrew Whimble and the staff of John Calmann and King. We would like to thank also the owners and staff of the houses we have visited, where without exception we have been met with courtesy and helpfulness. Finally, we would like to thank the staff of the following institutions for all their assistance in our researches: the Bodleian, the Bristol Fine Art and Reference Libraries, the Bristol University Library Special Collections, the National Monument Record.

We are particularly indebted to *Country Life* for permission to quote from early articles and to Ray Desmond's *Bibliography of British Gardens* for many leads to published material.

We gratefully acknowledge permission to quote from several modern texts: B.T. Batsford for Sacheverell Sitwell's *British Architects and Craftsmen*, Constable & Co. for Barbara Jones's *Follies & Grottoes*, Macdonald Orbis for *Sacheverell Sitwell's England*, John Murray for John Betjeman's *Summoned by Bells*, Octopus Publishing for Christopher Hussey's *English gardens and landscapes*, Penguin Books for Nikolaus Pevsner's *Buildings of England*, Michael Russell for *John Loveday of Caversham*, Alan Sutton for *Excellent Cassandra*, Taylor & Francis for van Spaen van Biljoen in the *Journal of Garden History*, and Thames and Hudson for *The diary of Baron Waldstein*.

To Caroline and Keith

PREFACE

Visiting other people's gardens is not a twentieth-century phenomenon. Garden tourists have a long and distinguished pedigree and, far from being profane intruders on private arcadias, they have been the *raison d'être* of many a show-piece. Some owners felt a certain *noblesse oblige* towards their visitors. The 6th Duke of Devonshire instructed his staff that the waterworks were to be played for any visitor irrespective of social status; at Castle Howard and Stourhead inns were provided by the owner for the benefit of tourists, and at Nuneham picnic huts were available for river trippers from Oxford. Privileged visitors were sometimes taken round landscaped gardens in 'a commodious garden chair' or might even have a portable camera obscura set up for them to study the view. Head gardeners were often allowed to run a lucrative business in guided tours and a Frenchman complained that at Blenheim at least six ciceroni, old servants as well as gardeners, appeared to extract their 2/6d from him. On public holidays gardens like Mount Edgcumbe and Chatsworth were crowded with day-trippers from the neighbouring cities. The painting of the fête at Petworth (Plate 1) shows the cheerful atmosphere of a peopled landscaped park; photographers nowadays tend to go out of their way to suggest a hallowed quality and avoid any human content in their pictures.

There is now much interest in garden history and, like art and architectural history, it is seen as a subject of study in its own right. Since the publication by English Heritage of the registers of parks and gardens of special historic interest in England following the 1983 National Heritage Act, historic gardens have been officially recognized as belonging to the national heritage. It was not until the late nineteenth century, however, that tourists visited gardens for the sake of their history. Previously garden visitors invariably dismissed what was 'old fashion' or in the 'taste of our fore-fathers' and preferred, like Celia Fiennes, things 'as the mode now is'. But in describing the new styles these visitors were inadvertently writing history and in their words we can trace the tides of taste directly.

The English Garden Tour presents each garden through the eyewitness accounts of tourists down the years with contemporary comments from landscape gardeners and owners, at least one of whom wrote his own guidebook. Their reports are invaluable in that they illuminate ways of seeing which might otherwise be lost to us and highlight the effects gardeners and designers were seeking which might today be misinterpreted or escape our notice. Travellers often made searching enquiries and bring life to estate records and maps. From Thomas Jefferson we learn that 200 people were employed in the grounds at Blenheim,

about 50 of whom were in the pleasure gardens, and that the turf was mowed once every ten days. In 1833 J. C. Loudon lamented that Blenheim had fallen into disarray through the new owner's personal extravagance and neglect. Sometimes the tourist's account captures the very moment when the garden is being altered to conform with a change in taste or family circumstance and, with him, we witness 'a Chinese House now building in the Park', trouble with a new fountain, 'a grotto in the making', an exotic flower blooming for the first time in England, or a village being moved in the making of a landscaped garden. The traveller might be lucky enough to have the Wilton waterworks demonstrated by their creator Isaac de Caus himself, or to bump into Repton or another professional improver on site. Sometimes the traveller comes with an introduction to the owner who tells him of his intentions for new garden buildings or plantations and what it has all cost him. Discussions with the head gardener might give a different picture, however, and we read in one travel diary of an encounter with a head gardener in tears at his new master's improvements.

Although many of the gardens have continuous and changing lives, the main focus for each garden is on the period when it was in its heyday: Wilton in the reign of Charles I, Hampton Court under William and Mary and Chatsworth in Victoria's day. The book therefore has an overall chronological sequence, ending with Athelhampton, a late nineteenth-century revivalist garden, which has now become a historic garden in its own right.

The present state of the chosen gardens varies enormously. Some are all-but archaeological sites, while others retain many of their historic features, some are restored to near their former glory, while others are complete recreations. Some restorations (notably Wrest Park, Kirby Hall and Studley Royal itself) give the opportunity to enjoy that 'respectable pause for anticipation between the conception of a project and its realization' which work in progress was said to have offered the Aislabies of Studley. All, whether royal parks, country parks, public open spaces, whether owned privately or by museums, colleges, trusts, hotels the National Trust, English Heritage or County Councils, are accessible to the modern garden tourist either wholly or in part.

1. *Fête in Petworth Park*, 1835, by William Witherington. The painting hangs in the North Gallery at Petworth and shows the cheerful atmosphere of a peopled landscaped park.

1
THE GARDEN TOURISTS

2. Stourhead in the early nineteenth century in one of a series of watercolours by Francis Nicholson, 1813–14. Here, as elsewhere, visitors have always been an integral part of the English garden scene. (British Museum, London)

Over the centuries travellers have had a variety of reasons for their journeys. They have been pursuing antiquarian, agricultural, naturalist, picturesque, social and sentimental interests and have always been imbued with a sense of curiosity. Few travellers before the eighteenth century were specifically looking for gardens, but they often commented on them *en passant*. The earliest of these was John Leland, Henry VIII's antiquary, who travelled widely in search of manuscripts and 'notid yn so doing a hole world of things memorable', including the building of many new mansions with 'fair made' walks, gardens and orchards.[1] Elizabethan travellers from abroad, chiefly from Germany and Switzerland, came out of curiosity to see how Protestant England was faring and although they were not specifically garden tourists they visited the gardens of the royal palaces and of the great houses built by the queen's councillors to show the loyalty of their owners. If they were noble or enterprising enough to cross the Channel they would usually gain easy entry and could even, like the young Baron Waldstein from Moravia, Paul Hentzner, the Brandenburg lawyer who was companion to a young Silesian nobleman, or Thomas Platter, who had studied medicine at Montpellier, have an audience with the queen or see an entertainment in the royal garden.

The foreign travellers give us the first accounts of real gardens, as opposed to the largely symbolic descriptions, in poetry and romance, of the gardens of the Middle Ages, when travellers were usually wayfarers or on a pilgrimage. Sometimes even foreign ambassadors, often on spying missions, would describe new garden fashions in their reports home.[2] As roads improved in the seventeenth century there was more opportunity for travel, if not actually for tourism, but some of those travelling on duty, of whom Lieutenant Hammond was the most informative, did deviate to see noble gardens. He made a 'delightful garden Journey' to Wilton and 'made a little bold to transgresse my ranke' to see Woodstock, and visited Kenilworth, Warwick and Petworth, energetically pacing distances and numbering features with military precision.

The early tourists were guided by William Camden's *Britannia*, which was published in Latin in 1586. Although Leland's *Itinerary* had been seen in note form by Camden and by William Harrison for his *Description of England* in 1577 it was not published until 1710 and so was not available to seventeenth-century travellers. Many gardening books appeared in the seventeenth century but these were herbals and profitable treatises on gardening based on expertise gained from the writers' own gardens. The first of the garden tourists as such was the great virtuoso, John Evelyn, who not only wrote or translated gardening treatises but from 1654 visited gardens at home and abroad, which he noted in his diaries. His intention had been to produce a great garden compendium bringing together scientific and practical knowledge and descriptions of gardens seen on his travels, to be called the 'Elysium Britannicum', but, unfortunately, this still remains largely in manuscript.[3] Tourists still had to rely on the antiquaries for topographical information, when Ogilby's new strip maps of 1675, based on his own journeys on foot, beckoned the traveller on.

One of the most intrepid of these was Celia Fiennes who toured the country on horseback, riding more than 3,000 miles between 1685 and 1703, for her health. At a time when the Grand Tour was fashionable for men she recommended that by travelling at home both sexes would 'form such an idea of England, add much to its Glory and Esteem in our Minds and cure the evil itch of over-valueing foreign parts'.[4] She disclaimed any intention of publishing her journal, but her remarks often seem to be addressed to a wider audience than her near relations. Her curiosity was unbounded and she was well aware of the latest fashions and liked 'exact fine gardens'. Her vivid and detailed descriptions of William and Mary gardens make her one of the most informative, if unintentional, garden historian tourists. At the same time there was a revived interest in horticulture, especially when there were new opportunities for obtaining plants through Dutch trade with the East Indies, and a new breed of expert garden visitors on the look-out for 'curious' plants corresponded with each other.

The eighteenth century, the Age of Taste, saw the dawn of real country house visiting at a time when tourists were being bombarded with new theories of aesthetics and standards for appreciating architecture and landscape. Gardens were seen to be associative and could arouse ideas in 'the mind of the beholder', an expression that often appears in accounts of landscaped gardens following Addison's influential 'Pleasures of the imagination', published in 1712 and translated into French in 1720. The right way round in a thematic garden was important and the gardener or the guide directed visitors on their first experience; regular visitors and guests at the house could presumably do it their own way, for, as Thomas Love Peacock commented, how was a visitor expected to react to this manipulated management of surprises the second time round?[5] French visitors, who hitherto had tended to compare the

3. The north and west sides of the Great Court at Nonsuch, c.1620. As in Hentzner's day, Nonsuch, like other palaces and great houses, was 'encompassed with parks full of deer'. (Fitzwilliam Museum, Cambridge)

English style of gardening unfavourably with their own, began to see the new landscaped gardens as part of the Enlightenment with its improved ideas on agriculture.

The German *Sturm und Drang* Romantics wrote most enthusiastically of the English naturalized gardens and Prince Franz Anhalt-Dessau, who brought three gardeners with him, returned to give Wörlitz one of the earliest English gardens on the Continent in 1765. Foreigners are always hampered on whirlwind visits by the English weather and, like the King of Saxony, taken to see the famous view of the villa-studded landscape from Richmond Hill, could only suppose that it was 'no doubt very pleasing and pretty in fine weather'.[6] They appreciate the English genius for park buildings, which they feel rival Italian statues and fountains—no doubt for shelter as much as effect.

English landowners travelled to see other improvements, particularly the work of the amateurs at Stourhead, the Leasowes, Studley Royal and Painshill, to get ideas for their own estates. Topographical poems in praise of gardens began to appear in the 1730s[7]; the first guidebook to a garden was produced for Stowe in 1744, and the field quickly attracted competing publishers.[8] There was a new language of aesthetics based on Burke's *Philosophical enquiry into the origin of our ideas of the Sublime and the Beautiful* and after 1757 these became emotive catchwords which often appeared in guidebooks and were applied by visitors to garden scenes in their travel journals. In 1770 Thomas Whately's *Observations on modern gardening* is the first gardening book to describe individual gardens in detail; although not

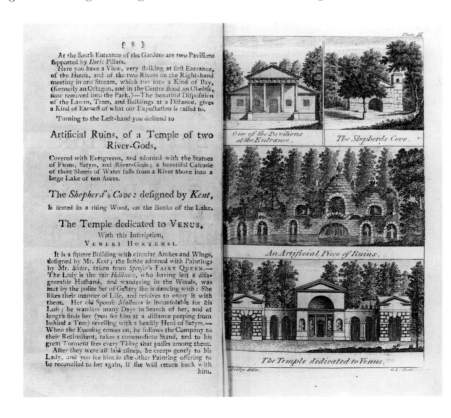

4. A page from Benton Seeley's *Description of the gardens of Lord Viscount Cobham at Stow*, the first tourist guide to a garden.

5. An engraving of Kew Gardens including Decimus Burton's palm house built in 1844. Kew Gardens in the nineteenth century catered for their visitors' new enthusiasm for horticulture.

comprehensive it was very influential and went into five editions as well as being translated into French.

The new word on every tourist's lips in the 1780s was 'picturesque'. Gilpin's popular picturesque Tours taught everyone to look at scenery like Jane Austen's fashionable Tilneys, who were seen to be 'viewing the country with the eyes of persons accustomed to drawing, and decided on its capability of being formed into pictures, with all the eagerness of real taste'.[9] Garden scenes had to be worthy of painting as well and the landscaping of ruined abbeys was particularly frowned upon. Travellers' descriptions took on the language of the Picturesque and the many illustrated books on picturesque seats and beauties of Britain gave a fresh impetus to country house and garden visiting. It now became the popular thing to 'make a Tour' and 'write it',[10] and there was no excuse for a tourist like poor Catherine Morland 'not to know what was picturesque when she saw it'.[11] In 1826 Fosbrooke produced a *Tourist's grammar*, bringing everybody up to date on picturesque thinking.

The nineteenth century saw a revived interest in horticulture, reflected in the formation of the Royal Horticultural Society in 1804, and the numerous gardening magazines opened new horizons for informed garden visiting.[12] At the end of the century came a mood of revivalism in gardens as part of the Arts and Crafts movement. Alicia Amherst researched the history of gardening in all its aspects and in 1892 Reginald Blomfield published his *The formal garden in England* in which he enumerated all the features that could profitably be copied in modern 'old-fashioned' gardens. The magazine *Country Life* first appeared in 1897 with splendid photographs of new Arts and Crafts gardens and well-informed articles on the history of old ones, which added a new interest to garden visiting. Pevsner's *Buildings of England* series, the post-War indispensable guide for architectural historian tourists, included descriptions of landscaped gardens, and county gardens guides were soon to follow. The National Trust led the way with guides to individual gardens and today's visitors can be well provided with information on most of the important historic gardens.

2
MEDIAEVAL
GARDENS

6. Aerial view of Leeds Castle. The castle with Queen Eleanor's gloriette on the lake is romantically offset by its deer park, which was landscaped in the eighteenth century.

The idea of the mediaeval garden has captured romantic imagination, but we have no intact monastery or castle garden to tell us what these gardens were really like and those depicted in art and literature are largely symbolic. In religious terms the garden was an *hortus conclusus*, an enclosed Mary garden celebrating the Virgin with mystic symbols based on the Song of Solomon, and in secular terms the garden was a symbol of earthly love, typified by Guillaume de Lorris's thirteenth-century poem the *Roman de la rose*, an allegory of man and an enclosed garden, where the lover endeavours to reach the rose which symbolizes his lady's love.

The best description of mediaeval gardens is given by Chaucer, who travelled widely in the king's service. Chaucer calls the garden a yerde or yard (as it is still called in many parts of America or as in the Pond Yard at Hampton Court), signifying an enclosure or garth. In *Troylus and Cryseyde* he speaks of garden beds being divided by 'wands' or railings and of green arbours and sanded paths, and in his translation, *The romaunt of the rose*, the gardens are enclosed 'by mesuring, right even and square in compassing'. In the poem we feel all the mediaeval delight in the freshness and fragrance of the garden, contrasting with the stuffiness and the stench of the insanitary houses. The garden 'pleasances' were essentially 'bowers of bliss' for the ladies in the tales of romance, and as we see in the illustrations there were 'flowery meads' or fragrant carpets to be sat on and dallied upon.

> Ther sprange the violete al newe,
> And fresshe pervinkle, riche of hewe,
> And floures yelowe, whyte, and rede;
> Swich plentee grew ther never in mede.
> Ful gay was al the ground, and queynt,
> And poudred, as men had it peynt,
> With many a fresh and sondry flour,
> That casten up ful good savour.

Leeds Castle is everybody's idea of a mediaeval castle, evoking days of troubadours and chivalry, romantically offset by a lake and a deer park landscaped in the eighteenth century. It became a royal palace when, in 1272, Edward I acquired it from a Norman baron's family and gave it to his queen, the Spanish princess, Eleanor of Castile, as a dower. For 300 years it was the 'lady's castle' of eight of England's mediaeval queens. It was the ladies who hankered after garden pleasances and other niceties, particularly the French and Spanish queens, who were used to more refinements in castle accommodation.

Although she had been prepared to accompany her husband on the rigours of the crusades, Queen Eleanor was clearly a woman of fastidious taste. She did not find the English fruit, wine and cheese to her liking and craved the luxuries to which she had been accustomed. 'At madam's command' grafts of the Blancdurel apple, pears, olive oil, cherry wine and Brie cheeses were brought over.[1] The queen is known to have sent for gardeners from Aragon to work at King's Langley and it is thought that it was she who introduced the hollyhock, then called the Spanish rose, to England.[2] Spain had inherited Moorish traditions of paved courtyards and fountains together with their advanced horticultural skills. From

7. A fifteenth-century illustration from the *Roman de la rose* showing a Chaucerian railed 'yerde' with carpets of 'flowery meads' in the tower of a mediaeval castle. (Bodleian Library, Oxford, MS. Douce 195 fol.6r.)

Spain also came the gloriette, a word of Arabic derivation. It was a pavilion away from the main building which could be used as a bower or summer-house. The tower gloriettes also served as look-outs for defensive purposes or as hunting stands. At Leeds Castle a gloriette was built for Queen Eleanor on the inner island of the lake which surrounded the castle. Vines were ordered and fishponds and a park made for her frequent visits. Gardens were laid out in preparation for her visits to other castles. A herber was hastily made at Conway Castle in 1284 upon notice of a royal visit to Wales. Two carts brought green turves and 3d was paid for watering the herber for one night.[3] In 1285 the Bishop of Winchester, who had no ladies' pleasance, made a 'herbarium' in the keep at Farnham Castle for the queen's visit; it cost him one pound and eleven pence to have soil carted up to the top.[4]

Leeds Castle also became a favourite place of Edward III and Queen Philippa of Hainault, who had the chambers of the gloriette redecorated, extended the park and rebuilt the castle boat for sailing on the lake to enjoy its scenic delights. Like Queen Eleanor before her, Queen Philippa was a keen gardener and introduced rosemary to England, cuttings of which probably found their way to the herber at Leeds Castle.[5]

At Leeds Castle we can visualize ladies in pointed hats looking out of the windows of the gloriette and Queen Eleanor sitting in a vine arbour in her long vanished privy garden, listening to a minstrel playing, but to see what her garden might really have looked like we must go to Winchester, where, outside the Great Hall, a mediaeval garden has been created on a most unpromising site. Winchester Castle was not a royal retreat in the country, like Leeds Castle, but a busy administrative centre with a large complex of buildings connected by a maze of alleyways. Queen Eleanor of Castile and her mother-in-law Eleanor of Provence, wife of Henry III, who built the castle, stayed there as the court moved from castle to castle. The building accounts show that Henry III had installed glazed windows, oriels, garderobes and gardens for the queen and her elegant Provençal ladies.

Nothing is known about any thirteenth-century gardens at Winchester Castle except for

the order 'Let three herbaria be made', presumably wherever possible in the odd leftover spaces between the buildings. The recreated herbarium is in a wedge-shaped space outside the Great Hall, its present shape being dictated by impinging modern building, rather than mediaeval layout. The garden features have been copied from illuminations and from local thirteenth-century architectural details: an oak-tiled pentice; a limestone fountain column surmounted by a bronze falcon, the water from which pours through leopard masks into a narrow stone channel; a trellised tunnel arbour and turf seats. In the corner by the wall is the queen's herber with a stone table backed by a trellis of roses on which a game of chess might have been played.

This garden, the inspiration of the Hampshire Gardens Trust, is the first attempt to reproduce a mediaeval garden and it is most successful. All the plants would have been grown in Queen Eleanor's time: Madonna lilies, German flag iris, peonies, soapwort, everlasting pea, columbines, mullein, hollyhocks and pot marigolds. In the turf speedwell, wild strawberries, violets and harebell make a Cluny-like millefleurs tapestry effect. Queen Eleanor's garden was opened in July 1986 by the Queen Mother and of the occasion Sylvia Landsberg, the creator of the garden, wrote: 'Even in the thirteenth century gardeners and flower arrangers would have been up at the crack of dawn – as we were – sweeping the last leaves from the paths, gathering petals of *Rosa alba* and *gallica* which had fallen overnight on to the turf seats, tying back a persistent honeysuckle from the Queen's path, making posies and garlands of roses, lilies, cornflower and heartsease; placing a bowl of cherries on the Herber table'.[6]

At the other end of the social scale, Sylvia Landsberg has created a garden for the *circa* 1500 Wealden house, known as Bayleaf, at Singleton Open Air Museum in West Sussex. Here she has planted what was available from the hedgerow or the manor house in the way of vegetables needed for the family. The Wealden house has now become rooted to the soil and no longer looks like a transplanted museum piece. Inside a pottage made from the bailiff's wife's vegetable garden brews on the open fire.

Before the Dissolution there were between 500 and 600 monastic and religious houses in England; in Yorkshire alone there were 66. Monasteries were largely self-sufficient and the garden, in which the monks did manual work, supplied the needs of a vegetarian diet. The physic garden attached to the infirmary comes nearest to the idea of a pleasure ground as benches were placed in a sunny corner for the infirm brethren. The Infirmarer's garden, where herbs including comfrey, cumin, betony, elecampane and fennel would have been dried as 'drugs', is being excavated at Westminster Abbey and a record of 1305 shows that benches were put outside the hall door above the pool.[7] Much is being learned of mediaeval medical and pharmacological practice from the excavation of infirmary waste at Soutra, an isolated

10. Vegetables, beehives and a rough sitting out area for the family in the garden created for the Wealden house, called Bayleaf, at the Singleton Open Air Museum.

mediaeval hospital 17 miles south-east of Edinburgh, which was dedicated to the care of the sick, the infirm and travellers, who included the vast invading armies of Edward I and Edward II across the border. A thorough study is being made of medical treatises including those of John Arderne, royal military surgeon in the reign of Edward III. Evidence of large-scale discarding of blood into the earth after letting has been found. On certain days visitors can see the advanced techniques used in the Soutra excavation, but are warned not to touch the soil for fear of unknown mediaeval infections.[8]

Mount Grace, licensed by Richard II in 1398, is the only Carthusian priory in England with substantial remains and its buildings and individual gardens bear witness to a different way of life. Charterhouse monks combined the life of the hermit and a community under a rule. They would meet in church and chapter house but lived in individual cells around a large cloister where they recited their offices, worked, ate, gardened, exercised and were looked after when they were sick. The monks received only basic deliveries from the communal brewhouse and bakehouse through a serving hatch with a right-angled bend so that the monk made no contact with the server. The vegetables for their pottage and remedial herbs were grown in their individual gardens. The garden of Cottage No. 9, including the privy at the end of the plot, is at present being excavated and may give us more information as to what the Carthusian monk grew and ate from his separate plot.

As with all Cistercian monasteries water and seclusion determined the sites of Rievaulx, Roche and Fountains Abbey. In France there were the Clairfontaine and Froidefontaine

11. Mount Grace: Individual cell garden plots typical of Carthusian monasteries.

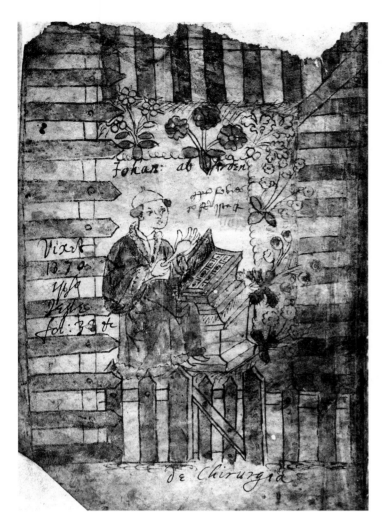

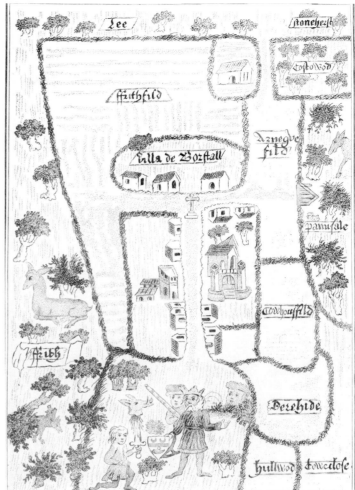

12 (above left). An infirmary garden with John Arderne, royal military surgeon, at work preparing medicines in the reign of Edward III. (University Library, Glasgow, MS. Hunter 112 fol.v)

13 (above right). The Saxon king gives the brave forester a coat of arms bearing a hunting horn and land for a mansion and park in the royal forest of Boarstall, Buckinghamshire. (Drawn from a carving at Boarstall House and reproduced in *Archaeologia* III)

Cistercian abbeys and the Yorkshire Fountains had not only the river Skell but six springs rising within the abbey. It was a particularly beautiful site and the gardens and orchards by the infirmary ran down to the river and must have afforded the infirm brethren much pleasure. Ruined abbeys were the *pièce de résistance* of any eighteenth-century landscaping scheme. Fortunate indeed were the improvers, like the Duncombes, Lord Scarbrough and the Aislabies who had the ruins of Rievaulx, Roche and Fountains within their sight.

William Camden on his antiquarian tours in 1598 was amazed to find how much of England had been allowed to lie waste for deer parks. At the height of enclosure for hunting parks in the reign of Henry II the ground covered was probably a third of the country. The king sometimes gave his feudal barons and bishops a licence to 'impark' or form a pale to make a chase. 'Pearroc' was the name given by the Anglo-Saxons to a piece of fenced land. A carving in the ancient tower of Boarstall shows the outlines of such a park, given by Edward the Confessor to a forester who had slain a huge wild boar in the royal forest. Woodstock is one of the oldest hunting parks, having been fenced in as a game preserve for Saxon kings before the year 1000. By 1110 Henry I, the youngest son of the Conqueror, had enclosed the park by a stone wall seven miles round and stocked it with wild beasts.[9] It was as well that these had been replaced by deer by the time Henry II's mistress, Rosamond Clifford, was installed in her bower in the park. This was the bower that was the inspiration of all the pleasance features known as Rosamondsbowers in mediaeval garden records.[10]

A hundred years of Barons' wars, after the relatively peaceful reigns of the three Edwards, took their toll on garden pleasances. The Tudor peace, when, in Shakespeare's words, 'every man shall eat in safety under his own vine what he plants',[11] brought new delights to gardens, except those attached to monasteries since these had been dissolved by Henry VIII. There were now many more travellers, antiquaries, topographical artists and surveyors to give eyewitness accounts of Tudor England. Foreign visitors were meant to be impressed by Henry VIII's palaces and gardens as the new Tudor image he tried to create was of a monarch who outshone all his subjects in sheer splendour rather than military power.

Henry VIII began to build his new palace of Nonsuch in April 1538, the thirtieth anniversary of his accession, when spoil from the monasteries was bringing him considerable wealth. He had already made Hampton Court, which he had acquired from Cardinal Wolsey in 1525, into a magnificent palace, but he wanted a nonpareil to excel those of rival princes, particularly Francis I, who had entertained him at the Field of the Cloth of Gold and upstaged him with his Renaissance palace at Fontainebleau with its fountains, mazes, galleries and pavilions. Hampton Court chase was joined to the parks around the palaces of Oatlands and Nonsuch, putting a major part of Surrey together with Windsor Forest under forest law to indulge the king's passion for hunting. The illustrations and travellers' descriptions of Nonsuch date from after Henry VIII's death in 1547, when the palace was still uncompleted. Only John Leland reported on the palace in Henry's lifetime and his is the first of a long series of rapturous references to its unrivalled magnificence. To him is ascribed the couplet:

14. Panorama drawing of Hampton Court by Anthonis van Wyngaerde, c.1558, showing the Pond Yard, Mount garden (removed by William III) and Privy garden with its numerous heraldic beasts on poles. (Ashmolean Museum, Oxford)

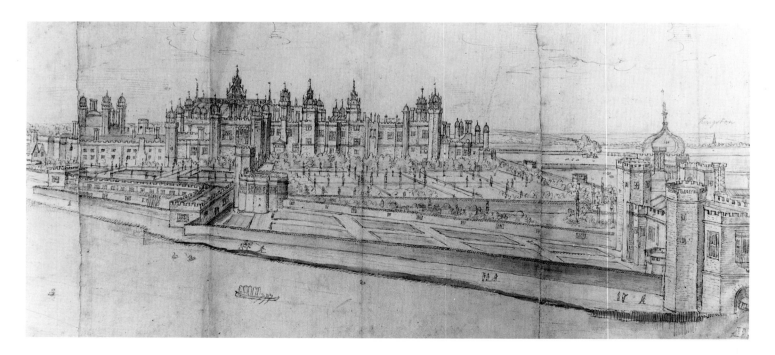

15. Engraving from a corner of Speed's map of Surrey, 1610, giving a compressed layout of the knot shapes, columns and heraldic devices.

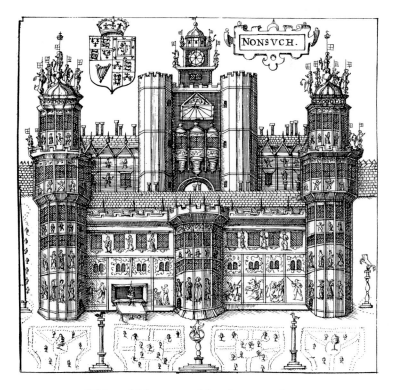

This, which no equal has in art or fame,
Britons deservedly do Nonesuch name. [12]

In his map of Surrey John Speed has tried to compress as much information about the palace into his drawing as possible and has taken an imaginary viewpoint from above the Privy garden wall. Only a fraction of the depth of the garden is shown and seemingly only half the knot shapes, described by Anthony Watson, the rector of Cheam, as 'plants and shrubs mingled in intricate circles as though by the needle of Semiramis'. [13]

The Elizabethan visitors were full of praise for the Tudor gardens. Paul Hentzner found Nonsuch 'encompassed with parks full of deer, delicious gardens, groves ornamented with trellis work, cabinets of verdure'. [14] In his drawing of Hampton Court, Anthonis Wyngaerde, who visited England in 1558, showed the heraldic beasts on poles that adorned all the royal gardens. The only remaining features of the Tudor gardens at Hampton Court, apart from the park walls, are the replanted Pond Yard and one of the tiltyard towers. The site of Nonsuch was excavated in 1959 and two years later John Dent published his outstanding *The quest for Nonsuch*. In 1988, to celebrate the 450th anniversary of the building of the palace, Martin Biddle, who was in charge of the excavations, devised the Nonsuch Walk. This starts at the Mansion House, where Thomas Whately lived in 1743, and reconstructs the routes taken by the Elizabethan travellers. Today's visitors following the numbered posts and leaflet descriptions can discover the gardens, wilderness, Grove of Diana and site of the banqueting house, which also served the king as a grandstand to watch the hunting in the Little Park.

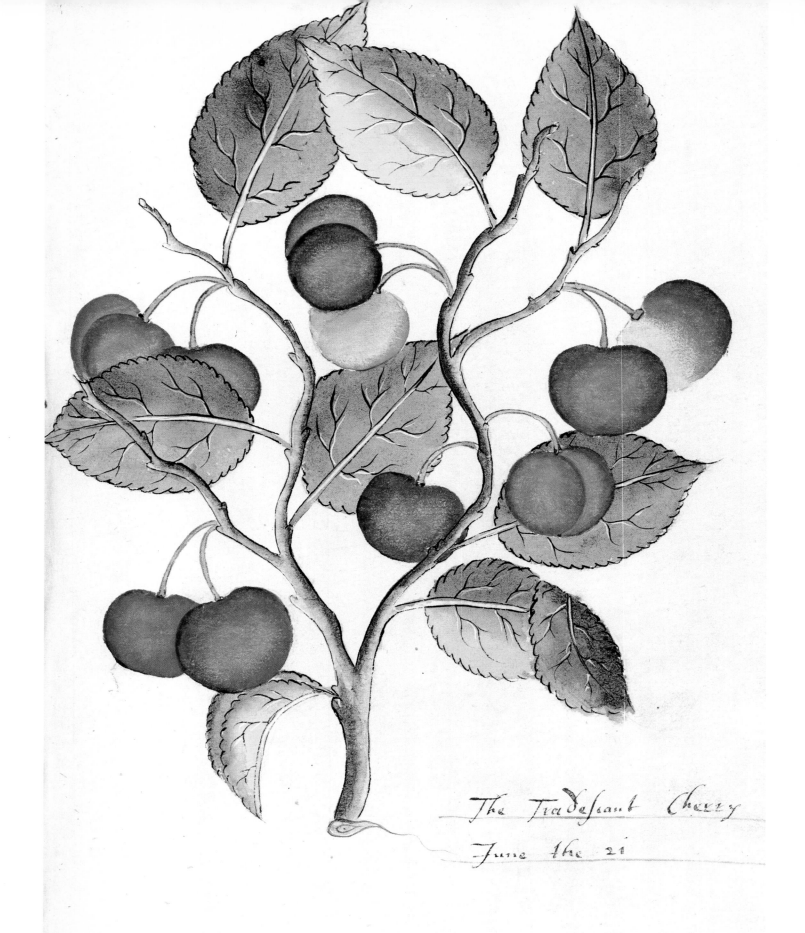

The Tradescant Cherry
June the 21

3
TUDOR
AND STUART
GARDENS

16. A plate from 'Tradescant's Orchard' of a cherry believed to have been grown at Hatfield. The Elizabethans took great delight in their 'growing banquets'. (Bodleian Library, Oxford)

Queen Elizabeth, who succeeded to the throne in 1558, did not build new palaces as her father had done, but encouraged her courtiers to vie with each other in improving their houses and making gardens for her entertainment. The queen delighted in gardens, especially when her courtiers paid compliments to her as Oriana or Diana through allegorical pageantry and permanent garden buildings, fountains, statues and grottoes. Outdoor entertainment on a lavish scale was provided for her and we have a particularly detailed account, by courtiers in attendance, of the pageantry associated with her famous visit to the Earl of Leicester at Kenilworth, later to be romanticized by Sir Walter Scott.

The travellers appreciated the English landscape, the country estates, the prevalence of deer parks, the green grass, the orchards and the gardens. They noted many features of the great gardens in detail and give us a record of Elizabethan gardens which would otherwise have been lost. They describe the wildernesses, groves, walks, mazes, ornamental fishponds, topiary works, fountains, mounts, aviaries, menageries, banqueting houses, canopied trees and arbours and the privy gardens with flower beds and pillars with heraldic beasts on top of them. Thomas Platter from Switzerland marvelled at the topiary figures at Hampton Court which he described as 'men and women, half men and half horse, sirens, serving maids with baskets, French lilies . . . all true to life and so cleverly and amusingly interwoven, mingled and grown together that their equal would be difficult to find'.[1]

Elizabethan gardening was transformed by new Renaissance ideas of design. The Earl of Leicester and other castle owners had had dealings with France through their various offices and would have seen the way that gardens were being built outside the walls at castles such as Amboise. The formal gardens shown in Du Cerceau's *Les plus excellents bastiments de France*, published in 1597, were a source of inspiration to many noblemen designing gardens. A detail of a design from Du Cerceau's book is the basis of the early seventeenth-century garden recreated in the Queen's Garden at Kew in 1969. The Elizabethan feel for linear design and the love of matching conceits and symmetry in frets and knots extended to garden terraces, paths and axially aligned gateways so that there was less of the haphazard mediaeval relationship of house and garden.

The availability of the new plants brought back by those who sailed in the queen's name to discover new lands, and recorded in Gerard's *Herball* of 1597, also transformed English gardens. After the Dissolution of the monasteries plant husbandry had passed to the great country houses and their gardeners. Lord Burghley, William Cecil, who had John Gerard as his herbalist and garden adviser at Burghley, and his son, Robert Cecil, who laid out the influential garden at Theobalds, were the greatest patrons of gardening and plant exploration. William Harrison reported on the 'manie strange hearbs, plants and annuall fruits . . . dailie brought unto us from the Indies, Americans, Taprobane, Canarie Iles, and all parts of the world'.[2]

James I and his queen, Anne of Denmark, continued the tradition of Elizabethan progresses, which encouraged courtiers to improve their houses and make new gardens for them, but, unlike Queen Elizabeth, they themselves also entertained on a lavish scale and

17. The frontispiece to Gerard's *Herball*, 1597, depicting visitors to his London garden. Elizabethan gardens were transformed by plants from new lands.

were patrons of the arts. The Burghley influence in statesmanship, building and gardening was continued by Robert Cecil, who became 1st Earl of Salisbury in 1605. He bridged the two reigns by retaining his offices of Secretary of State and Lord Treasurer, which he took over in 1598 when his father died. The 'magnificent' Theobalds, so admired by the Elizabethan travellers, was taken over by James I in exchange for the old palace at Hatfield, where Robert Cecil set about building a new house in 1606. The Hatfield gardens came to be admired by seventeenth-century travellers as much as the Elizabethans had praised those at Theobalds.

Visitors to Jacobean gardens observed changes in fashion. The new houses were no longer a series of courtyards, like Hampton Court and Theobalds, but were outward-looking, giving more scope for unity with the gardens by means of a terrace on the principal garden front. Not only did the Venetian ambassador note in 1618 that there was much new to be seen in English horticultural practice, particularly in fruit growing, but what also struck him as 'worthy of note' were the new designs in gardens. He reported on the square, geometrical nature of the gardens near the house formed by cross walks with central features of statues and fountains, the balustraded terraces, ornamented with pyramids and balls, the very close grass on the slopes leading down to the lower gardens and how 'walking on the terrace one has a good view of the general arrangement, the fountains and all the designs'.[3] John Taylor, who visited the Jacobean gardens at Wilton, found the walks in one of them so geometric that he compared them with the rings of an onion. The shapes in the knot patterns became much influenced by Flemish strapwork, so often seen in the carvings inside Jacobean houses.

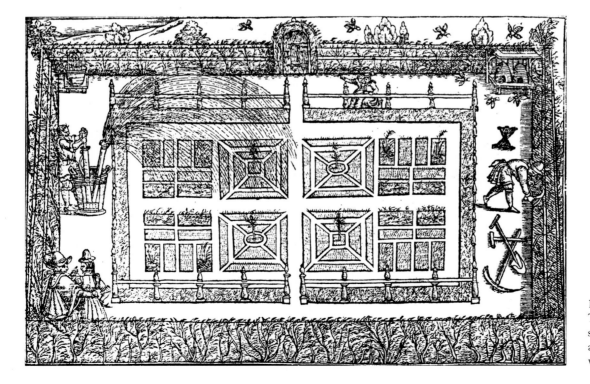

18. An illustration from Hill's *The gardeners labyrinth* of 1577 showing typical knots, tunnel arbour, pots, beeskips and watering devices.

19. Festival design by Inigo Jones, 1611. The masques of Ben Jonson and Inigo Jones, often staged *en plein air*, had a considerable influence on the architectural element in early seventeenth-century garden design. (Courtesy of the Trustees of the Chatsworth Settlement)

Improved skills in engineering and hydraulics gave new dimensions to the terracing and waterworks, most notably after Salomon de Caus arrived in England about 1610 and worked at Richmond, Greenwich and Hatfield and his brother Isaac later at Wilton.

There was a new theatrical quality in gardens, particularly associated with grottoes and waterworks complete with sound effects, moving statues and tricks of light, which had been influenced by the popularity of masques. The masque, which for Elizabeth had been an elaborate peripatetic pageant, became a much more highly finished dramatic performance for the Stuart court owing to the collaboration of Ben Jonson and Inigo Jones. King Charles I and Queen Henrietta Maria were royally entertained by Jonson's patron at Bolsover Castle in a specially created garden into which they were led to see the performance of *Love's welcome to Bolsover* by an elaborate Venus fountain. The gardens at Wilton were the ultimate in fantasy gardening with grottoes and waterworks which fascinated all seventeenth-century visitors.

Henrietta Maria, the daughter of Henry IV and Marie de' Medici, was accustomed to great gardens in the palaces in which she had been brought up. The Luxembourg gardens in Paris were made for her mother inspired by the famous gardens of her home at Boboli in Florence. When Henrietta Maria first came to England as Charles I's queen she brought over her father's Fontainebleau gardener, André Mollet, to work at St James's Palace and Wimbledon House. Inigo Jones completed the Queen's House for her at Greenwich and was engaged on many other royal works. At the queen's Somerset House, the great Arethusa fountain, later called the Diana fountain and now in Bushy Park, was installed. Time, however, was running out for court architecture and princely gardens and when the Civil War broke out Inigo Jones was sent to the Marquis of Winchester's Basing House in Hampshire to help strengthen the defences, as many of the queen's friends had taken refuge there. Inigo Jones was still there at its final surrender to Cromwell after a heroic siege, and today a 1640s garden is being recreated at Basing House to commemorate the historic event.[4]

KENILWORTH CASTLE
KENILWORTH, WARWICKSHIRE

Kenilworth, which was granted to Robert Dudley, later the Earl of Leicester, in 1563, was recorded by the Parliamentary Survey as 'the like both for strength, state and pleasure not being within the Realme of England'. It is now, thanks to Cromwell, one of England's most impressive ruins. Its situation on a sheet of largely artificial water, spread over 111 acres, according to the survey, must have rivalled that of Leeds Castle. Henry V had made a retreat called the pleasaunce in the marsh at the far end of the lake,[1] but this pavilion was demolished by Henry VIII who had a new 'Pleasaunce' made between the inner and outer walls of the castle near the Strong Tower. The Earl of Leicester, Queen Elizabeth's favourite, turned Kenilworth from a fortress into a palace and entertained his sovereign there in 1565 and 1575. The famous pleasure garden he made to the north of the castle below the Keep is known, not so much from travellers' descriptions, household records or illustrations, but from two famous accounts of Queen Elizabeth's visit in 1575 by Robert Laneham, a courtier, and George Gascoigne, the court poet, who were in attendance.

Laneham thought it so 'very pleasantlie appointed' with 'great art, cost, and diligens' that 'Diana herself myght have deyned thear well enough too raunge for her pastyme' with a terrace walk along the castle wall, obelisks, spheres and white bears 'all of stone upon they curioouz bases', fountains, arbours and all the sensual pleasures of an Elizabethan garden, 'whearby at one moment in one place, at hande without trauell to have so full fruition of so many Gods blessinges, by entyer delight unto al sencez at ones: for Elysium of the woord woorthy to be called Paradys'.[2] There was lavish entertainment for the queen lasting nineteen days with music, hunting, fireworks and a great water pageant and masque. On arrival she was greeted by the Lady of the Lake, surrounded by her nymphs, paying homage on a floating island. Like her father, the queen delighted in hunting and all the ritual of venery was performed at her standing in the park. The huntsmen would present the deer fumets (droppings) found that morning for her inspection so that she could choose which hart should be driven towards her for the kill, the queen knowing that 'the moystness showes, what Venyson he beares'.[3]

Few of the masques performed before Queen Elizabeth have survived but the Kenilworth masque is preserved in Gascoigne's *The princely pleasures at the Castle of Kenelwoorthe*. The last act contains the usual eulogy to the Virgin Queen, to whom Leicester is said to have proposed:

> *The Countrey craves consent, your virtues vaunt themselfe*
> *And Jove in heaven would smile to see Diana set on shelfe.*

The Kenilworth pieces by Laneham and Gascoigne were reprinted in 1788 by John Nichols in his *Progresses and public processions of Queen Elizabeth* and were read by Walter Scott with great interest. They appeared again in 1821, together with Dugdale's history of Kenilworth, in an antiquarian publication called *Kenilworth illustrated* printed by Merridew of Coventry. Sir

Walter Scott's name appears in the list of subscribers and the romantic illustrations must owe something to his novel, just published. Scott visited Kenilworth, which he had seen before, in 1815, but this time with particular curiosity as the poet had just begun to turn his attention to novel writing. Scott was the inspiration not only of a new genre of historical novel but of a new type of romantic traveller in search of historic associations. According to Elihu Burritt, the American consular agent in Birmingham in the 1860s, its namesake novel was worth £10,000 a year to Kenilworth and the hotel visitors' book showed how people came from all over the world to see the scene of Scott's romance. 'Take away that famous novel, and, with all the authenticated history that remains attached to them, not one in five visitors they now attract would walk around them with admiration. In fact they are more a monument to the genius of the great novelist than to the memory of Elizabeth and the Earl of Leicester'.[4]

Scott was himself interested in old gardens and in his *Kenilworth* revelled in describing Leicester escorting Queen Elizabeth from her chambers to the pleasance building between the inner and outer walls near the Strong Tower and down the terraces to the pleasure garden he had made for her:

> She had scarcely made one step beyond the threshold of her chamber ere Leicester was by her side, and proposed to her, until the preparations for the chase had been completed, to view the Pleasance, and the gardens which it connected with the Castle yard. To this new scene of pleasures they walked, the Earl's arm affording his Sovereign the occasional support which she required, where flights of steps, then a favourite ornament in a garden, conducted them from terrace to terrace, and from parterre to parterre.[5]

Scott's *Kenilworth* is now only obtainable in secondhand bookshops and few of today's visitors

20 (below left). The page from Turbeville's *The noble art of venerie or hunting*, 1575, showing Queen Elizabeth inspecting the deer fumets in her standing in the park.

21 (below right). A romantic view of Kenilworth in 1821, from Merridew's *Kenilworth illustrated*, which was inspired by Walter Scott's recently published novel.

22. Leicester's garden as replanted in 1973. The area is now being replanned by English Heritage.

have read it. It seems, however, that we owe the initial protection of the ruins to Scott's novel and the romantic travellers, as in April 1828 he wrote in his journal: 'Well! the last time I was here in 1815 these trophies of time were quite neglected', but now are 'preserved and protected. So much for the Novels'.[6]

Today the interest in the castle, now in the care of English Heritage, is provided by their guidebook and the historical presentation in the Tudor stables. The Ancient Monuments policy of stabilizing and preserving the ruins is now well established, but the treatment of the surroundings of the monument, particularly the gardened area, has not yet been satisfactorily resolved. A preliminary attempt was made to recreate the Kenilworth garden to an authentic formal design of the period, but this is now being changed. It is not possible to reinstate Leicester's grand garden with its elaborate marble fountain and obelisks topped with the earl's heraldic bear and ragged staff, and a mere pattern book box design with thin planting to fit Dugdale's ground plan in his *Antiquities of Warwickshire* conveyed none of the splendour and sensual delights of the garden in which Queen Elizabeth walked. Furthermore, the congruity of ruins and cared for gardens is open to question; it is something that the picturesque eye or the romantic heart would have frowned upon. The overwhelming fact of Kenilworth is that it was destroyed after the Civil War and left a ruin, and its surroundings should reflect its history. William Gilpin, seeking the Picturesque, saw the area that was 'formerly floated' grazed by a herd of cattle, which he felt 'were a great addition to the scene, and reminded us of some of Berghem's best pictures, in which cattle and ruins adorn each other'.[7] John Byng, Viscount Torrington, was also intrigued by the idea that 'the lake is now a firm meadow; no longer affording themes for the fiction of poetical parasites, whose ladies give place to cows'.[8]

It is the reinstatement of the lake, drained when the Parliamentarians destroyed the dam to create acres of farmland, which would bring back landscape history and romance to Kenilworth and reflect a splendid ruin, but this is almost certainly not possible today.

Victorian visitors, bred up on Scott's novels and picturesque engravings of ruins, 'turned aside to the mouldering gates of our ancestors as a pilgrim turns to some favourable shrine' and Kenilworth was hailed as one of the most evocative of our ruins:

> *Illustrious ruin! hoary Kenilworth*
> *Thou hast outlived the customs of thy day;*
> *Yet though thy halls are silent, though thy bowers*
> *Re-echo back the traveller's lonely tread,*
> *Again imagination bids these rise.* [9]

Henry James on a passionate pilgrimage in Warwickshire deplored the 'cockneyfication' of romantic sites and wrote in 1905 that Kenilworth was best seen from a distance 'with purple shadows and shifting lights', rather than with hawkers, 2d pamphlet sellers, beery vagrants and the 'usual squares of printed cardboard suspended upon venerable surfaces'. [10] Perhaps it is the romantic option, with due concern for guardianship but leaving room for the imagination to work, which is the best solution for the management of the surroundings of Kenilworth, and today's visitors should see it as Prince Pückler-Muskau did: 'with Sir Walter Scott's captivating book in my hand I wandered amid these ruins, which call up such varied feelings . . . a gloomy but sublime memorial of destruction'. [11] The evocation of the garden made for Queen Elizabeth, in Laneham's words, 'woorthy to be called Paradys', is perhaps best left for the exhibition display.

23. The imaginary reconstruction by Alan Sorrell of the castle and gardens at the time of Queen Elizabeth's visit to Kenilworth.

THE TUDOR GARDEN
TUDOR HOUSE MUSEUM, SOUTHAMPTON, AND ERNEST LAW'S RECREATED TUDOR GARDENS

An authentically recreated Tudor garden, but not on the princely scale of Nonsuch or Kenilworth, can now be seen in Southampton at the Tudor House, Bugle Street, one of the city's museums. Like Queen Eleanor's garden at Winchester, it was designed by Sylvia Landsberg and it shows how a contemporary garden can enhance a building and its sense of history. There is now in museums a new understanding that historical presentation should extend to the garden. Before the new garden in the Tudor House Museum was made, the ground had been laid out as a small amenity area to the house with seats and waste-bins, lawns and bedding-out like any municipal park. The new Tudor garden, which has become an important educational asset, is a collection of features of ornamental gardens recreated from sixteenth-century texts and illustrations using only plants known at the time in the way they would have been grown.

Henry VIII's Lord Chief Justice of England, Sir Richard Lyster, inherited the house about 1520 and his wife Jane continued to live in it after his death in 1554. From the parapet looking over the city wall at the end of the garden the family could watch galleons coming up Southampton water and they may have entertained the king himself when he visited Southampton. Little is known of the families who followed the Lysters, but doubtless they too enjoyed the enclosed garden by the city wall which only altered in detail through the long Tudor reign.

Knot gardens had begun to be popular in Henry VIII's reign and were very fashionable during the Elizabethan age. A strong historical link in the Tudor garden is that the planted knot is an echo of a door carving in the hall of the house, as it is known that designs for carvers, glaziers, embroiderers and gardeners were taken from common Renaissance pattern books. One of the features of a knot garden which delighted the owner was that it was green all the winter, the plants which edged out the shapes being low-growing thyme, hyssop, cotton lavender or box. This last was not so popular as it had a sour smell, while the clippings of the sweet-smelling herbs could be used for strewing floors in the house. Sometimes the interstices of the knot shapes were filled with gravel, crushed bricks, powdered tiles or mineral substances.

Of the hundred plants selected for the garden half are native British plants or garden forms developed from them. The rest, including most of the herbs, are native to Europe and many of them may have been brought to Britain by the Romans. It was unlikely that any of the 'outlandish' plants from the New World destined for the great gardens would have found their way to the Southampton garden. Nevertheless there is much seasonal colour and fragrance to be enjoyed in the recreated Tudor garden: daffodils, primroses, cowslips, violets, clary, columbine, gillyflowers, wallflowers, fleur-de-lys, lilies, marigolds, heartsease, peonies,

24. A view of the garden showing the rose and vine arbour and the heraldic beasts.

25. The Tudor garden has been recreated from texts and illustrations using only plants known at the time.

26. An illustration of Ernest Law's recreated Shakespeare garden at New Place, Stratford, with features copied from Hill's *The gardeners labyrinth* (see Plate 18).

periwinkle, poppies, maiden pinks, rose campion and sweet williams. The Apothecary's rose, damask rose, the musk rose, Provence rose and *Rosa mundi* all grow in the garden. Raised and boarded herb beds for the manifold duties of the housewife contain costmary for ale-making, wake robin for starching ruffs, wormwood for keeping off fleas, feverfew for fevers and horehound for coughs as well as culinary herbs. Thomas Tusser's *Five hundred points of good husbandry* told the sixteenth-century housewife when to plant 'the seedes and herbs for the kitchen' and what herbs and roots to plant for using in salads and sauces and 'to boile or to butter'. Most of the herbs are familiar to today's cooks, but many of the vegetables listed would be considered weeds, and flowers such as marigolds, 'pot marigold', are not usually considered to have culinary uses.

At the end of the garden under the wall is the kind of tunnelled arbour canopied by vines and climbing plants made fashionable by the French. Thomas Hill, in his *The gardeners labyrinth*, 1577, describes the purpose of these shady covered walks:

> The commodities of these Alleis and walkes serve to good purposes, the one is that the owner may diligently view the prosperities of his herbes and flowers, the other for the delight and comfort of his wearied mind, which he may by himself or fellowship of his friends conceyve in the delectable sightes and fragrant smelles of the flowers, by walking up and downe.

Features in the Southampton Tudor garden, reminiscent of what the Elizabethan travellers saw at Nonsuch and Hampton Court, but on a minor scale, are the topiary figures trained on wire and twigs, the fountain and the heraldic ornaments. Although these heraldic emblems, such as Leicester had at Kenilworth, were now for garden pageantry, such badges had originated as essential distinguishing markers for knights in battle who all looked alike in armour. The mounted wooden beasts and painted railings in the Tudor garden are based on the famous painting of 1545, showing parts of the Great Garden at Whitehall Palace, where Baron Waldstein had admired the 'pillars with figures of animals on them'.[1]

To realize just how much of the true historical sense is missing when modern plants are used in would-be Tudor gardens the visitor should sit in a honeysuckle bower in the Southampton garden, preferably with a lute playing, and enjoy the feathery texture of the herbs in patterns and the overwhelming feeling of the fragrance of the plants, with the bees coming and going from the skeps in a wall niche just as they did when the Tudor Lord Chief Justice and his wife refreshed themselves in the garden. The recreated Tudor garden is truly a pleasance in the midst of modern Southampton.

The first recreated Elizabethan garden was for New Place, Stratford-upon-Avon, Shakespeare's last home, where he lived in retirement and died in 1616. It is now vested in the Shakespeare Birthplace Trust. Ernest Law, a Shakespeare scholar and historian, designed the garden, which was opened to the public in 1920. Only flowers mentioned in Shakespeare's plays were to be used, supplemented by Gerard's *Herball* of 1597, which the poet must surely have known. Law felt that Shakespeare may even have met the herbalist, as Gerard rented a piece of ground as a nursery garden from Queen Anne of Denmark at Somerset House where Shakespeare was in attendance as Groom of the Chamber in 1604. When it was first made authentic flowers for the garden were sent from places with Shakespeare associations: Greenwich, Windsor, Hampton Court, Wilton, Charlecote, Gorhambury, Knole, Cobham and Burghley and from mediaeval castles mentioned in the plays: Glamis, Cawdor, Warwick

27. The Hampton Court knot garden beneath Queen Elizabeth's bay window dated 1568. The garden is as recreated by Ernest Law but now has modern planting.

and Berkeley, as well as from Warwickshire cottage gardens. The walls were made of Tudor bond bricks and the paths with old stone from Shakespeare's mother's home. The trellis railing was made from Warwickshire elm from a pattern in Hill's *The gardeners labyrinth* and at the end of the garden a bank of wild flowers mentioned by Shakespeare was planted.[2]

A 'curious knotted garden' modelled on the New Place garden was also designed and laid out by Law at Hampton Court Palace with interlacing bands of thrift, dwarf lavender and thyme and with the interstices planted with daffodils, fleur-de-lys, marigolds, gilly-flowers and snapdragons in season.[3] Unfortunately, to give a greater and longer flowering effect, plants such as calceolaria, begonias and modern pansies are now used in both of Law's Elizabethan knot gardens, even though it would be of great interest for today's visitors to see the flowers enjoyed by Shakespeare in his own garden and by Queen Elizabeth when she looked out of the Hampton Court bay window which bears the date 1568 and her initials ER.

HATFIELD HOUSE
HATFIELD, HERTFORDSHIRE

At Hatfield, the modern tourist can see one of the best examples of a Jacobean house with some of its gardens restored to the period. Although the original gardens were largely wiped out in the eighteenth century, they were romantically revived in the nineteenth; and now, under the direction of the present Lady Salisbury, recreated with considerable authenticity.

Hatfield was built between 1607 and 1612 for Robert Cecil, James I's prime minister and later 1st Earl of Salisbury. Cecil had inherited the magnificent Theobalds from his father, Lord Burghley, but it was so much admired by James that Cecil was obliged to hand it over. In return he was given the old fifteenth-century episcopal palace at Hatfield. This he proceeded to have demolished and replaced with a more fashionable and grandiose creation. Only one range of the original palace was left, while the new house went up to the south-east. Fittingly splendid gardens were created, most notably on the sloping ground east of the house, where he employed Montague or Mountain Jennings, the gardener from Theobalds, to draw up plans.

The garden comprised a series of terraces running down to the river via flights of painted wooden steps. The lower part of the garden was planted with 'goseberies Rasberies Roses straberies & flowares',[1] and the river was used to form two now vanished water features, the Island and the Dell. The Dell was diamond-shaped and cut through with straight channels. In its centre was a pavilion, and in its canals hydraulic sea-monsters played. Both Dell and Island were planted with shrubs like white thorn and sweet briar, with alleys of 'garnished' hedges.

Cecil employed John Tradescant the Elder to supervise the planting, and Tradescant travelled to the Continent to purchase rarities for the garden. In 1611 a vineyard was laid out north-east of the house on both sides of the river, stocked with 30,000 plants from the wife of the French ambassador. West of the new house Cecil also laid out a garden in place of the old

28. Hatfield in an oil painting of *c*.1740. Much of the great formal layout disappeared during the eighteenth century, first neglected and then landscaped. (Hatfield House, courtesy of the Marquess of Salisbury)

palace's garden, though the site of Lady Salisbury's knot garden probably remained undeveloped. In the accounts references to the west garden include 'balisters . . . framing the walks'; 'quartares walkes & bordares'; a mount with water pipes leading to it; stairs garnished 'with French termes and vinealls'; and the 'nessorie [or nursery] below'.[2]

No account of the garden at this early stage is known. There is an elegant but rather vague description of the vineyard in 1640 by Thomas Fuller, who wrote in his *Worthies* of 'a place called the Vineyard, where Nature, by the midwifery of art, is delivered of much pleasure'.[3] John Evelyn noted in his diary a visit to Hatfield in 1643, 'where the most considerable rarity besides the house (inferior to few for its Architecture then in England) was the Garden & Vineyard rarely well water'd and planted'.[4] When writing on water-gardens in his great unpublished treatise on gardening, 'Elysium Britannicum', he advises his reader that the channels be 'so cutt, as not to glide altogether in a straite line, but in frequent meanders & serpentings so as now and then to forme *Ilands & peninsuls* an example whereof we have in the vinyard at *Hatfield* in *Hartford*-shire'.[5] Samuel Pepys enjoyed Hatfield, and visited several times. In 1661 he notes all too briefly that the Vineyard 'is now a very beautiful place again'. At Hatfield, he declared, are 'gardens such as I never saw in all my life; nor so good flowers, nor so great goosburys, as big as nutmegs'.[6]

The 2nd Earl had managed a remarkable feat of political balancing during the Civil War,

and as a result lived at Hatfield throughout it and the Commonwealth. While this was not a time to encourage new extravagances in the garden, planting continued and his father's layout was maintained. So it was substantially the Jacobean garden which Samuel de Sorbière, historiographer royal to Louis XIV, visited in 1663 and described in considerable detail. His account concentrates on the east gardens: the Dell is vividly evoked; an aviary is noted; and interestingly the pleasure of the view out into the countryside is stressed. From the house, he writes, 'you have a Prospect of nothing but Woods and Meadows, Hills and Dales, which are very agreeable Objects that present themselves to us at all Sorts of Distances'. Immediately below the east front was 'a Greenplot with Two Fountains in it, and having Espaliers on the Sides, but a Balister before it, upon which there are Flower Pots and Statues'. There were two further parterres below this one. Below them all was 'the great Water Parterre', in which the river 'as it were forms the Compartments': the water 'rises and secretly loses itself in an Hundred Places'. The banks were neatly boarded, and where the river entered the parterre there were 'open sorts of Boxes, with Seats round, where you may see a vast Number of Fish pass to and fro'. Sorbière concluded, 'I never saw a more engaging Retreat than this'. Beyond was a meadow 'where the Deer range up and down, and abbutting upon a Hill, whose Top ends in a Wood, and there bounds the Horizon to us'. 'There are also Arbours or Summer-Houses, like *Turkish* Chiosks, upon some of the Eminences, which have a Gallery round, and are erected in the most Beautiful Places, in order to the Enjoying of the Diversified Prospects of this Charming Country'.[7]

During a large part of the eighteenth century Hatfield went into a kind of hibernation. The 6th Earl, who inherited in 1728 and died in 1780, spent little time at the house, and the great tides of change passed the gardens by. In 1770 the young Irishman John Parnell described Hatfield's air of romantic decay, but deplored 'the Excessive neglect of the Parts Immediately Reaching to the court walls in Hattfeild Park the whole being overrun with molehills Rushes &c Lord Salisbury spends little or no time here'.[8] The 7th Earl embarked on improvements, Thomas Pennant remarking in 1782 on his journey from Chester to London, 'the grounds disposed in the modern taste; a considerable tract of road is going to be removed to a proper distance from the park'.[9] However, judging by Prince Pückler-Muskau's scorn in 1829, the introduction of the modern taste at Hatfield was not particularly successful. He saw 'a park rich only in large avenues of oaks and in rooks; otherwise dreary, and without water, except a nasty green standing pool near the house'.[10] Of a visit in 1825 J. C. Loudon later noted in the *Gardener's Magazine* that the gardens were well maintained, but, he concluded, 'there is . . . little evidence of such a love of gardening in the proprietor, as would be sufficient to stimulate and encourage his gardener'.[11]

29. The East Garden at Hatfield, designed by the present Lady Salisbury.

30 (left). An anonymous drawing showing the fanciful nineteenth-century recreation of the formal gardens. (Hatfield House, courtesy of the Marquess of Salisbury)

All that was to change once the 2nd Marquess set about creating a garden which would be in keeping with the Jacobean house. During the mid-nineteenth century a series of highly elaborate formal gardens was created, including the maze below the East Garden. In 1874, six years after the marquess died, the correspondent of the *Gardeners' Chronicle* described the Rosery (now Lady Salisbury's knot garden in front of the Old Palace); the Lime Tree or West Garden with its four ancient mulberry trees; a South Garden; the East Garden, of course; the Lake 'recently remade and extended'; the Parterre or Lord Burleigh's Garden; the Croquet Ground; an arcade of Roses one hundred yards long; and finally the Garden of Perfumes, below the East Garden, which contained only sweet-scented flowers and herbs.[12]

In recent years, the present Marchioness of Salisbury has done much to continue and develop the 2nd Marquess's work on the formal gardens. His layouts, a Victorian vision of the Jacobean style, have been redeveloped, with a greater awareness of historic authenticity. The Vineyard is not open to the public; but a knot garden has been created in front of the old Tudor palace using only plants grown in England during the fifteenth, sixteenth and seventeenth centuries, while in the East Garden, authentic planting, box-edged beds, rows of evergreen oaks clipped into balls, and a formal central axis marked with young yews, recreate the atmosphere of the Jacobean layout. Most recently Lady Salisbury has planted an orchard south of the East Garden using early varieties of fruit trees.

John Tradescant, the 1st Earl of Salisbury's gardener, was one of the most important figures in garden history, and recently a memorial to him has been created at St Mary's, Lambeth, the church where he and his son are buried. The new plants which Tradescant brought back from the expeditions he made for Lord Salisbury, made Hatfield horticulturally

31 (top right). The knot garden at the Museum of Garden History, Lambeth, designed by the present Lady Salisbury in honour of John Tradescant, who is buried in the churchyard.

32 (bottom right). The parterre on the west front at Hatfield.

famous. Lists of his purchases survive in the house, and 'Tradescant's Orchard' in the Bodleian Library contains drawings of fruit possibly grown at Hatfield (see Plate 16). In 1617 Tradescant became a member of the Virginia Company and this enabled him to introduce many North American plants, including spiderwort, *Tradescantia virginiana*, and Virginia creeper, *Parthenocissus quinquefolia*. John Tradescant the Younger also made expeditions in search of new plants, and both father and son had a keen eye for all sorts of natural curiosities. They collected shells, fauna and precious stones, which were then displayed in the Ark or Cabinet of Rarities at their Lambeth house.

In 1977 the Tradescant Trust was formed to save the church of St Mary-at-Lambeth and to found a museum of garden history. The tomb of the Tradescants, father and son, was restored, and a seventeenth-century garden was planted in the churchyard, growing only the plants known to the Tradescants. It seems fitting that the knot garden created in their honour was designed by Lady Salisbury herself, and that the first museum of garden history should be at Lambeth, where the Tradescants had their public museum alongside their nursery garden.

CAMPDEN HOUSE
CHIPPING CAMPDEN, GLOUCESTERSHIRE

Campden House was, like Hatfield House, a stylish house built in the first years of the reign of James I, but it was burned down in the Civil War and never rebuilt. Its elaborate Jacobean gardens are preserved in a remarkable series of earthworks, which have recently been investigated by Paul Everson for the Royal Commission on the Historical Monuments of England.[1] The evocative outbuildings that escaped destruction, the ogee domed gatehouses, the two banqueting houses, the coach house to which the dowager had to retire after the fire, the screen walls and Lady Juliana's gateway have always intrigued visitors, not only for their fine building, but as an indication of what the great house itself must have been like. Bishop Pococke visited Chipping Campden on his tour of 1750 and recorded:

> Near the church is a gate with a porter's lodge on each side; going down to the town
> and entering a court are two piles of offices with handsom door cases; then we came
> to the terrace which was behind the house, at each end of which there was a
> banqueting house built with 3 clos'd arches and a basement and rooms above, the
> chimnies are as twisted fluted pillars with a stone in appearance laid on them, and a
> rose at each corner. Here seems to have been a terrace round a grass plat.[2]

When he returned in 1764 very little was left of the shell of the house, but Dr Pococke, like all other antiquarian visitors to the nearby church of St James, could not fail to be impressed by the tomb of the builder of Campden House, Sir Baptist Hickes, later Viscount Campden, who died in 1629. The tablet recorded in Latin that it was he who had built the great (*amplus*) house and splendid (*nitidus*) gardens and his wife added an inscription in English to record that

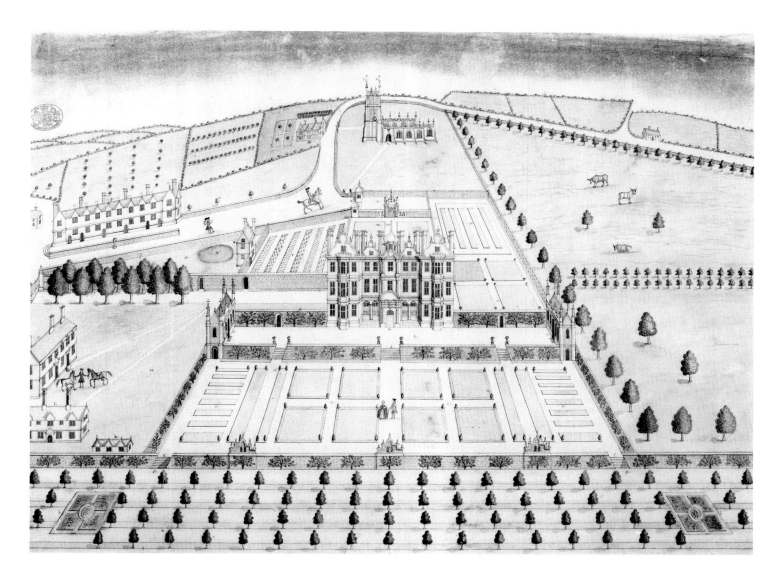

33. Campden House seen in a drawing by William Hughes, c.1750. The lower garden containing the water features is not shown. The eastern banqueting house has now been restored by the Landmark Trust. (British Library, London)

'Baptist, Lord Hickes, Viscount Campden, born of a worthy Family in the City of London, who by the Blessing of God on his ingenious Endeavours, arose to an ample estate, and to the aforesaid Degree of Honour'. Lady Campden seemed justly proud of her husband's relatively humble origins and achievements. His family came from Tortworth in Gloucestershire and his father was a prosperous Cheapside shopkeeper. Baptist himself became a mercer and one of the chief purveyors of silks to the court, and provided 'velvets damasks and satins of the colour crimson' for James I's coronation. He became wealthy through money-lending and even the king was in his debt to the tune of £16,000 in 1605. He was knighted in 1604 and set about finding an estate in his native county. In about 1609 he bought the manor of Chipping Campden, a little market town that owed its prosperity to the wool from Cotswold sheep. As well as building his great house he played the part of the benefactor to the town by providing a water supply, building almshouses, a market hall, parsonage and grammar school, and giving the church a new pulpit and lectern.

Ralph Bigland, visiting about 1784, saw a plan of the house which gave him the opportunity to describe 'the most sumptuous house with accompaniments of corresponding magnificence' in his history of Gloucestershire:

> From an accurate Plan and Elevation still extant, it appears to have been an Edifice in the boldest Style of that Day. It consisted of four fronts, the principal towards the Garden, upon the grand Terras: at each Angle was a lateral Projection of some Feet, with spacious Bow Windows; in the Centre a Portico with a series of Columns of the 5 orders (as in the Schools at Oxford) and an open Corridore. The Parapet was finished with pediments of a capricious Taste; and the Chimneys were twisted Pillars with Corinthian Capitals. A very capricious Dome issued from the Roof, which was regularly illuminated for the Direction of Travellers during the Night. This immense Building was enriched with Frizes and Entablatures most profusely sculptured; it is reported to have been erected at the Expense of £29000 and to have occupied, with

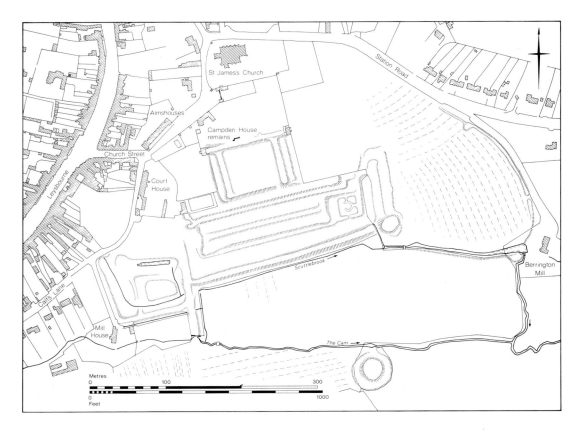

34. Survey drawn up for the Royal Commission on the Historical Monuments of England. (Crown Copyright)

its Offices, a Site of 8 acres. Part of a Wall, discoloured by Fire, and the two Banquetting Houses which terminate the Terras, are the Remains most worthy Notice, of this magnificent pile. Beside there is the grand Entrance adjoining the Church-yard composed of two low Pavilions connected by a Skreen with Pediments of a form which defies Description. Without doubt, the munificent Founder employed the most eminent Architect that Age afforded but whom is not known.[3]

The plan Bigland saw is now lost but a bird's-eye view was later drawn up which gives the layout of the estate including the gardens in some detail. This and a much extended layout has been confirmed by the recent RCHME survey. The technique of non-excavational field survey has given a new dimension to garden history. Formal gardens need structural features such as terraces, mounts, dams and ponds to create their effect. When these are abandoned and not removed by later land use they remain as earthworks in the landscape. Those of the abandoned Jacobean garden at Campden House are outstanding, because the house was never rebuilt and so there was no chance that its grounds would succumb to changing fashions; nor was the land ever ploughed up, but in the terraces, orchards and dried up ornamental water features Cotswold sheep have grazed for centuries, unconsciously preserving an historic garden. No family papers survived the fire and there are no plans or accounts for the garden, so that the garden designer as well as the architect is unknown. A descendant spoke of the family tradition of the 'nitidus' garden: 'this garden must have been as princely any Bacon could have desired. Terrace below terrace there is; then comes a brook which, doubtless, had its part in the scene. Beyond the brook the ground rises again and the horizon is a narrow one. On the other side of the house, next the church, is a space which legend calls the Italian garden and the remains of a courtyard, with arched gateway and lodges'.[4]

One significant fact is that Sir Baptist Hickes's brother Michael was a secretary in William Cecil's household and a friend of his son Robert, of Fulke Greville and of Francis Bacon and was, therefore, intimately acquainted with Gorhambury, the gardens of Theobalds and with the new gardens at Hatfield, which were being laid out at the same time as his brother's at Campden House.[5] Even though the newly-knighted Sir Baptist could never hope to entertain his sovereign, the site shows many of the features of the princely Cecil gardens. There was an upper terrace with banqueting houses at each end leading by three flights of steps to the Great Garden arranged in parterres. This was enclosed by walls with curved and finialled gables at the south end. At each end stairs led down to the great orchard bounded by a long canal. A large mount was situated at the angle of the canal and a narrow causeway led out to an island to which the visitor might perhaps 'have the pleasure of going in a boat and rowing between the shrubs', as did Hentzner at Theobalds.[6] Like the Hatfield water parterre it was probably lined with coloured pebbles in which the river 'as it were forms the Compartiments'. Campden House seemingly had the naturalistic features of 'Ilands and peninsuls' recommended by Evelyn.[7] At the west end the Scuttlebrook stream has been dammed to feed a spiral water feature and there were mills associated with the brook which may also have been ornamentally featured as at Theobalds, where Waldstein saw in the gardens 'two wooden water-mills built on a rock'.[8]

The Landmark Trust has restored the eastern banqueting house, so that visitors will now be able to sample the delights of a holiday in a garden building which was intended as a place in which to take banquets. A banquet was a dainty post-prandial meal of sweetmeats sometimes combined with an entertainment in the garden. It would have included such mouth-watering conceits as candied violets, marigolds, roses, borage, almonds, musk, ginger and comfits of all kinds, apples, roasted wardens, sliced oranges and lemons, washed down with a laced fruit cup called Ipocras; with so much syrup and juicy fruits the servants were in constant attendance with basins and silver ewers of rose water. The pleasure of eating fruit, according to Sir Hugh Platt, was greatly increased if you had first walked through your 'growing banquet' in the orchard, and in the height of summer flowers could be candied as they grew, three hours being sufficient for the sugar and rose water confection to set upon them.[9] At Kenilworth preparations were made for Queen Elizabeth to 'taste of delicious strawberries, cherries and other fruits even from their stalks'. Perhaps Platt's *The art of preserving and candying* should be placed on the bookshelves to give Landmark Trust visitors the true flavour of the pleasures of living in a banqueting house.

35. The humps and bumps of the lower garden at Campden House. These have recently been investigated and surveyed (see Plate 34).

BOLSOVER CASTLE
BOLSOVER, DERBYSHIRE

The walled garden at Bolsover is the site of one of the most elaborate court entertainments ever staged. The garden rooms built into the wall still survive, as does the elaborate Venus fountain, which was the centrepiece of the entertainment. The formal layout of beech hedges is a nineteenth-century creation, but the garden's seclusion, surrounded by the rippling gables of the castle, still creates the kind of dramatic effect that must have struck the guests in 1634.

In 1633 on his journey northwards for his Scottish coronation, Charles I had stopped at Welbeck and been entertained by William Cavendish, Earl of Newcastle, in, as Clarendon describes it, 'such a wonderful manner, and in such an excess of Feasting, as had scarce ever before been known in *England*'. But Newcastle went on to stage 'a more stupendious Entertainment' for the king and queen in the following year, whose excess Clarendon thanked God was never imitated.[1] That 'stupendious Entertainment' was staged at Bolsover and it is impossible to describe the garden without it for that was the garden's very reason for being.

Bolsover Castle was acquired by William's father, Sir Charles Cavendish, in 1610 from Gilbert Talbot, Earl of Shrewsbury. He demolished the remains of the old twelfth-century

36. The Duke of Newcastle with Bolsover in the background. An engraving for the duke's *Méthode et invention nouvelle de dresser les chevaux*, 1658, based on an earlier drawing, c.1620.

castle and replaced it with the present 'Little Castle'. With the architect and builder John Smythson, he conceived one of the most fantastic of all Jacobean houses. In fact it was less a house than a castle of Romance. The last years of the sixteenth century and the early years of the seventeenth century saw an extraordinary flourishing of tournaments and tilts, a self-conscious recapturing of the spirit of mediaeval chivalry. Elizabeth had fostered it with her 'Accession Day' tilts in which favoured knights would joust in her honour. Although the jousting was dangerous enough, these were in essence highly artificial and mannered fêtes; like Spenser's *Faerie Queene* they invoked a poetically inspired golden age. Perhaps the most famous of these tournaments was in 1581, when the queen herself took part. She occupied a pasteboard 'Castle of Perfect Beauty' and was besieged, unsuccessfully of course, by the 'four Foster Children of Desire', Lords Arundel and Windsor, Sir Philip Sidney and Sir Fulke Greville. James I had continued to encourage this craze with his 'King's Day' tournaments. Charles Cavendish, a famous horseman and swordsman, conceived his new castle in the same romantic vein.

The keep was started between 1610 and 1613, but Cavendish died in 1617, and was succeeded by his son William. It is not known precisely when the garden was created: its thick walls seem to have been formed from the original inner bailey, with the new castle's forecourt on the site of the old keep. Certainly Charles left much unfinished, and it was William, from about 1629 onwards, who did most to develop the building. William Cavendish was described by Sir Philip Warwick as 'a Gentleman of grandeur, generosity, loyalty, and steady and forward courage', but, 'his edge had too much of the razor in it: for he had a tincture of a Romantick spirit, and had the misfortune to have somewhat of the Poet in him'.[2] That romantic spirit, and that misfortune, are both evident in the entertainment at Bolsover and its garden setting.

When, after the entertainment at Welbeck in 1633, the king decided to return in a year's time with Queen Henrietta Maria, Cavendish chose to hold the entertainment at his romantic castle, which was as yet barely half-built. The 'Little Castle' was quickly completed and work was begun on the terrace range and riding school. He commissioned Ben Jonson to write a masque for the evening, and as it was to celebrate the love of the king and queen, it seems most likely that it was now that the garden, with its presiding statue of Venus, was created. It was here that *Love's welcome to Bolsover* was staged for the royal guests.

By the time of the entertainment the terrace range was still unfinished—part of Jonson's masque is a dance of mechanics or workmen. After the feasting, Jonson tells us, the king and queen 'retir'd into a Garden and are entertain'd'. They 'repos'd themselves', and 'in a fitt place, selected for that purpose, two Cupids present themselves'. Thus the masque in the garden began, the two cupids descending on wires out of clouds made from blue silk. One of the characters tells the audience, who watched the masque from the terrace on the garden walls: 'The Place . . . you are now planted, is the divine School of Love'.[3] Such a masque would have been inconceivable in the gardens of Elizabeth's time, where the pageantry centred on the cult of the Virgin Queen. The imagery at Bolsover was not altogether reverent however: the ageing Jonson did not miss the opportunity to take a

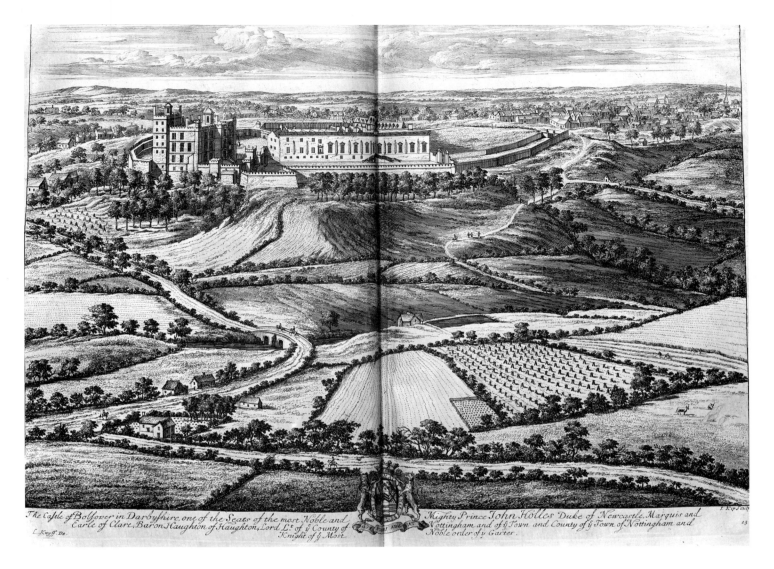

The Castle of Bolsover in Darbyshire, one of the Seats of the most Noble and Mighty Prince John Holles Duke of Newcastle, Marquis and Earle of Clare, Baron Haughton of Haughton, Lord Lt. of ÿ County of Nottingham and of ÿ Town and County of ÿ Town of Nottingham and Knight of ÿ Most Noble order of ÿ Garter.

L. Knyff De.   I. Kip Sculp.

37. Bolsover in the early eighteenth century, an engraving by Johannes Kip.

swipe at his erstwhile collaborator Inigo Jones, whom he here mocks as 'Iniquo Vitruvius'.

The evening of *Love's welcome to Bolsover* was the garden's great moment. That one night cost the prodigal Cavendish over £13,000. He did go on to complete his terrace range, but only a few years later the Civil War swept away the Caroline court, and Cavendish returned from exile in 1660 to find his castle 'much out of repair'.[4] He retired to Bolsover with his wife, and the process of rebuilding was begun. They continued to write their courtly poems, plays and essays, but their era had passed: Pepys summed up the couple as 'a mad, conceited, ridiculous woman, and he an ass'.[5] The rebuilding does seem to have been finished some time before Cavendish died in 1676, but the world in which Bolsover had been conceived remained a ruin.

As for the garden, what was actually there in Cavendish's time may well have been fairly simple, given its primary function as a stage. The glimpses we have of it in the early drawings and engravings, show the fountain standing in an apparently bare court. The fountain has lost some of its more elaborate features: there used to be statues of griffins and satyrs astride eagles in the angles of the basin, from which jets played, while in the arched niches were alabaster

busts of eight Roman emperors. The alcoves in the wall with their stone benches seem to date from the original garden; and the three garden rooms are also contemporary with the fountain, although their function is mysterious. Certainly the west room with its fireplaces and ornamental doorway must have been pretty sumptuous. It is tempting to wonder if it was intended as the 'fitt place' from which the king and queen watched the masque, but there is no evidence of that.

The garden we see now is the work of the nineteenth-century tenants of the Little Castle, the Reverend John Hamilton Grey and his wife. In 1894 it was described by A. J. Foster in his guidebook *Round about the crooked spire*, as 'a delightful little old-fashioned garden once the inner yard or bailey, but now containing prime flower borders arranged around a dry fountain, which is surmounted by a nymph of Rubens-like proportions'. Grey, gardening in the late nineteenth century, seems to have planted the formal beds and beech hedges in the revivalist spirit, attempting to evoke an 'old-fashioned' garden. The fountain garden as it is now represents a Victorian version of a Caroline garden, and for Foster this had a melancholy effect: 'The fountain presided over by the unclad nymph of stout proportions, in the inner garden, no longer flows. Bolsover castle where once was feast and revel is silent and desolate'.[6]

The Little Castle was abandoned as a residence after a serious fire in 1897, and in 1945 it was given to the nation by the 7th Duke of Portland. It is now maintained by English Heritage, but the words of an early twentieth-century tourist, Sacheverell Sitwell, describing the Venus fountain, and the 'strange little rooms with fireplaces' in the garden wall, may still apply for the romantic tourist of today: 'the whole feeling is that this is the court of love . . . . Nothing else, like this, keeps the love songs of the Cavaliers and their ladies, and still echoes, to our imagination, with the trembling of the lute string'. For Sitwell, Bolsover was 'dead, dead, as the Mayan ruins of Uxmal or Chichen Itza, and as remote from us, but with a ghostly poetry that fires the imagination, that can never be forgotten, and that never cools'.[7]

WILTON HOUSE
WILTON, WILTSHIRE

39. Leonard Knyff's topographical painting of Wilton, *c.*1700, combining a bird's-eye view with insets of the south side of the house, a waterfall, the stables, the grotto's interior, the loggia and the pavilion. (Wilton House, courtesy of the Earl of Pembroke)

Since 'black Will Herbert', later created 1st Earl of Pembroke, acquired the lands of Wilton Abbey at the time of the Dissolution of the monasteries, the estate has been a centre of great power and culture. Wilton was admired in the nineteenth century for its Italianate garden, and in the eighteenth for its landscaped garden; but its heyday was undoubtedly in the early seventeenth century when Isaac de Caus' elaborate formal garden was created. What remains today of this mythical garden was described by Inigo Triggs in 1902: 'lawns cover the site of De Caux's gay parterres. . . . Here and there a column, or a sundial . . . may still be seen, and opposite the orangery are certain pieces which formed part of the fountains in the old garden. A grotto, probably designed by Inigo Jones, and now used as a school-house, formed

one of the attractions in former days; but beyond these few relics nothing remains'.[1]

It was black Will's son, married to Sir Philip Sidney's sister, Mary, who made Wilton, in John Aubrey's phrase, 'an Arcadian place and a paradise'. They were great patrons of poets and playwrights, and in their time 'Wilton House was like a College, there were so many learned and ingeniose persons'.[2] The garden in the late sixteenth century was probably quite similar to that seen by the eccentric John Taylor, the 'Water Poet', who described his visit in 1623. He praised the 'paines and industrie' of the gardener, 'an ancient Gentleman Mr *Adrian Gilbert*':

> (much to my Lords cost and his own pains) . . . there hath he made Walkes, hedges, and Arbours, of all manner of most delicate fruit Trees, planting and placing them in such admirable Artlike fashions, resembling both diuine and morrall remembrances
> . . . he hath there planted certaine Walkes and Arbours all with Fruit trees, so pleasing and rauishing to the sense, that he calls it *Paradise*, in which he plaies the part of a true *Adamist*, continually toyling and tilling.[3]

Encouraged by Charles I 'upon making this magnificent garden and grotto' which the king 'did love . . . above all places',[4] the 4th Earl, who succeeded in 1630, was responsible for the greatest phase of the garden's history. Pembroke commissioned de Caus to design and lay out

40. View of the gardens drawn by Isaac de Caus in the late 1630s, published in *Le jardin de Wilton*, *c*.1645. (Worcester College Library, Oxford)

an immense formal garden, stretching 1,000 feet southwards from the house and across the river. In 1635 Wilton was visited by Lieutenant Hammond, one of the earliest tourists to visit country houses. The garden seems to have been almost finished although the famous grotto was evidently still being worked on. Hammond was accompanied by de Caus himself, to whom he refers as 'the fat Dutch Keeper . . . a rare Artist'.

He first describes the central walk, 'a curious broad Alley of 500. Foot long' leading to 'a fayre House of Freestone'. This was the banqueting house, its façade decorated with white marble bas-reliefs. De Caus evidently explained his proposals, for Hammond describes in some detail 'that rare Water-worke now making, and contriuing by this outlandish Engineer'. From the banqueting house, 'on either side the whole breadth this Garden, is rang'd double rankes of pleasant greene walkes, one aboue another, and sett all along with Pots of Flowers of the best kind'. Nearest the house were four square parterres, with central fountains, ornamented with statues, Venus and Cupid; 'Diana, with her bathing sheet'; 'Susanna pulling a thorne out of her Foote'; and 'Cleopatra with the Serpent'. Across the stream of the Nadder were two large square pools, 'with stately high Rockes in the middst of them, and golden Crownes on the Tops, and 4. lower Rockes about them, which by turning of Cockes that are close by, the water flyes spouting out, at the top of the Rockes; turning, and whirling the Crownes, and so fall powring into the Pooles'.[5]

Of all the bizarre and wonderful grottoes of the seventeenth century Wilton was widely thought the masterpiece. It survives today only in a few scattered fragments, the plans drawn by Isaac de Caus, and the tantalizing accounts of tourists, the best of whom must be Celia Fiennes:

> In the middle roome is a round table, a large pipe in the midst, on which they put a crown or gun or a branch, and so it spouts the water through the carvings and poynts all round the roome at the Artists pleasure to wet the Company . . . on each side is two little roomes which by the turning their wires the water runnes in the rockes you see and hear it, and also it is so contrived in one room that it makes the melody of Nightingerlls and all sorts of birds which engaged the curiosity of the Strangers to go in to see, but at the entrance off each room, is a line of pipes that appear not till by a sluce moved it washes the spectators, designed for diversion.[6]

The grotto was moved in the early eighteenth century, but survived until after 1733, when the ninth earl finally 'Destroyed the old rediculous Water works and whims'.[7] The garden was progressively simplified, as shown in drawings by Knyff in 1700 and the antiquarian William Stukeley in 1723.[8] The only addition was a straight avenue, extended from de Caus' central axis to the brow of the hill, and an equestrian statue—now to be seen over the north entrance.

Today there are only the most fragmentary remains of de Caus' grotto and garden. If you look out across the meadow towards the hill, you may, if the sun is low, discern suggestive lumps and bumps and the boundary ditch of the de Caus layout. His stables, admired by Aubrey, are the largest fragment, south-west of the house beyond the river: 'of Roman architecture, built by Mons. de Caus, [they] have a noble avenu to them'.[9] The statues in the

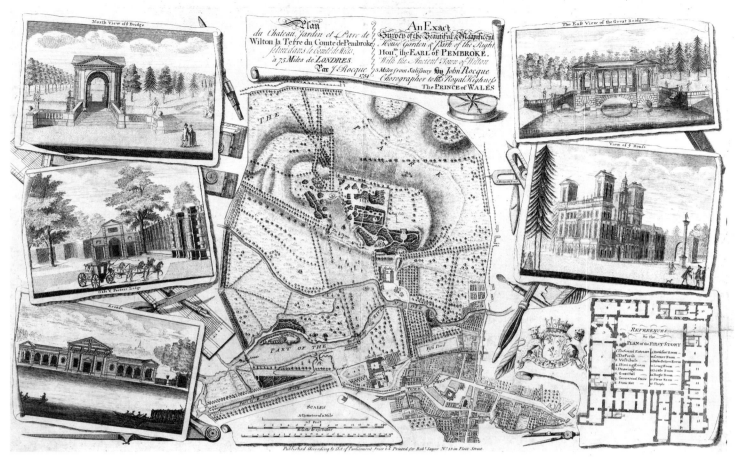

41. John Rocque's plan of Wilton, 1746, showing the informal English Palladian landscape.

north forecourt are those described by Hammond in the four-square parterre. An appointment is necessary if you want to see the arcaded loggia in the Italian garden, which is decorated with marble bas-reliefs of sea gods and goddesses from the grotto; similarly with the two rusticated columns, by the nineteenth-century orangery, which were originally the 'stately high Rockes' in de Caus' 'Coronet Fountains'. The best remnant of the grotto is alas not accessible at all: Park School House, between the main house and the Garden Centre, incorporates an internal stone façade, carved with the most amazingly intricate swirls of foliage, faces, and flowers, all now further adorned with a velvety covering of grey lichen. In its garden is a temple decorated with reliefs of Tritons and mermaids which also must be refugees from the grotto.

The 9th Earl was, like his Elizabethan ancestors, a notable patron of the arts. A friend of Burlington, Pope and Kent, it was he who was responsible for the landscaping of the gardens in the 1730s. He was known as 'the Architect Earl', and, with the help of the professional architect Roger Morris, he designed the Palladian bridge in 1737. The 1738 edition of Defoe's Tour, reports that 'the present Earl . . . is making a further Improvement with regard to prospect . . . throwing down the Walls of the Garden, and making instead of them the newly-introduced Haw-Haw Walls, which afford a boundless View all around the Country from every Quarter'.[10]

The eighteenth-century landscape is depicted in the views by Richard Wilson, but a later age found the 'pretty river' and 'gently sloping lawns dotted with plane-trees [and] cedars of Lebanon'[11] to be in doubtful taste. The agriculturist Arthur Young, who in his scientific tours shows a well-trained eye, thought the 'much esteemed' bridge 'rather heavy';[12] and it was Wilton which inspired William Gilpin on his Western Tour to pronounce 'Garden-scenes are never *picturesque*'. He too criticized the Palladian bridge, as 'a species of bombast in architecture'. It was, he decided, offensive: 'it offends at least the simplicity of the picturesque eye'.[13]

In the early nineteenth century there was a revival of formality when the Italian garden was laid out to designs by Sir Richard Westmacott. This was decorated with numerous statues, urns and vases, and the 'Holbein Porch', a survival from the sixteenth-century house, was made a feature. Westmacott also designed the short formal gravel walk from the east front to the stone seat and formal yew enclosure. J. C. Loudon thought this 'very improperly placed . . . conveying the idea that there is a public road, or some interruption, or object to be concealed behind', but he considered that the 'architectural flower-garden is the best of its kind' and admired the view from the loggia, while censuring the owners for denying the traditional right of way along the river to the villagers.[14]

In 1971 the present earl commissioned David Vicary to design a layout for the forecourt. His formal garden, with pleached limes, fountain, straight paths and the seventeenth-century statues, is only the latest addition to this most layered of gardens.

42. The meadow beyond the river, under which the formal layout is buried. Aerial photographs taken by the Royal Commission on the Historical Monuments of England during the dry summer of 1989 clearly show its outlines.

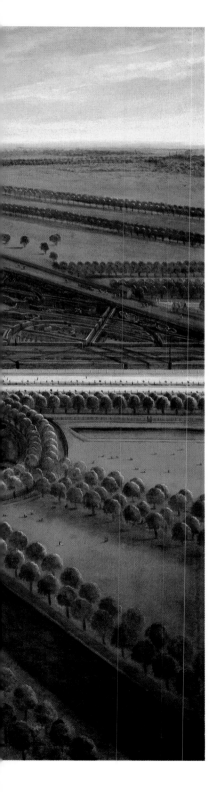

4
RESTORATION GARDENS

43. Bird's-eye view of Hampton Court painted by Leonard Knyff, showing the grand layout begun by Charles II at the Restoration with parterres designed by Marot for William III. (Royal Collection, reproduced by Gracious permission of Her Majesty the Queen)

Royalist houses and gardens suffered different fates during the Commonwealth. Where the palaces and great houses were destroyed in the Civil War or its aftermath and not rebuilt, as at Theobalds, Kenilworth and Basing, the gardens were abandoned or used for other purposes. Few have survived fossilized as earthworks like those at Campden House. Not all the royal gardens were neglected, however, and the parks belonging to the London palaces were maintained for public enjoyment. Cromwell decided to spend his weekends at Hampton Court and brought the great Arethusa fountain over from Henrietta Maria's Somerset House and set it up in what was now his Privy garden. Many royalist landowners, like Sir Christopher Hatton of Kirby, went into voluntary exile with the court abroad, and although there was no attempt at new gardening their gardens were maintained in their absence. Two of the once most loyal families, the Cecils and the Pembrokes, broke with the Stuarts, became members of Cromwell's Parliament and continued to live on their estates at Hatfield and Wilton.

The mood of dreamworld fantasy in gardens had been drastically changed by the realities of a bitter civil war. The days of *Love's welcome to Bolsover* or the enchantments of 'Arcadia' at Wilton were over. Pleasures to be derived from gardens became more intellectual and scientific. Ideas from France brought the baroque grand manner to England when Charles II

44. A parterre de broderie design from André Mollet's *Le jardin de plaisir*, 1651.

and his court returned in 1660. André Mollet, whom Henrietta Maria had first brought to England, was appointed Royal Gardener in 1661. He had not lost touch with England during the Commonwealth and returned with his nephew from Sweden where they had worked for the queen. He had recorded the principles of French garden design formulated by a whole dynasty of Mollet family gardeners in *Le jardin de plaisir* in 1651 and it was through him that the *parterre de broderie* was introduced to England.

The great house and its garden was to become part of a layout conceived as a whole and not a building with unconnected gardens. The Renaissance ideas of symmetrical gardens within boundary limits had been replaced at Versailles by central axes and the extension of vistas by the use of *claires-voies*, perspective and optical illusion. Monsieur de Sorbière, visiting Hatfield, which still had its delightful Jacobean garden, was quick to note that, in 1663, it lacked the baroque nature of the French gardens. Although he was clearly enraptured by the 'enchanted castle', particularly the naturalistic Island and Dell, he compared it with the formal type of water feature on the central axis which Le Nôtre would have given. 'Our Nobility, and even those of a more inferior Degree, would have made use of the Waters here, for some excellent Uses and Inventions'.[1]

The Glorious Revolution brought Dutch influence to English gardens, most notably in the royal gardens laid out by William and Mary, who were both keen gardeners. This was most apparent at Hampton Court, where the more intimate and horticultural Dutch gardening was superimposed on Charles II's French layout, and in their gardens at the newly-built Kensington Palace.[2] Daniel Defoe praised King William for having revived 'the love of gardening in his kingdom' by these examples. The National Trust has restored a Dutch-style canal garden at Westbury Court in Gloucestershire. One remarkable topiary garden, laid out at the end of the seventeenth century and now of outsize growth, can be seen at Levens Hall in Cumbria. Ideas from France continued to dominate garden design at the turn of the century and can still be seen at Melbourne in Derbyshire and at Wrest Park in Bedfordshire.

John Evelyn is an important commentator on late seventeenth-century gardens. During the 1640s he travelled widely on the Continent, meeting up with other virtuosi getting away from civil war, and called on the exiled Henrietta Maria and her court in France. He was interested in reporting the state of the arts, particularly gardens, and returned home in 1653 to live quietly under the Protector at Sayes Court, Deptford, where he made a notable garden. His most famous book, written at the Restoration, was *Sylva* for the newly founded Royal Society. He advised his friends, amongst whom he counted Charles II, on planting and especially advocated extending avenues into the countryside in the French manner. He first used the word avenue specifically for trees, as hitherto it had only signified an approach. Evelyn's diaries contain valuable comments on gardens such as Ham and eyewitness accounts of the laying out of royal gardens, particularly Hampton Court for Charles II and later for William III.

Although not himself a gardener like Evelyn, in his diaries Samuel Pepys often describes new trends in the gardens he visits. Grander spatially designed Restoration gardens were noted in July 1666 as 'our present fashion of gardens to make them plain, that we have the best

45. Detail of an engraving of Wrest Park by Johannes Kip. Such engravings show the 'exacte and complete' appearance of complementary houses and gardens favoured by Celia Fiennes and other tourists.

walks of gravell in the world, France having none nor Italy; and our green of bowling allies is better than any they have'.[3] Pepys was content that the grass plots should contain only statues or ornaments and that flowers would spoil the borders but 'are best seen in a little plat by themselves'. John Worlidge thought that plainness could be taken too far and that Restoration layouts were guilty of banishing 'out of their gardens Flowers, the Miracles of Nature, the best Ornaments that were ever discovered to make a Seat pleasant'.[4]

Horticulture was not, however, neglected by the gardening virtuosi of whom John Evelyn was the most notable. The Oxford Physic Garden, founded in 1621, and the Chelsea Physic Garden in 1673, were rallying points for the 'curious' plant seekers. The Tradescants' Lambeth garden was well visited even before the Civil War and at the Restoration many more new nursery gardens were opened with an international trade in plants. From 1681 the Brompton Park nurseries set up by George London, with Henry Wise becoming a partner in about 1688, supplied the royal gardens and most of the great gardens including Melbourne. They are still remembered for the double Brompton stock. Garden makers such as Christopher Hatton of Kirby visited other 'curious' gardeners to exchange plants and information. Kirby, which is at present being restored by English Heritage, had its great garden of grass parterres and statues such as Pepys noted, but the Privy garden and other areas were set aside for the 'best ornaments'—flowers.

The Duchess of Chandos saw much horticulture to admire in gardens such as Badminton and Melbourne on her tours.[5] For garden and social history, however, the most informative travel journal was undoubtedly that of Celia Fiennes, which was published in 1888 under the title of *Through England on a side saddle in the time of William and Mary*.[6] She relished new fashions and admired the Wren-style houses with a 'visto through the whole house' and their complementary courts and gardens giving them an 'exacte and compleate' appearance. The 'neate' gardens of the period are best known from the bird's-eye views and one can walk into a Kip engraving with Celia Fiennes and 'discover the curiosities' she admired—flower gardens, topiary, movable plants, waterworks, ornamental orchards, vistos and greenhouses. After so many engraved views the amount of colour comes as a surprise when she describes iron and stone work and statuary 'painted proper'. 'Blew with gilt tops', as seen at Ham today, was a favourite colour for railings; she approves of such 'grates to look through' which enable a traveller to see into the gardens. When country house visiting she expected to be taken up on the leads of the house where the designed shapes and 'thro glides and vistos of trees' could be seen to advantage as in a bird's-eye view. This is a rare privilege today but can be enjoyed at Celia Fiennes's ancestral home at Broughton Castle, near Banbury, where an Arts and Crafts recreation of a garden 'cutt into flower deluces' such as she describes in her journal can be seen from the leads.

GREENWICH PARK
GREENWICH, LONDON

Greenwich is one of the finest examples of the grand baroque concept of integrated buildings and landscape. For views of the capital, John Macky recorded in 1713, 'neither Frescaty near Rome, nor St Michael del Bosco near Bologna, so much admired for their prospects, affords near the Variety of this'.[1]

Greenwich was the first of the now public royal parks to be enclosed when, in 1433, Henry VI granted his uncle, Humphrey, Duke of Gloucester, a licence to enclose 200 acres bounded by the river. The boundaries of the royal park extending to the edge of Blackheath remain as they were five and a half centuries ago; the Tudor wooden paling was replaced by a wall built for King James I which is basically the same wall as today. It became Henry VIII's favourite palace within easy river distance from Whitehall. Here he married Catherine of Aragon, Anne Boleyn and Anne of Cleves and here his two daughters were born. Queen Elizabeth also loved Greenwich and conducted many festivities here including going on board the *Golden Hind* to knight Drake in 1580.

Much of the Tudor building was demolished in 1616 when the Queen's House, the dowry of King James I's queen, Anne of Denmark, was begun by Inigo Jones and after her death completed to the original plans for Queen Henrietta Maria in 1635. The Queen's House was offset with a Salomon de Caus garden which included an impressive fountain and a grotto aviary. During the Commonwealth horses were stabled in the state rooms of the Queen's House and the gardens left to decay. The palace itself had housed prisoners from the Dutch wars and was demolished at the Restoration. Charles II intended to build a new King's House fronting the river with formal gardens joining it to the Queen's House, but this was never finished and stood amongst the ruins of the old Tudor palace until it was incorporated into King William's great naval hospital.

Charles II lost no time in replanting to replace the trees felled during the Commonwealth. His Superintendent of Greenwich Park, Sir John Boreman, planted about 600 elms,

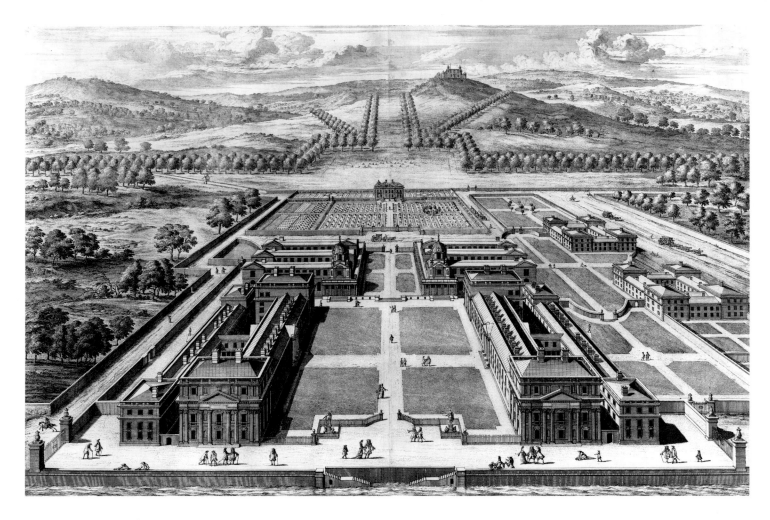

formed the east and west wilderness coppices and completed the chestnut avenues (some of the sweet chestnuts still survive in Great Cross Avenue) in 1664.[2] This was the year that John Evelyn, the king's neighbour at Sayes Court, wrote that he 'planted the homefield and West field about Says Court with Elmes, being the same year that the Elmes were also planted by his Majestie in Greenwich Park'.[3]

Evelyn may well have advised on the king's replanting. The Royal Society had just published his most influential book on arboriculture *Sylva or a discourse of forest trees*, which was dedicated to Charles II. John Evelyn strongly approved of the formal landscaping ideas, giving unity to the house and park, that the king had acquired in France. While in exile during the Commonwealth Evelyn had also greatly admired French gardens and had visited the young king and his mother in 1649 at her former home at St-Germain-en-Laye admiring the 'extraordinary long Walkes set with Elmes and a noble Prospect on the Sienne towards Paris'.[4] Henrietta Maria had returned to the Queen's House as the Restoration Queen Mother and took a great interest in the redesigning of Greenwich Park.

It seems practically certain that the Mollets, whom Henrietta Maria had originally brought to England, worked at Greenwich, which was laid out at the same time as their recorded commission for St James's Park. The three avenues radiating from a double semicircle of elms forming a huge *patte d'oie* was a favourite Mollet design. André Le Nôtre was

46. Kip's view of Greenwich shows Charles II's park layout on which Evelyn advised. When the seamen's hospital was built Queen Mary insisted that the view from the Queen's House should remain open.

certainly consulted, however, but the extent of his involvement is unclear. Louis XIV had granted permission for his most famous landscape architect, then working on Versailles, to visit England, and, although it was often said that Le Nôtre came, there is no evidence that he did so. However, a working sketch of 'Grenuche' *circa* 1662 for the garden of the Queen's House was discovered amongst Le Nôtre's papers in Paris in 1955. The banked outline of its baroque shape can still be traced but it is not known whether this garden ever contained a broderie parterre.

It may have been thought that Le Nôtre's presence was needed to relate this design, so important for the immediate setting of the Queen's House, to the extended vistas and grand concept of the park. There is no doubt that some of the layout already existed, since the most notable feature of the design, the twelve grass steps 40 yards wide, taking the eye and the legs up the steep gradient to the Blackheath terraces, was already in position and aligned on the Queen's House. Pepys, one of the many Londoners who frequently visited and appreciated the novelty and grandeur of the new royal park at Greenwich, first comments on the steps in April 1662, which was before Charles II wrote to Louis XIV about Le Nôtre. Running up and down

47. Canaletto: *Greenwich Hospital from the north bank of the Thames.* The grand concept of integrated buildings and landscape can still be seen from Wren's chosen viewing point. (National Maritime Museum, London)

the giant steps was greatly enjoyed by the young and carefree and even great ladies suitably paged made sedate ascents to the top of the hill:

> June 1662. Thence to my house, where I took great pride to lead her [Lady Carteret] through the Court by the hand, she being very fine, and her page carrying her train . . . then to Greenwich park; and with much ado she was able to walk up to the top of the hill, and so down again she being much pleased with the ramble in every particular of it.[5]

The views from Greenwich towards London seen across the bend of the river where so many sailing ships were harboured were described by Evelyn: 'the Prospect, which (after Constantinople) is doubtless for Citty, river, Ships, Meadows, hill, Woods and all other distinguishable amenities, the most noble the whole World has to shew'.[6] These views became even more breath-taking when Wren rebuilt St Paul's and the city churches on the skyline after the Great Fire of London. Within Greenwich Park Wren built the Royal Observatory in 1675 and, after the great naval victory at La Hogue, he was commissioned by King William to build a hospital for seamen on the riverside site originally intended by Charles II for a palace. Queen Mary insisted that the view from the Queen's House to the river

48 (left). A view from the Queen's House up to the Observatory showing the giant green steps that delighted Londoners in the days of Pepys.

49 (right). Visitors and inmates of the naval hospital disabled in the Napoleonic Wars enjoying the delights of the park with its superb unspoilt views of London. Painting by G. Arnaud. (Private Collection)

should be retained and that the block of the King's House that had been begun should not be demolished as it formed part of the grand design of building and park. According to Hawksmoor, writing in 1727, the queen maintained that 'this wing, Part of the Grand Design intended by her Uncle King Charles II, was both beautiful and durable . . . and it was proved to answer the regular Designs of that most admirable person Monsieur Le Nôtre, in the Esplanades, Waller, Vistar, Plantation and Lines of that beautiful park'.[7]

Queen Mary did not live to see the full effect of Wren's masterly solution. Canaletto painted the scene from the spot on the opposite river bank, which Wren had indicated should be kept as a viewing platform for his work. This site on the Isle of Dogs (where the kennels from the palace were originally kept) became the Island Gardens in 1895. Today it is close by the terminus of the Docklands railway so visitors can still have the breath-taking view across the river of Wren's naval hospital and Inigo Jones's Queen's House (converted into a naval school with wings and colonnades added in 1806) set back, with the royal park rising up the hill and the Observatory slightly to the right of the main vista.

In the 1970s it was decided in principle that the layout of the park, including the giant steps, should be restored as nearly as possible to the seventeenth-century plan, but this was indefinitely postponed.[8] Londoners may be too ready to take Greenwich for granted but the much travelled and hard to please Zacharias von Uffenbach was prepared to say in 1710: 'I think there can be no more agreeable place in the world than this Park'.[9]

HAM HOUSE
RICHMOND, LONDON

Ham House, 'a house King Charles II used to be frequently at, and was exceedingly pleased with', according to Defoe,[1] is one of the most authentic period pieces in England. The house, furnishings and gardens, restored by the National Trust, are largely unchanged since the great days of the Lauderdales in the 1670s. At the entrance the gate piers to the blue and gold painted gates surmounted by urns dated 1671 set the scene. The avenues, seen through wrought-iron screens, extending into largely unspoilt countryside and 'Ham's embowering walks' along the river, extolled by the poet James Thomson, have always helped to preserve a strong feeling of Evelyn's seventeenth century. The oil painting in the White Closet showing the duke with the duchess on his arm in the garden, gives us the view of Ham, which John Evelyn described in 1678 as one of the grandest places then to be seen:

> After dinner I walked to Ham to see the house and garden of the Duke of Lauderdale, which is indeed inferior to few of the best villas in Italy itself, the house furnished like a great Prince's, the parterres, flower garden, orangeries, groves, avenues, courts, statues, perspectives, fountains, aviaries and all this at the banks of the sweetest river in the world, must needs be surprising.[2]

50. Detail of an oil painting attributed to Hendrik Danckerts, c.1675, showing the Lauderdales walking in the garden. (Ham House)

The Duke of Lauderdale was the L in the powerful CABAL (Clifford, Ashley, Buckingham, Arlington, Lauderdale) of Charles II's ministers, but his wife, who appears in many portraits in the house, was in every sense mistress of Ham, and it was she who was largely responsible for the house we see today. As Elizabeth Dysart she had inherited the house from her father the Earl of Holderness, a favourite of James I, and obtained the title of Countess of Dysart in her own right. Her first husband, Sir Lionel Tollemache, was not ambitious enough for her liking and she formed a close friendship with the Earl of Lauderdale, whom she married six weeks after his wife's death in 1672, the year he was created duke. They immediately set to work to enlarge Ham House and improve the gardens, and a suite of rooms was set aside for the queen on the south front overlooking the gardens.

The virtuoso and amateur architect, Roger North, who was often entertained at Ham, approved the way in which the alterations had been made to the Jacobean house 'esteemed one of the most beautyfull and compleat seats in the kingdome'. Seventeenth-century travellers, including Celia Fiennes, approved of a 'compleate' seat, where house and garden neatly complemented one another, and at Ham House Roger North appreciated the way in which 'the plantations about it give a great complement and gardens (made with unlimited cost and excelent invention) perfection to the whole'.[3] The 'grand and beautiful Plots of Parterres in the gardens of Ham House' were commended by Batty Langley and greatly to be preferred to those at Hampton Court.[4]

When the duchess died in 1698 Ham became the property of Lionel Tollemache, 3rd Earl of Dysart, her son by her first marriage. By all accounts he was as parsimonious as his mother had been extravagant. The splendid furnishings were put in store and, according to John Macky, the house was neglected but the gardens Evelyn had admired were still well kept.[5] In 1724 this type of garden, hedged and walled into compartments, was still in fashion, but by the time Horace Walpole saw them in 1770 they were a rarity. It was forty years since William Kent had 'leaped the fence and saw that all Nature was a garden'.

Walpole's niece Charlotte had married the 4th Earl of Dysart, who was apparently as close-fisted and inhospitable as his grandfather. Walpole on his first visit denigrated the owner ('a strange brute'), his ancestors, the approaches to the house (like 'an old French fortified town'), the furniture and, above all, the old-fashioned gardens:

> I went yesterday to see my niece in her new principality of Ham. It delighted me and made me peevish. Close to the Thames, in the centre of all rich and verdant beauty, it is so blocked up and barricaded with walls, vast trees, and gates, that you think yourself an hundred miles off and an hundred years back.[6]

However, his friend Miss Agnes Berry found the gardens in 'the style of Charles II' delightful:

> I was much pleased with the house and its situation, surrounded as it is by large avenues of trees, with its terraced gardens, and its great bowling green; and it needs only to cut down a few trees to enjoy a most smiling scene, yet as perfectly quiet and secluded as if the house were placed in the furthest country from London.[7]

Queen Charlotte who, in 1809, stayed in the apartments set aside for Charles II's queen also enjoyed the gardens and found 'this little retreat is quite a little Earthly Paradise'.[8]

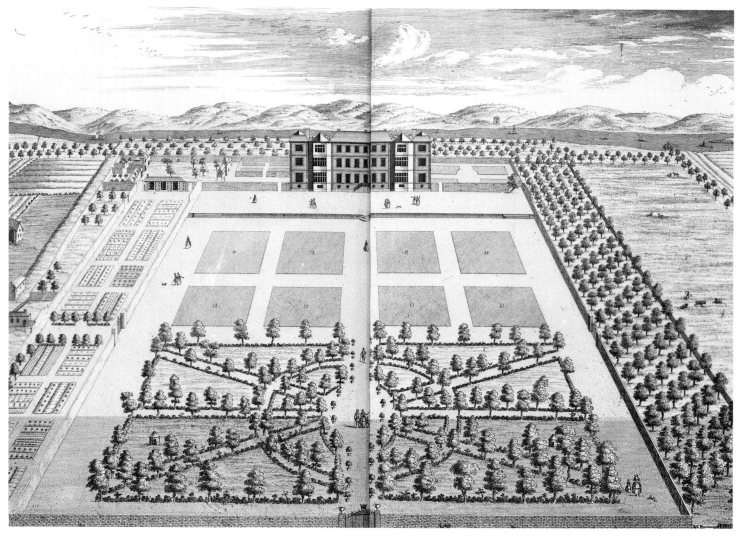

51. Bird's-eye view c.1730. This was used by the National Trust as the basis for restoring the gardens in 1975.

Having survived the landscaping era, the 'paternal entrenchments of walls and square gardens' which Walpole so deplored were allowed to remain and were remarkably intact in 1948 when Mr Cecil Tollemache presented Ham House to the National Trust. The restoration of the gardens was begun in 1975, based on a plan of the layout in the 1670s. The fountains, statues and aviaries Evelyn saw had disappeared, although in the house the volury room where the caged birds were taken in winter is still so named. The seventeenth-century red brick orangery still stands, with very slight alterations to the exterior, and now serves as a tea-house. It is not clear, however, whether Evelyn was referring to a structure when he mentioned the 'orangeries' at Ham. To the east of the house, where the 'cherry garden' led out of the White Closet, a parterre of box-edged beds diagonally divided is filled with silver cotton lavender and lavender and accentuated with pyramids of box in the corners and diagonals.

It is the wilderness restoration that arouses the greatest interest as this is an unique example of a most popular feature of the seventeenth century which can usually be seen in any Kip engraving. The wilderness was essentially a formal and not a wild place; it was a designed grove, like the French bosquet, with alleys running mazelike between hedges of trees and shrubs, forming different shaped garden rooms. The wilderness was not itself a maze, although this feature might occur in the grove, and the spaces within the hedges were large enough for summer-houses or bowling alleys. Books of the day talk of the spaces as cabinets, halls of verdure, green arbours, galleries and apartments within the wilderness. The tall trees, as can be seen in the Ham painting, only grew at intervals in the clipped hornbeam hedges and the tops of the flowering trees, lilacs, syringas, cherries and suchlike in the next compartment, could be seen above the hedges. Celia Fiennes describes 'a very fine wilderness with many large walks of great length, full of all sorts of trees sycamores willows hazel chestnutts walnuts set very thicke and so shorn smooth on the top which is left as a tuff or crown',[9] and the Duchess of Chandos tells of honeysuckles and sweet briars running up 'ye bodys of ye Trees' and how she was able to shelter from the rain in the arbour-like walks of wildernesses.[10]

The Ham wilderness was designed by John Slezer, a German engineer, and Jan Wijk, a Dutch painter, centrally aligned on the house and the grass plots in front of it. When the National Trust began the restoration the wilderness was overgrown by rhododendrons and sycamore scrub but the paths radiating from a circular clearing seen on the plan have now been recovered.[11] The boxes of flowering shrubs and the cockleshell backed seats seen in the seventeenth-century painting have been copied and reinstated in the main alley and in two of the green rooms, where cowslips and bluebells grow wild, delightful wilderness huts have appeared again. The sheltered wilderness rooms are in feeling akin to the numerous small secluded closets within the main house for playing cards or drinking tea, away from the more public places of parade.

52 (below left). The restored 'cherry garden' which led out of the White Closet.

53 (below right). The restored wilderness, a popular seventeenth-century garden feature seen in most Kip engravings.

OXFORD BOTANIC GARDEN
OXFORD

Delightful scientifick Shade!
For Knowledge, as for Pleasure made.

Visitors have indeed for centuries been delighted and would-be gardeners enlightened by Oxford's botanic garden. Although it is a part of the university it has always been available to the public. The earliest botanic gardens for teaching medical students about the properties of plants were established in Italy in the sixteenth century at Pisa, Padua, Florence, Rome and Bologna and the idea soon spread to the rest of Europe. John Gerard, herbalist and gardener to Lord Burghley, suggested that his employer should establish a physic garden in Cambridge, where he was chancellor.[1] The whole world of plants was made for the use and benefit of man 'for medicine to recover health', according to Gerard, and even the 'very brute beasts' had found out their hidden virtues. Lord Burghley died in 1598 soon after receiving Gerard's request and it was not until 1621 that a physic garden was founded by the Earl of Danby in Oxford and planted with 'divers simples for the advancement of the faculty of medicine'. John Ayliffe in 1714 summed up its aspects of ornament and use:

> For the Use and Honour of the University; serving not only for Ornament and Delight and the pleasant Walking and Diversion of Academical Students and of all Strangers and Travellers; and of great use, as is easily found, among all persons willing to improve their Botanical inclinations and studies and for the pleasant Contemplation and Experience of Vegetative Philosophy, for which is here supposed to be as good Convenience as in any Place of Europe (if not the best) and also for the service of Medical Practitioners, Apothecaries, and who else shall have occasion for things of that nature with what is right and true, fresh and good for the service of Health and Life.[2]

Lord Danby leased from Magdalen College five acres of meadow land outside the city walls, which until 1290 had been the cemetery of the Jews in Oxford. It was low lying and 4,000 loads of 'mucke and dunge' were used to raise the land above the Cherwell flood plain and prepare the ground to receive the plants. The founder had decreed that the walls were to be as 'well fair and sufficient as All Soules Colledge walls, Magdalen Tower, or any of the fairest buildings in Oxford both for truth and beauty'. The gateways to the Oxford Botanic Garden, known as the Physic Garden until renamed in 1840, are as fine as those in the finest country house and were built by Inigo Jones's master mason Nicholas Stone. The pedimented archways terminating the walks are similar to those built by Stone at Kirby Hall in Northamptonshire.

John Tradescant was appointed the first keeper of the Physic Garden, but he was already in failing health and unable to take up the post.[3] Danby finally decided in 1642 when staying at the Greyhound Inn opposite Magdalen that the tenant, Jacob Bobart, a retired German soldier, would make an ideal Horti Praefectus and could live in his own house. Bobart rose to the occasion and became greatly skilled as a gardener. Dr Plot described him as 'an excellent gardener and botanist'[4] and the Reverend John Ward, who later became a botanist of some standing, wrote with enthusiasm of what he had learned from Bobart before a professor of botany was appointed.[5]

John Evelyn and other distinguished visitors took 'hortulan refreshment' in the Physic Garden and on 25 October 1664 Evelyn recorded in his diary that he had seen 'some rare Plants under the Culture of old Bobart'. Bobart also produced a catalogue of plants growing in the garden which was available to visitors. Sir John Lauder was favoured with a copy when he visited in the 1660s:

> Next day I went to the Physick Garden not far from Marlan Colledge. The gardener (a German by nation) gave me their printed Catalogue of all the hearbs, which may be about some 7000 in all . . . . Saw African Marigolds, the true Aloes trie; all the wals cloathed with very big clusters, tall cyprusses, Indian figs, etc. the students can enter when they please.[6]

Charles II had appointed Robert Morison, whom he had met when in exile he was in charge of gardens at Blois and studying botany under Vespasian Robin, as the king's botanist. It was Morison who was responsible for the formal plan of the Oxford Physic Garden as seen in the Loggan plan. Bobart had had his own system of planting the 'curious' plants that came to his care but Morison designed more sophisticated plots such as he had been used to for setting off his rare plants for the Duke of Orléans at Blois. The professor gave lectures three times a week reading from a table in the middle of the garden and many distinguished visitors including Evelyn went to hear him: 'July 8 1675. I had in the morning early heard Dr Morison Botanic Professor reade on divers Plants in the Physic Garden.'

Bobart died in 1679 and Robert Morison soon afterwards in 1683. Bobart's son first succeeded as keeper of the garden and then as professor of botany. The younger Bobart was as diligent and eccentric as his father and Oxford took his uncouth appearance in its stride, but the idea of a gardener-professor greatly disturbed the German savant Zacharias von Uffenbach when he visited the garden in 1710:

> We entered the Hortus Medicus and Professor Bobart was waiting for us. I was greatly shocked by the hideous features and generally villainous appearance of this good and honest man. . . . His clothing and especially his hat were also very bad. Such was the aspect of the Herr Professor that no one would have taken him for anything but a gardener.[7]

Uffenbach was also critical of the classification used and thought that the number of items did not approach the interest of either the Leiden or Amsterdam botanic gardens. Italians, whose country had pioneered botanic gardens, could, like the Grand Duke of Tuscany in 1699, be even more superior, dismissing Oxford's which 'from the smallness of its size, irregularity, and bad cultivation scarcely deserves to be seen'.[8]

Nevertheless there were many satisfied European visitors to Bobart's garden and none more so than Dr Hermann of Leiden who was overjoyed to find there a plant he had collected

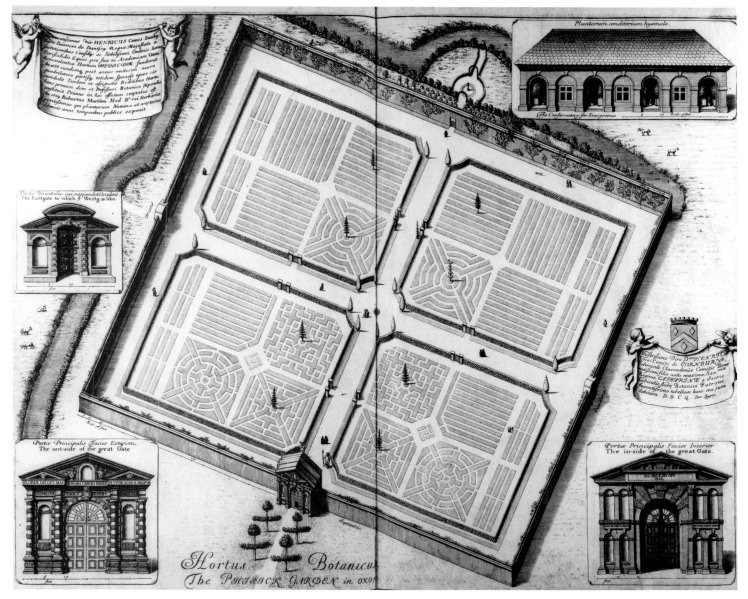

The following text appears on the engraving:

Plantarum conditorium hyemale.

(The Conservatory for Evergreenes)

Portæ Orientalis, cui respondet Occidens.
The Eastgate to which ye Westg is like.

Portæ Principalis Facies Exterior.
The out-side of the great Gate

Portæ Principalis Facies Interior.
The in-side of the great Gate.

Hortus Botanicus
The PHISICK GARDEN in OXON.

54. Loggan's plan of the Hortus Botanicus in 1675. The 'conservatory for evergreenes' in the top right corner was probably the first green house in England.

in India but had had hi-jacked by a French privateer on the way back.[9] Bobart immediately dug it up and gave it back to him. Abel Evans of St John's College recognized the true worth of the professor of botany and in 1713 praised him as 'Horticulture's Sapient King':

> Nothing in Africk, Asia shoots
> From Seeds, from layers, Grafts, or Roots,
> At both the Indies, both the Poles,
> Whate'er the Sea, or Ocean rolls,
> Of the Botanick, Herbal kind,
> Lies open to thy searching Mind.

Bobart circulated the first seed lists to invite exchanges and sold seeds himself to many owners of famous gardens such as Kirby, then in the making. An undergraduate from Cambridge, where there was no such physic garden, admired Bobart's work enviously and noted that 'whoever brings a new plant, one of whose species there is not in the Garden, is entitled to a handsome reward'.[10] Like all other visitors he enjoyed the Bobarts' well-known topiary 'yewmen of the guard', which can be seen just inside the Danby gate in the Loggan engraving,

and was told that the Duchess of Marlborough had offered £500 to have them transplanted to Blenheim.

Celia Fiennes was particularly pleased by her visit to Bobart's garden, where she tasted the sage and pinched the sensitive plant (*Mimosa pudica*), whose sensitive reactions had also intrigued John Evelyn:

> The Physick Garden afforded great diversion and pleasure, the variety of flowers and plants would have entertained one a week, the few remarkable things I tooke notice of was the Aloes plant which is like a great flag in shape leaves and coullour . . . there is also the Sensible plant, take but a leafe between finger and thumb and squeeze it and it immediately curles up together as if pained, and after some tyme opens abroad again, it looks in coullour like a filbert leafe but much narrower and long; there is also the Humble plant that grows on a long slender stalke and do but strike it, it falls flatt on the ground stalke and all, and after some tyme revives againe and stands up, but these are nice plants and are kept mostly under glass's, the aire being too rough for them.[11]

The first conservatory for tender plants, which Celia Fiennes mentioned, was built in Oxford in 1670, and is illustrated on the Loggan plan; its south wall backing the High Street still survives but its successors, which house tropical plants, succulents, orchids, insect-eating plants and water-lilies, are now on the opposite side of the garden. Today there is also an alpine garden, a fernery, grass garden, herbaceous borders, a water garden and a collection of historical roses. Outside the entrance, a rose garden commemorates Oxford's contribution to the science of antibiotics through the discovery of penicillin. The memorial garden designed by Dame Sylvia Crowe echoes the traditional long regular plots inside the Botanic Garden, where originally the professor stood at the head and lectured to medical students lining the sides of the systematic herb beds.

55 (left). The founder's gate and Magdalen tower with the long narrow garden beds in the foreground.

56 (right). The High Street garden designed by Dame Sylvia Crowe to echo the original physic garden in commemoration of the wartime discovery of penicillin.

KIRBY HALL
near GRETTON, NORTHAMPTONSHIRE

Kirby Hall, the home of the Hatton family, was one of the outstanding Elizabethan prodigy houses. In the seventeenth century it became horticulturally famous. The house and gardens, in the care of English Heritage, have remained fossilized in the period of its golden age. Modern visitors' first impressions of Kirby as they approach along the avenue are not of an abandoned stately home, and it comes as a surprise to many that it is in fact a shell. English Heritage's commitment to the restoration of the seventeenth-century gardens of this substantial ruin, therefore, has none of the question marks that apply to proposed gardens at ruined Kenilworth Castle.

Sir Christopher Hatton, who was made Lord Chancellor in 1587, was one of Queen Elizabeth's favourite courtiers. He was a promoter of Drake's great voyage of 1577 and Drake renamed his flagship the *Golden Hind* in honour of Hatton whose crest was 'a hind statant Or'.

57. The great garden as laid out after the early excavation in 1935. Now, following extensive research and archaeology, the gardens at Kirby are being authentically restored to the 1690 phase.

58. Survey of Kirby, 1584, showing the original extent of the Hatton gardens.

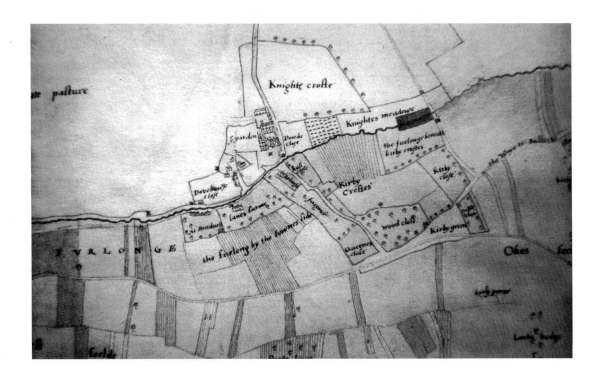

The house in which he entertained his sovereign was Holdenby, which he began to build in 1574 on a scale comparable with William Cecil's palatial house at Theobalds on which it was modelled. Holdenby was, like Theobalds, built to honour the queen. 'God send us both long to enjoy her for whom we both mean to exceed our purses in these buildings', wrote Cecil to Hatton. In spite of the great expense of building Holdenby, Hatton bought Kirby in 1576 after its owner, Sir Humphrey Stafford, died. He completed it and his son Christopher Hatton II entertained James I and Queen Anne there.

Surveys of the gardens at Holdenby and Kirby were made in the 1580s and they are shown to be quite different in scale. The Holdenby survey shows orchards, knot gardens, bowling alley, ponds, a wilderness, terraces and a banqueting house.[1] John Norden in 1610 found Holdenby 'a most pleasante, sweete, and princely Place with divers walks, manie ascendings and descendings replenished also with manie delightfull trees of Fruits, artificially composed Arbors, and a Distilling House'.[2] To achieve this spaciousness Hatton had swept away two small villages, leaving only the parish church to be incorporated into the garden. The Kirby survey of the same date shows only a garden to the west of the house and the site constrained by a church, cottages and village lands, but it was only a matter of time before this land was, as at Holdenby, also to be taken into the Hatton garden.[3]

There are few details about the Jacobean garden at Kirby. It was rectangular and enclosed by a terrace on the north and west sides retained by a brick wall; at the south end a free-standing brick wall linked the house and the west terrace. Pedimented gateways by

Nicholas Stone resemble those he erected in the Oxford Physic Garden in the 1630s. Christopher Hatton III went with the court to France in the Civil War and for most of the Commonwealth period but the Kirby gardens were maintained during his absence. Holdenby, on the other hand, was demolished in the Commonwealth and its gardens, which Norden thought would 'delight a prince', are now earthworks.

English Heritage will be restoring the 1690 phase of the Kirby gardens, when they were developed to their fullest extent and Christopher Hatton IV, who inherited in 1670, extended the garden south to develop a wilderness. The small mount seen today may be the remains of the church as John Bridges reported that 'where the mount now is, a cartload of bones was dug up about the year 1700'.[4] The distinct shape of the wilderness on the rising ground can be seen on the parish map of Deene. There was now a change of emphasis from the Jacobean rectangular garden in favour of open views out on to the newly acquired land, and the seat was no longer as Evelyn found it in 1654 'naked' without the avenues of approach he favoured.[5]

In terms of garden history the importance of this period, when Kirby was said to have 'the finest garden in England', is that Christopher Hatton was advised by his brother Captain Charles Hatton, a noted gentleman botanical collector. He was a friend of Robert Morison, the Oxford professor of botany, who called him 'a curious person, a great lover of flowers', and of John Ray of Cambridge, who dedicated his *Historia plantarum* to him in recognition of his great encouragement.[6] In *Acetaria* John Evelyn also bears testimony to 'the honourable and learned Charles Hatton, Esq. (to whom all our phytologists and lovers of horticulture are obliged, and myself in particular for many favours)'. John Morton, who wrote *The natural history of Northamptonshire* in 1712, said that the 'ingenious gentleman' Charles Hatton had first successfully propagated mistletoe from the seed on poplars round Kirby.[7] When Bridges visited Kirby in the 1720s he found 'the gardens here are beautiful, stocked with a great variety of exotic plants and adorned with a wilderness composed of almost the whole variety of English trees, and ranged in an elegant order'.[8]

Fortunately, Charles Hatton's voluminous correspondence with his brother about the 'curious' plants he was obtaining for Kirby is preserved, so that there is unusually accurate documentation of what was grown there. There was a new breed of curious traveller exchanging notes and plants with fellow garden enthusiasts with frequent mention by Hatton of Evelyn, Hans Sloane, Bishop Compton of Fulham Palace and Ashmole at Lambeth. Journeys were made by the virtuosi to see new flowerings and Hatton complained in 1688 that 'this year my Lord Mordant's tulipp tree flowered. My Lord Bishop justly complained of the stupidness of his gardener, who never gave notice to eny curious personns that it was in flower. It was a flower like a tulippe, but hung down like a Martagon . . . said to be a most beautifull flower'.[9]

In 1688 Charles Hatton reported on his visit to Bobart of the Oxford Physic Garden: 'I have settled a corrispondence with Mr Bobart and he hath in ye season promised me some curious plants that I design for your Lordship'.[10] The Chelsea Physic Garden, established in 1673, was another happy hunting ground for gardening virtuosi. In 1690 Hatton told his

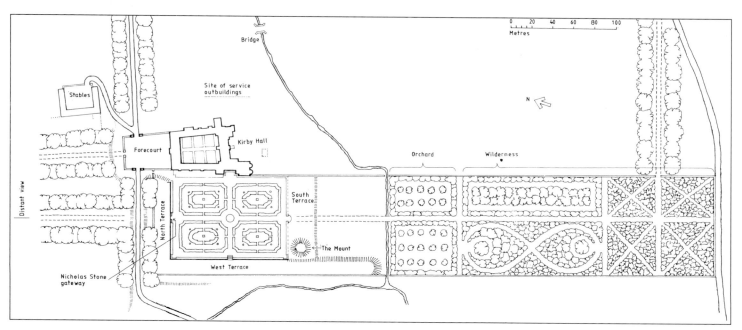

59. Plan of the garden as it is thought to have been in about 1700. The wilderness is on the right.

brother that 'I have been today at Chelsey garden and have made choice of two potts of the passion-flower, and am very confident your Lordship need not fear, but they will thrive very well . . . and if the gardener be careful to lay them well, by this time 12 month you may have 20 other'.[11] William and Mary's gardens at Hampton Court were a great source of inspiration and in 1694 Hatton was studying the glass cases there perpendicular to the sun's rays and with a subterranean system of heat and may have suggested these for Kirby.[12] Certainly in 1688, when the great gardener Henry Compton, the Bishop of London, visited Kirby, they were stoveless as Hatton wrote to his brother, 'if you desire very curious plants you must have a stove and I wish you would have a discourse with my Lord Bishop as to ye making, ordering and advantage of one'.[13]

Lists of the material Hatton obtained have been drawn up by English Heritage from the many sources and selected plants known to have been at Kirby will be used in the restoration, supplemented by those on a list drawn up by John Tradescant in 1656 which are still available in specialist nurseries.[14] By chance there is a connection with Castle Bromwich, which is also being restored according to archival and archaeological investigations.[15] In 1698 William Winde the architect wrote to Lady Mary Bridgeman, 'I shall tomorrow meet with Capt. Hatton, a very great vertuoso in gardening, to consult with him what plants or trees are most useful'.[16] Further archaeological investigation is needed to know where these exotic plants were grown at Kirby; it is assumed that those that did not require stoves were planted in the Privy garden, which has not yet been excavated.

The west or great garden has already been excavated. The excavation by George Chettle in 1935 was the first known example in this country of horticultural investigation by archaeology. It resulted in a plan of the paths and beds and the discovery of some of the stone edgings. In 1987 a much more detailed excavation has revealed details of the garden design and supplied information about the extent of levelling and earth-moving, drainage and revetment of the terraces undertaken in the creation of the famous Hatton gardens. An exhibition shows the work in progress and future plans for this exciting recreation of a Restoration garden by English Heritage.

HAMPTON COURT PALACE
HAMPTON, LONDON

Hampton Court has always been a show place and today it is, like the Tower of London and Windsor Castle, on every tourist's itinerary. 'This is the most splendid and most magnificent royal palace of any that may be found in England or indeed in any other kingdom' with 'many beautiful gardens both for pleasure and ornament', a much-travelled sixteenth-century visitor, the Duke of Württemberg, wrote in his journal.[1] The gardens of Hampton Court, even in Wolsey's day, were always at the height of fashion, indeed often led fashion until the eighteenth century. At the Restoration, Charles II, after his experience in exile of French gardens with their extended vistas, wanted to introduce the grand manner into the layouts of his palaces. After the king's marriage to Catherine of Braganza in May 1662 the royal pair spent three months at Hampton Court before their triumphal entry into Whitehall. A balcony in the queen's apartments had been gilded and on this the new French layout was

60. Aerial photograph (taken before the limes were felled) showing the bones of the Knyff layout (see Plate 43), with outsize yews in the *patte d'oie* and the Tijou screens bordering an unrecognizable Privy garden on the south front.

aligned. In June Evelyn noted 'the Park, formerly a flat, naked piece of Ground, now planted with sweete rows of lime-trees, and the Canale for Water neere perfected'.[2] As in the Mollet design at St James's Park the canal was the central line of the royal gardener's *patte d'oie*.

A much grander layout was planned when the Dutch King William and his wife Queen Mary made Hampton Court their principal residence in 1689 and directed Wren to extend and modernize the Tudor palace. William already had a most impressive Dutch royal garden with fifty fountains at Het Loo, said by Walter Harris to be 'a Work of wonderful Magnificence, most worthy of so great a Monarch'.[3] John Evelyn visiting Hampton Court 'about business' on 16 July 1689 saw that 'a spacious garden with fountains was beginning in the park at the head of the canal', which would be seen from the state apartments in Wren's magnificent new east front.[4] To complement his building Wren had retained the main elements of Charles II's scheme, the *patte d'oie* and the Long Water canal, although this was shortened to make the great semicircle outlined with an arcade of trees and radiating avenues. The king, not satisfied with grand spatial concepts alone, employed Daniel Marot, the Huguenot *émigré* who had been the king's designer in Holland, to design parterres to fill in the great semicircle. Jean Tijou designed the beautiful and elaborate wrought-iron screens originally intended for the Great Fountain garden, but now seen at the end of the Privy garden, which for Sir Sacheverell Sitwell were 'the absolute embodiment of the age . . . as personal as the tread of the courtiers, the cut of their clothes, or the accents of their voices'.[5]

The William and Mary gardens were much admired by visitors but most of the descriptions of the Great Fountain garden are of a later period when it was simplified by Queen Anne in a 'plain but noble manner' in Stephen Switzer's view, and it is not clear whether the elaborate Marot broderie parterre was carried out. Queen Mary died in December 1694 and William lost interest in Hampton Court. Virtually no work was done there until 1699, when in April he paid his first visit for five years, and before he left for Holland for the summer ordered that the palace should be made ready to receive the court, Whitehall Palace having been put out of action by a disastrous fire. One person who saw Hampton Court in the in-between period, when all the rooms Queen Mary had loved were shut and the gardens still uncompleted, was Celia Fiennes: 'the gardens were designed to be very fine, great fountaines and grass plotts and gravell walkes and just against the middle of the house was a very large fountaine and beyond it a large Cannal guarded by rows of even trees that runn a good way; there was fine carving in the Iron Gates in the Gardens with all sorts of figures, and iron spikes round a breast wall and severall rows of trees'.[6]

The parterre, if ever completed, was probably newly-finished for the Kip engraving in 1701, shortly after the court went into residence. King William died early in 1702 and Queen Anne dismantled the Great Fountain garden. According to Defoe the queen disliked the smell of box and had the edgings removed, but these were replanted by Queen Caroline. The plain Queen Anne parterre is described by Zacharias von Uffenbach, who saw in 1710 'a great garden in a semi-circle figure, consisting of nothing but grass-plots but with beautiful metal and alabaster statues in it'.[7] Celia Fiennes revisited Hampton Court in 1712, while Anne was still alive, and described from the leads the 'vast sight all about of the park and gardens'. The

61 (left). The Privy garden,
c.1697, by Sutton Nicholls with
its grass cutwork before it was
extended and redesigned by
Henry Wise in 1701. The
Arethusa fountain was moved to
Bushy Park in 1713.

Privy garden had by then been redesigned by Henry Wise into 'a cross which cutts the grass
plotts into four, which are cutt into flower deluces and severall devices with paths of gravell,
borders of mould in which are greens of all sorts, piramids and then round interchangeable'.[8]
The alternating clipped greens mentioned would have been dark green obelisk yews
contrasting with globes of silver or variegated hollies.

Queen Mary was greatly interested in flowers and always had cut flowers in her
apartments. The ground floor of the south front, which looked on to the Privy garden was, as
described by Daniel Defoe, used as an orangery: 'The Orange Trees, and fine Dutch Bays, are
plac'd within the Arches of the Building under the first Floor: so that the lower part of the
House was all one as a Green House for some Time'.[9]

Until Queen Mary's death in 1694 her Water Gallery with its special Delftware closet
was at the southern end of the Privy garden, and here 'she ordered all the little, neat, curious
Things to be done, which suited her own Convenience, and made it the pleasantest little
Place within Doors, that could possibly be made'.[10] She also had the pond garden area 'laid
out into small Inclosures, surrounded with Tall hedges to break the Violence of the Winds'
and a so-called 'glass case' garden where she grew her special florists' flowers, auriculas,
polyanthuses, finely striped tulips and Marvel of Peru. Captain Hatton on the look out for
plants for Kirby noted 'the finest collection of amaranths and hollyoke I believe were ever seen
in England, and besides severall very curious plants, a very rare and beautiful one, a tuberous

62. The beautiful wrought-iron
screens by Jean Tijou at the end
of the Privy garden were
originally intended for the Great
Fountain garden.

hyacinth with a blew flower but it hath noe smell'.[11] After Mary's death, when the Water
Gallery was demolished, the Privy garden was lengthened and in 1700 a small banqueting
house built out of an old Tudor garden tower for King William.

The Hampton Court was singled out by the natural landscape improvers as the bastion of
regularity, the clipped evergreens being particularly vilified. As the century wore on the
clamour got louder and one anonymous minor poet having deplored the long gravel walks,
'puerile knots of flowers' and 'tonsur'd bushes' thankfully escaped to the 'rural meads' outside,
finding 'what these gardens want, in them we meet'. Foreign visitors on the look-out for the
much vaunted English landscaped gardens were particularly surprised to find a royal palace, of
which so much was expected, still with a formal layout. Count Frederick Kielmansegge, over
for George III's coronation in 1761, found that 'the garden is not in the present English style,
being far too regular with its cut hedges and an artificial labyrinth'.[12] Capability Brown, who
as royal gardener lived at the Wilderness House, is said to have declined to naturalize the
famous royal layout 'out of respect to himself and his profession', but could not bring himself to
clip the evergreens formally. He is remembered for planting the Hampton Court vine in 1768.

The antiquaries turned the tide by pointing out the historical interest of the garden and
in 1892, Reginald Blomfield, the formal garden revivalist, lovingly dwelt on the various
features, the long canal, Tijou's wrought-iron screens, alleys, arbours and sundials, which
were worthy of emulation.[13] It was left to the historian Ernest Law, who lived at the Bowling
Green House, to make a positive appraisal of Hampton Court's garden history in 1890. He
worked through public records and revived the old names that had gone into disuse, the
Tiltyard, the Pond Yard and the Wilderness and in 1924 laid out an Elizabethan knot garden
against the Tudor brickwork modelled on his work for Shakespeare's garden at New Place (see
p.39). At his suggestion the Tiltyard was made into lawns and gardens and the one
remaining spectators' viewing tower converted into a tea-house. The Tijou screens which had
been sent to various museums in the nineteenth century were also rounded up and replaced as
part of the restoration.

Today Hampton Court is recognized as the country's most historic garden and much of
its historic layout does still remain, but it is not always apparent to the visitor, who looks
rather to the herbaceous borders along the brick walls in Broad Walk and the Tiltyard rose
gardens. Like Jerome K. Jerome's three men in a boat, everybody knows that Hampton Court
has a famous maze but few realize it is of late seventeenth-century origin or why the garden
round it is called the Wilderness. The planned baroque relationship between the palace
and the landscape still dominates the layout and planning applications to build high
rise developments at the end of the Long Vista have so far been refused. After public consul-
tation the misshapen limes in Wren's semicircular arcade were felled and replanted in
1986. The huge pyramid yews in the Fountain garden, which were intended to be small
obelisks in Marot's parterre, have a history of their own, having been clipped until the
mid-eighteenth century, when they were left to range freely, as Jefferson noted,[14] and then
in Law's day, when vastly overgrown, clipped into pyramids again. Along the Broad Walk,
where topiary has long been abandoned, the original heights of some of the hollies can

63. The banqueting house built for King William in 1700 by the original Pond Yard.

be seen by wrinkles on the bark showing where they were clipped into balls and obelisks.

It would be out of the question to restore the costly William and Mary Fountain garden with its parterres and fountains, and it is best left to the 'plain but noble manner' of the *parterre à l'anglaise* which displays the excellence of English turf and allows the eye to glide down the canal vista. The Privy garden is another matter as it was maintained in its original design for much longer and the essential historic features of the garden remain. The visitor can still walk along Queen Mary's long bower, where she loved to sit and sew with her ladies. The sundial outside the Upper Orangery overlooking the Privy garden bears William and Mary's cypher. The garden was lowered for King William to give a view of the Thames and the Barge walk beyond the Tijou screen from the orangery. This effect is completely lost today by overgrown planting and many visitors on the obvious circuit do not even see the magnificent wrought-iron screen. Henry Wise's parterre, seen by Celia Fiennes, is now obliterated by overgrown trees and shrubs, but its outlines still survive and, if restored, could be viewed to advantage from the surrounding terraces and bring back something of the spirit of the Wren age at Hampton Court.

LEVENS HALL
LEVENS, CUMBRIA

William and Mary's gardens at Hampton Court can now only be evoked through historical presentation, but at Levens Hall we can walk into a layout of the same period virtually intact. It was one of the first gardens to be admired by visitors as a historic garden and was indeed one of the few that, before the days of restoration and recreation, could be seen as a living survival of seventeenth-century gardening. 'Precious indeed, are the few remaining gardens that have anything of the character of this wonderful one of Levens: gardens that above all others show somewhat of the actual feeling and temperament of our ancestors', wrote Gertrude Jekyll in 1904.[1]

It was the feeling that gardeners had for two centuries clipped the same topiary shapes that Guillaume Beaumont had designed for Colonel Grahme in 1689, that awakened the visitor's historical sense. Lord Stanhope, the nineteenth-century historian, reacted with typical sentimentality: 'So complete has the change proved that at present, through the whole of England, there remains perhaps scarcely more than one private garden presenting in all its parts an entire and true sample of the old designs; this is at the fine old seat at Levens, near Kendal. There, along a wide extent of terraced walks and walls, eagles of holly and peacocks of yew still find each returning summer their wings clipped and their talons pared'.[2]

The *Country Life* reporter in 1899 was similarly enchanted by Beaumont's topiary surviving as the 'happiest example' that England possessed:

> It is an ideal and grotesque world we enter when we tread in the pleasure-place of Colonel Graham and of M. Beaumont, the gardener who came from France.
> Fantastic forms rise in yew, strange and remarkable, as far as the eye can reach—a peacock here, a huge umbrella-like construction there, an archway, a lion and a crown, a helmet bigger than any man could wear, and a host of other such creations, all shaped out of ductile yew, except that some of smaller adornments are in box. A bewildering world of gardening, some may say![3]

Beaumont might not have been altogether pleased that Levens came to be seen primarily as a topiary garden which through years of growth had turned into a 'grotesque world'. Early eighteenth-century visitors came to see more than 'fantastic forms'.

Although Levens garden was created in the year of William's accession, it was not, like the Duke of Devonshire's at Chatsworth, a result of newly won favours, for Colonel Grahme, who had been Privy Purse to James II, had been on the wrong side of the Glorious Revolution. He had also been made supervisor of the royal gardens in succession to Hugh May in 1683 and Guillaume Beaumont had acted under him.[4] Both found themselves out of a job in 1689 and Colonel Grahme took the Frenchman back to Levens, where they concentrated on laying out the park and gardens for the newly acquired property. Guillaume Beaumont was certainly a gifted gardener trained in the Le Nôtre tradition. Alicia Amherst, who researched seventeenth-century gardens for her *History of gardening in England*, published in 1895, recognized the Levens gardens as 'something unique' and referred to Beaumont as 'one of the French gardeners sent over when Le Nôtre, the great designer of Versailles, was supplying plans to Charles II'.[5] His portrait at Levens is inscribed 'Monsieur Beaumont. Gardener to King James II and to Col. Jas. Grahme. He laid out the gardens at Hampton Court palace and at Levens'. There is little record of what Beaumont did at Hampton Court before he was replaced by George London but there is extensive documentation for his work at Levens.[6] His layout as seen on the 'Map of Leavens garding' largely remains: the beech hedge and great circle and his designs for the garden and park with its great avenue. The garden was divided into compartments, the parterre with formal beds and topiary being one of them. Beaumont's design was kept intact by generations of owners and head gardeners for whom he was a legend.

Visitors flocked to see Levens in the eighteenth century from Kendal and from as far

64. The seventeenth-century garden at Levens from Joseph Nash's *Mansions of England in olden times*, 1849. The illustrations evoked 'historical atmosphere' for the benefit of sentimental tourists.

away as London and, as one note shows, permission to visit had to be obtained from Beaumont, who had his own house in one of the garden vistas, which was referred to locally as 'Beaumont's Castle'.

> To Mr Beaumont att Leavens   July the 23 1727
>   Sr the bearers hereof being part of my family hath a desire to se the Garden at leavenss if it may be a proper time to admittt them & their acquaintance itt will be taken as a great favour & will much oblige
>   Sr your humble servtt Robt Hubbersley   they are all honestt neighbours.[7]

Bishop Nicholson on a visit in 1704 admired 'the maze with Lime-trees, Chestnuts, beech etc'.[8] This may have been on a smaller scale than the Hampton Court wilderness in which Beaumont is thought to have had a hand.

The park in the beautiful Westmorland countryside delighted the eighteenth-century picturesque eye. West's *Guide to the Lakes* found it 'the sweetest spot that fancy can imagine', and William Gilpin, the ultimate Picturesque traveller, approved of the 'happy combination of everything that is lovely and great in landscape',[9] but he did not see the topiary gardens otherwise he might have deplored, as did Joseph Budworth, a disciple of Rousseau, 'the heavy taste of a man that had deformed the beauties of nature'.[10]

In the early nineteenth century nine miles of box hedging was replanted within the formal gardens and extensive restoration carried out. The contrast of the wild riverside parkland and the formality within the walled garden surrounding the house was something of a novelty for visitors from the south. When walls and hedges had been removed as part of landscape improvement such a contrast between untamed and tamed nature within the estate had largely been lost in England. Walled gardens had always prevailed across the border, however, and remote Westmorland would have had more in common with Scotland than with Hagley and Stowe or even Studley Royal. Gertrude Jekyll, who in her Surrey woodland home had advocated that a garden should melt imperceptibly into the landscape, was enthusiastic about the effect of contrast at Levens:

> The river Kent, a rock-strewn stream with steep wooded banks, flows within 50 yards of the house. The contrast is a great and delightful one. Wild parkland and untamed river without; and within the walls ordered restraint; then again, the quiet of the wide bowling-green, with its dark clipped hedges, and beyond it a long tree-shaded walk.[11]

Formal revivalist garden designers, of whom H. Inigo Thomas, who illustrated Levens for Blomfield's *The formal garden* in 1892, was one, relied heavily on the *Britannia illustrata* bird's-eye engravings by Kip for inspiration. The new *Country Life* magazine made the revivalist gardens one of their specialities and in 1899 in an article on Levens rejoiced that designers could actually visit an authentically old garden to pursue their studies, rather than rely on engravings:

65. Today, when historic gardens are being recreated after painstaking research, Levens is unique in having had continuous historic maintenance.

There are recent gardens of the old character, too. But go where we will, we shall find nothing in its kind to rival ancient Levens. No other place in England possesses so much old and curious topiary work. Elvaston, the seat of the Earl of Harrington, which we have illustrated and described, is perhaps as striking in its character, but there is this distinction between the two, that while Levens is an old representative garden, Elvaston is a wonderful creation of modern times.[12]

66. George Samuel Elgood's watercolour from *Some English gardens*, with commentary by Gertrude Jekyll, 1904. Levens Hall was much visited by lovers of gardencraft and the old-fashioned gardens. (Private Collection)

Early garden historians, such as Alicia Amherst, were a little puzzled as to whether Levens should be called French or Dutch style. Guillaume Beaumont may have been trained in the French tradition, but such concentration on the art of topiary was surely Dutch. Inigo Triggs, in his book *Formal gardens in England and Scotland*, agreed that 'the old Dutch garden at Levens Hall is probably the most perfect example, remaining in England, of a garden designed under the Dutch influence prevalent soon after the accession of William and Mary, although curiously enough the designer happened to be a Frenchman'.[13] It is now appreciated that there was a great overlap in French and Dutch garden design especially when the two influences reached seventeenth-century England together. Celia Fiennes was not bothered by continental influences. She took delight in what was appropriate and commendable in William and Mary gardens. Levens was off her route, but she would undoubtedly have found much to admire in Beaumont's garden in 'the mode that now is'.

WESTBURY COURT
WESTBURY-ON-SEVERN, GLOUCESTERSHIRE

Westbury Court's survival is unique: no other such water-garden of the late seventeenth century weathered the winds of change which swept away formal layouts in the succeeding century. Its survival after the 1960s is also remarkable: it was one of the first restorations—in the sense of being historically accurate—undertaken, and signalled a new awareness in modern treatment of historic gardens.

The estate's history—one of short-lived houses and a long-lived garden—is simple, given that after the early eighteenth century it seems to have been altered hardly at all. The core of the house shown in Kip's engraving published in 1712 was Tudor, built for Sir

67. Westbury with its water garden, shortly after completion, from an engraving by Johannes Kip, published in Atkyns: *Ancient and present state of Glocestershire*, 1712.

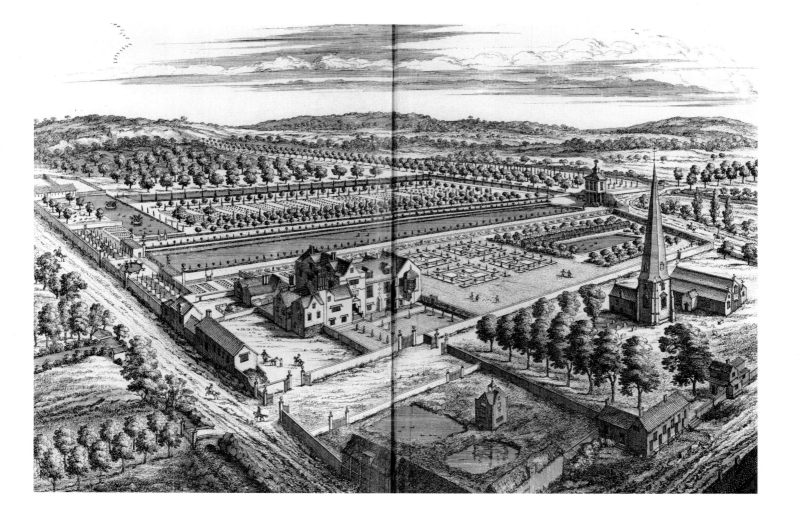

Alexander Baynham in the early sixteenth century. In 1619 it was bought by a lawyer, Nicholas Roberts, who made additions to it, and then in 1641 it passed to his nephew Richard Colchester. Colchester's son, Duncomb, was rewarded with a knighthood after the Restoration for his loyalty to Charles I, but by the time he died in 1694 little seems to have been done to either the house or garden. It was his son, Maynard, married to an heiress, who began to improve the estate. Interestingly, the garden rather than the house was his priority. His account books for the years 1696 to 1705 give a detailed record of its construction. The long canal was built in 1696, and the pavilion in 1702–3; payments in 1698 to 'Thos. Wintle for laying 87,850 bricks' (at 3/6 per thousand), and in 1699 for laying 120,800 bricks, indicate the dates of the walls, while the iron rails for the first *claire-voie* were paid for in October 1702.[1]

Colchester died in 1715 and was succeeded by his son Maynard Colchester II. He had the T-shaped canal built, along with the second *claire-voie*, the gazebo and little walled garden in the east corner. In the 1740s he also had the house rebuilt in the modern Palladian style, and it showed strong individual judgement so to have ignored the rule of taste as to preserve an old formal garden with such a house. It was judged a success by the Gloucestershire historian Samuel Rudder, who in 1779 described the ensemble as 'an elegant house, in modern taste, with beautiful canals, and extensive pleasure gardens'.[2]

That house was in turn demolished in 1805 when the family moved to their other estate at Micheldean. Then in 1895 they came back to Westbury and built a new house, not on the original site but attached to the pavilion in the south-west corner. In the early twentieth century the garden was in beautiful condition, as shown in the set of *Country Life* photographs of 1908,[3] but by 1960 when it was finally sold to a developer by Colchester's descendants it must already have been decaying. The house was then demolished, the pavilion damaged and the wall that ran the length of the canal was knocked down.

68. The canal and pavilion at Westbury, restored by the National Trust.

In 1962 Westbury was sought out by Miles Hadfield, a founder and later president of the Garden History Society, after he had read of it in the press. Hadfield later described peering through the grilles from the lay-by to see 'packed willow-herb, many years' accumulation of it, the height of a man. Beyond antique, distorted yews we could see the gem of a pavilion'. He and his companion broke in, and attempted to draw a sketch plan of the green, weed-filled canals and their rotting margins. 'An old deserted garden,' he wrote, 'has a compelling spiritual attraction'.[4] Publicity followed, and in 1964 the County and District Councils were prompted to buy the site. They erected much-needed old people's housing on the land north of the drive and offered the garden to the National Trust. The results of the garden's subsequent restoration by the Trust can now be judged by the modern visitor.

In the past Westbury seems to have been little visited by garden tourists. On the north shore of the Severn and backed by the Forest of Dean, it was off the route for tours of the south-west and during the eighteenth century the garden would have been too old-fashioned to lure people out of their way. But in the 1690s it was modern in style and it now shows, as no other surviving formal garden does, the influence of Dutch gardening in the time of William and Mary. At Westbury the canals, the steep pitched roof of the pavilion, the profuse use of evergreens, and the modest rectilinear design are all Dutch characteristics. In the 1890s Westbury was rediscovered by enthusiasts for the formal garden and Inigo Triggs, who classed it unequivocally as a 'Dutch garden', included a plan and two plates in his book, *Formal gardens in England and Scotland*.[5]

In the Kip engraving we can see along the canal the 'greens of all sorts, piramids and then round interchangeable' which William promoted.[6] The fashionable use of yew and box for hedging is well illustrated at Westbury and we can experience the intimacy and formal structure they create, preserving what Defoe called 'the figure of the place'.[7] In the hedged rectangle between the canals the Trust has also planted box 'cutt close in four squares down to the bottom, towards the top . . . enclined to a point or spire'.[8] The parterre which has been created beyond the T-shaped canal is modelled on that shown in Kip on the land now occupied by the old people's flats.

At Westbury too we can see, among other features typical of the late seventeenth century, how the vegetable garden was included in the ornamental layout. In the most fashionable gardens fruit trees were an integral part of the pleasure garden; a fashion made still more popular by King William who at Het Loo had dwarf apple trees planted round the parterres. Celia Fiennes would partake of 'apricock, peach, plumb, necktarine' as she strolled round the garden, and she describes seeing 'dwarfe trees of fruite and flowers and greenes in all shapes, intermixt with beds of strawberyes for ornament and use'. Now, on the west wall at Westbury the modern tourist can still see the kind of fruit Celia Fiennes would have eaten: Lemon Pippin, Golden Reinette and Catshead apples; Black Worcester and Beurre Brown pears, greengages and Fotheringham plums, all 'nail'd neate' in espaliers, in the way she admired.[9] Also in the beds along this wall are tulips and other flowers of the type grown when the garden was laid out. The species and cultivars now at Westbury represent a seventeenth-century collection.

The iron railings in the wall at the ends of the canals are fine examples of *claires-voies*. The first, at the end of the long canal, was made for Maynard Colchester I, with delicately-wrought alternate straight and twisted rails, flanked by piers topped with imposing pineapples. The second was built by Maynard II, probably soon after 1715, and is less ornate. These 'grates to look through' were designed not only to 'discover the curiosities' within the garden to passers-by, but also to reveal 'open views into the park' from within the walled garden. Colchester had an avenue planted in the field across the road to draw the eye out still further from the enclosure and to extend his 'visto'. Celia Fiennes remarks of one garden in Somerset, 'its capable of being very handsome if made with open grates to let one out to see the orchards and woods beyond'.[10] Having been told by Horace Walpole that it was William Kent who 'leaped the fence and saw that all nature was a garden', we may be surprised to discover how seventeenth-century garden enthusiasts like Celia Fiennes and, evidently, the Colchesters enjoyed open views out of the garden.

69 (left). The newly made parterre at Westbury, based on the design shown behind the old house in Kip's view.

70. The wall to the public road at Westbury, showing the *claires-voies*, which 'discover the curiosities' within.

CASTLE BROMWICH HALL
BIRMINGHAM

On the eastern fringe of Birmingham, just off the M6, Castle Bromwich Hall pokes its eaves and tower above a rare spot of greenery. Within that greenery, beneath a rampant tangle of neglected undergrowth, the buildings, paths, walls and hedges of a complete early eighteenth-century formal garden have slept largely undisturbed. Now they have been discovered by more erudite explorers than tramps and local children, and a trust has been set up to restore as authentically as possible this unique survivor.

The garden which is now re-emerging dates mainly from the time of Sir John Bridgeman I and his wife Lady Mary. Bridgeman bought the hall in 1657 from the Devereux family, who had built it in about 1599. Lady Mary consulted her husband's cousin, the soldier turned architect, William Winde, about the design of the garden. Apart from advice on planting and layout, he supplied ornate dolphin-patterns for the parterres in the 'Best Garden' adjacent to the house, to be made with coloured sand and gravel. The small garden north of the house was to be ornamented, according to one of his letters to Lady Mary, with 'a statue in ye middel & flower pottes on ye sydes, or Else Cypress Trees or as yr Ladp shall beste please yr selfe'.[1] There was evidently a close collaboration between Winde and the owners.

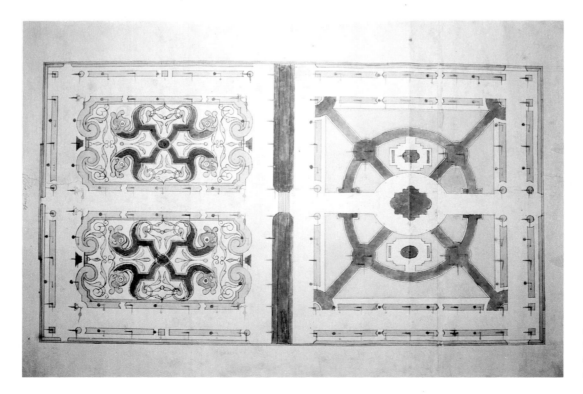

71. William Winde's dolphin design for the Best Garden at Castle Bromwich. The delicate colours would have been picked out in coloured sand and gravel.

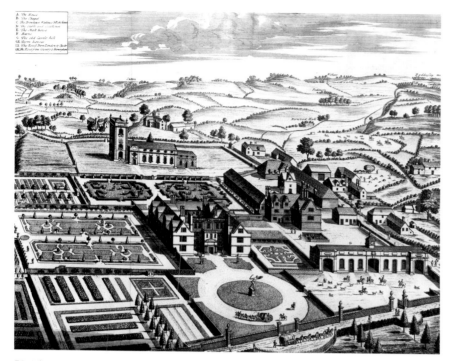

72 (above left). Henry Beighton's bird's-eye view of Castle Bromwich, 1726. The newly acquired land to the west is not included, presumably because garden work was not yet complete.

73 (above right). The newly restored orangery at Castle Bromwich. The restoration at Castle Bromwich is painstakingly authentic. When complete it will show the garden tourist precisely what an early eighteenth-century formal layout looked like.

Winde also introduced the Bridgemans to various other experts, including George London, whom he described as 'ye beste gardiner in Endgland', and Captain Charles Hatton, brother of Viscount Hatton of Kirby Hall. Winde corresponded with Charles Hatton on the design of the wilderness which was planted on the terrace now bounded by the holly walk, while London supplied two alternative designs to Winde's for the Best Garden parterre.

The wilderness, far from being wild, was planted with exotics in hedged enclosures. Hatton suggested that apart from the 'Hag-Berry' (rowan) and the 'quicken' (hawthorn), the Bridgemans should plant 'all manner of Exotick ever Green'. He listed among others bay, laurel, pyracantha, laurustinus and gilded phillyrea. These, he wrote, should be combined with flowering shrubs—laburnum, lilacs, jasmines, roses, the spindle tree (for its berries, 'being of a pretty coulour and phantastic shape'), woodbines, dwarf almond, hypericum and sumac.[2]

Sir John died in 1710 and his son, also John, inherited the hall and the estate. He extended the gardens westwards, down to their present boundary, where he built the ornate west wall. He laid out the Holly Walk, with the Orangery and Music Room at either end. It is not certain yet what he planted in the lowest section: there were certainly vegetable beds laid out to either side, but the maze, although its pattern is a London design, is first referred to only in the nineteenth century. Of his planting here only four ancient yews survive—a tantalizing fragment. Elsewhere, in 1733, he reported to his son, 'I am making in my Garden House (in the Best Garden) a Cold Bath, and adjoyning to it, have a room with a fire place in it'.[3] It is into this room that the door in the north wall of the Best Garden leads. A possible influence on Sir John's outlook is Joseph Addison, author of the *Spectator* essays on gardens as a 'pleasure of the imagination'. He had married a cousin of the Bridgemans, and his daughter was made their ward. His home at Bilton Grange, near Rugby, was close enough to allow him to make visits, and given the family connection such visits seem quite likely.

The garden was depicted in a print of 1726 by Henry Beighton, although he does not include the newly acquired area to the west, presumably because its laying out was not at that time completed. The illustration shows that the gardens emerging from the jungle are little changed in nearly 250 years.

In 1719 Bridgeman's son, Orlando, married into the family of the Earls of Bradford and, as a result of various deaths without issue, the Bradford estates passed to the Bridgeman family in 1762. These included Weston Park in Staffordshire, and the family promptly left Castle Bromwich for Weston, which has remained their home to this day. It was perhaps to this move above all that Castle Bromwich's survival is owed, because at Weston Sir Orlando's son employed Capability Brown to improve the garden. Some ripples of the new style did reach Castle Bromwich: yews were felled in the wilderness, and old hedges were dug out, but little was done to alter the symmetrical, axial layout.

As an uninhabited, unimproved old house, Castle Bromwich was passed over by eighteenth-century tourists. In an age of sweeping new styles, there was little interest in an old-fashioned garden. Richard Jago in his topographical poem of 1767, *Edgehill*, contrasted Bridgeman's 'fair Scenes' with the 'smoaky Scene' of Birmingham, but was prevented by 'envious Time' from entering upon a description.[4] Viscount Torrington in 1790, looking back on the day's travel noted that at Castle Bromwich 'there is, seemingly a good inn—with a fine old mansion of Sir Hy. Bridgman (now to be let); one of those venerables—the seat of ancient hospitality; which perhaps I ought to have seen'.[5]

In the later nineteenth century, however, a new historical awareness, albeit often a romanticized and fanciful one, made survivals like Castle Bromwich once more a place to visit. In 1872 the *Gardeners' Chronicle* included the garden on one of its tours:

> To pass into the quiet of the courtyard of the fine old Elizabethan mansion is to go back three centuries. Nothing seems changed. Were one to meet courtiers in slashed hose and broad-toed velvet shoes the sight would scarcely create astonishment. The garden is quite in keeping with the mansion; it is of the old style—old. The terrace walks, the geometric beds, the rose arcades, the clipped hedges, the dense shrubberies, all speak of a bygone age, and produce a feeling of melancholy. One may wander about here as in a dream, and ignore the existence of such things as telegraphs and railways, and the feverish haste of the 19th century.[6]

The garden at this date was not, however, just a quaint and fossilized remain. From 1870, with one break between 1898 and 1915, Lady Ida Bridgeman, wife of George Bridgeman, 4th Earl of Bradford, lived at the hall until her death in 1936 and devoted much of her time to the gardens. She replanted hedges, and made new beds for the parterres, and while her work was not restoration as such, she did aim to recapture the spirit of the old garden. In 1891 Lady Ida wrote an account of the hall and gardens for the *Pall Mall Magazine*: she led the reader from the house, into the centre of the Best Garden, 'which is laid out in four sets of formal beds', to 'a large stone vase, and on either side are arches over which are trained Noisette roses, red, white and pink.' From here she takes us down the steps, between thick box hedges into the next garden, where 'all is given up to shrubberies and lawn. Grassy paths intersect the shrubberies, which are filled with flowering shrubs and trees of all kinds'. Beyond this, 'a wide

74. Castle Bromwich in Lady Ida's time; photograph from *Country Life*, 1900.

grass glade, known as the Archery Ground, bounded on the lower side by variegated holly hedges, about thirty feet high'. Across the wide gravel walk between them, we are led to 'the third and lowest terrace of the Garden', with its shrubberies 'radiating' from 'an ancient stone vase', 'with grassy paths intersecting'; and its maze 'planted in holly and quick and . . . laid out on the same plan as the one at Hampton Court'.[7] The garden she is showing the reader around is full of shrubs and flowers which she has planted, but the predominant feeling is of the past.

A *Country Life* article of 1900 is illustrated with beautiful photographs of Lady Ida's garden: its quaint formality made it of great interest to an age which was rediscovering the formal garden in England, under the guidance of Alicia Amherst, Inigo Thomas, Sir Reginald Blomfield and others.[8]

After Lady Ida's death, the hall was abandoned by the family for good. In 1947 the gardens were covenanted to the National Trust, but during the 1970s they suffered greatly from neglect and vandalism. In 1985 Castle Bromwich Hall Gardens Trust was launched, supported by local authorities, the present Earl of Bradford, and various charities and expert bodies. Its aim is an authentic restoration of the garden to the period 1680–1740. The restoration is based not only on archival research but on extensive archaeological fieldwork. Although the gardens are now open to visitors, it will probably not be before the mid-1990s that the work is finally completed. Then, incredibly, a formal garden of the early eighteenth century will bloom newly planted at the dawn of the twenty-first.

MELBOURNE HALL
MELBOURNE, DERBYSHIRE

Melbourne is the only surviving Queen Anne garden laid out by the royal gardener Henry Wise, his other work at Hampton Court, Blenheim, Chatsworth and Longleat having been obliterated. The garden was made for Queen Anne's Vice-Chamberlain Sir Thomas Coke, a man of taste and an amateur architect. Sir Thomas had no sons and the hall passed down the line to daughters who lived elsewhere and were content for the garden to be kept up as it was in the days of Queen Anne. The only concession to fashionable landscaping that took place was allowing Wise's stunted trees to grow freely, so that it was all there for garden historians, lovers of the Queen Anne style and formal revivalists to discover at the end of the nineteenth century. The plan that Inigo Triggs made and published in *Formal gardens in England and Scotland* in 1902 did not differ greatly from the estate plan of 1722 and visitors today still see much of what Alicia Amherst described as 'not only one of the most beautiful gardens of which the date is ascertained, but a perfect example of a garden laid out by the designers London and Wise, famous in their day'.[1] Many of Coke's garden bills and notes survive to give a detailed picture of the laying out of the garden.

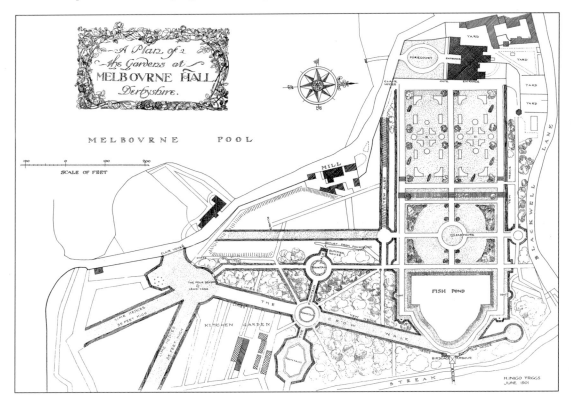

75. The plan of Melbourne in 1901 by H. Inigo Triggs from his *Formal gardens of England and Scotland* does not differ greatly from the estate plan of 1722.

76. The birdcage built by the local blacksmith Robert Bakewell had just been finished when the Duchess of Chandos visited in 1706.

The garden was adapted from an earlier one, with formal terraced walks, flower gardens and square fishponds with planted islands, which complemented the Jacobean house with its Stuart portraits and furnishings which had belonged to Sir John Coke, the Secretary of State to Charles I. Thomas Coke, who was to build on a new east wing to the house and remodel the gardens, succeeded in 1692. He lost no time in ordering plants: 'dwarf apples grafted on Paradise stocks from Brompton Park [the London and Wise nursery] and trees I saw at the Bishop of London's [Fulham Palace]; liburnam, flowering maple of Virginia'. In the garden books he gives delightful instructions for 'things to be done whilest I am away . . . to make a bed behind ye espalier but close to it of violetts . . . severall sorts of hony Suckles, heehocks, Seringos and in ye middle a close arbour'.[2] Coke was also probably responsible for the yew walk tunnel which Blomfield found to be 120 paces long and 12 foot wide which he said was like Queen Mary's wych elm tunnel at Hampton Court. The Van Nost figures in lead, Perseus, Andromeda, Mercury and Psyche, which give such character to the garden groves were bought in 1699. This garden with its wilderness of sweets obviously delighted Thomas Coke's sister Betsy even before the improved Henry Wise plan was implemented: 'I don't know what to say of your garden, but as I used to do—mighty pleasant and sweet', she wrote after the improvements.[3]

The contract for the garden had been signed in 1704 after Wise had sent two proposals; the one to be carried out, according to Coke, was said 'to suit with Versailles'. Betsy had been left to superintend the works while her brother was in London so it was with some relief that she wrote in the summer of 1705: 'All the dust and noisy works of your garden is finished. . . . I believe you will be much pleased with them and these late rains have refreshed the turfs and the trees, that you will find it in great beauty'.[4] Queen Anne presented a lead vase of the Four Seasons by Van Nost for one of the rond-points in the new garden which Blomfield described as 'the most magnificent lead vase in England. It stands on a stone pedestal some 5feet 3 from the ground. The vase itself, which is 7feet high, is supported by 4 monkeys and richly ornamented; its modelling is admirable'.[5]

When the Duchess of Chandos visited, the crowning glory of the French birdcage built by the local blacksmith Robert Bakewell had just been added in 1706, 'the most extraordinary observed in ye garden—an Arbour or Summer House made of very neat ironwork'.[6] The intention was that inside the wrought-iron treillage should be 'a Venus coming out of the Sea, standing on a piece of rockwork and four nymphs at ye corners of ye rock. Ye rockwork to be like that under Neptune at Vaux Le Vicomte', but this never emerged. The Birdcage was always greatly admired by visitors and is the centre-piece to the garden, the eye being led from it up a climbing grass avenue of trees to the skyline.

How much the Melbourne garden really owed to France, in spite of Coke's 'to suit with Versailles' choice of proposals for his ten-acre site, is open to question. It would be interesting to know the views of Marshal Tallard, the French prisoner of war, who visited Melbourne. He was entertained by Betsy Coke who was afraid that 'I must make a simple figure where I could not speak nor understand properly',[7] but we do not know whether he recognized Melbourne as a French garden. The Cokes had sent champagne to Marlborough's defeated Blenheim

77. Melbourne in a painting by George Samuel Elgood, 1894. The yew tree alleyed walks, statues, pools and fountains were much admired by Blomfield and the formal garden revivalists. (Private Collection)

general at the Nottingham house he had been given, where Wise had been allowed to give him a French garden. According to the plan in London and Wise's *The retir'd gard'ner* of 1706 the Tallard parterre was much more French than that shown in the Melbourne plan of 1722.

Blomfield was the first to puzzle whether Melbourne was French or, on its restricted scale, Dutch in origin. He decided in the end that the gardens of Melbourne were 'much more influenced by French than Dutch examples' and were in fact:

> a perfect instance of the French manner in England on a moderate scale . . . from designs by Henry Wise. . . . The ground is of irregular plan, but the difficulties are met by the design in a most masterly manner. Some alterations were made to the garden about fifty years ago. Otherwise the original design is substantially perfect, and is a very valuable instance of a garden laid out when the French influence was still dominant in England.[8]

Gertrude Jekyll also praised the ingenuity of the French design adapted to a restricted site and the value of Melbourne as garden history, but she saw it, not as Blomfield, purely as a matter of design, but, as she also remembered Levens, as showing 'something of the actual feeling and temperament of our ancestors'; to her the French influence seemed to speak of the elegant garden gallantry of Watteau rather than of baroque design, which was eloquently borne out by Elgood's paintings in their book *Some English gardens* in which she said:

> Wise's plan shows how completely the French ideas had been adopted in England, for here again are the handsome pools and fountains, the garden thick-hedged with

78. *Le Bosquet de Bacchus*, engraving after Watteau. Gertrude Jekyll felt it might have been painted at Melbourne.

yew, and the bosquet with its strange paths, green-walled, leading to a large fountain-centred circle in the thickest of the grove. The whole space occupied by the house and grounds is not of great extent; it is irregular and even awkward in shape, and has roads on two sides. The treatment is extremely ingenious; indeed, it is doubtful whether any other plan that could have been devised would have made so much of the space or could have so cleverly concealed the limits. The pleasure ground of Melbourne is a precious relic of the past. The tall trees inclosed by massive yew hedges, the pools and fountains, the statues and other sculptured ornaments, all recall, with their special character of garden treatment, the times and incidents that Watteau loved to paint. Such a picture as his Bosquet de Bacchus, so well known by the engraving, with its gaily-dressed groups of young men and maidens seated in a grassy shade and making music of their lutes and voices accompanying that of the fountain's waters, might have been painted at Melbourne. For here are the same wide, green-walled alleys, the pools, the fountains and ornamental details of the great gardens of courtly France of 200 years ago acclimatised on English soil; not in the dreary vastness of Versailles, but tamed to our climate's needs and on a scale attuned to the more moderate dimensions of a reasonable human dwelling.[9]

The most discerning visitor who first studied the archives was Henry Wise's biographer David Green. As the Blenheim archivist he had always been intrigued by difficult-to-please Duchess Sarah's statement that at Blenheim 'for the gardening and Plantations I am at ease, being very sure that Mr Wise will bee diligent', which led him on to a study of his life and methods for his book *Gardener to Queen Anne*. The archives he studied were housed in Thomas Coke's gazebo-muniment room and his verdict that the Frenchness of Melbourne is so acclimatized that it is almost unrecognizable should perhaps be the last word that today's visitor hears before setting out for the delights of Melbourne:

> Yet one has only to go there and look at it (and no garden is more delightful to walk in) to see how very English, how very unFrench it is . . . a mild and tranquil garden, a Wilderness of Sweets, with statues, urns, and arbours set off by the incomparable green of English grass and the solemn black-green of yew. There is a complete absence of formality; there is not even a parterre. Nevertheless, the original outline, three-quarters smothered, is still there, and shadowy though it is, on the strength of it, Melbourne may qualify as the nearest England now has to an unrestored garden of the late 17th or early 18th century, in the Le Nôtre manner. It is in fact the perfect compromise, the formal garden grown informal and English: the bob-tailed sheep-dog that was at first taken to be a poodle.[10]

WREST PARK
SILSOE, BEDFORDSHIRE

Wrest has much more of the grand baroque manner of Le Nôtre than more domestic Melbourne had set out to achieve and this can still be seen in spite of later landscaping by Capability Brown. Avray Tipping commented that 'if it were desired to let a stranger of rather more than average taste learn for himself what the great country houses and their parks and gardens mean to the country districts of England, we should be inclined to think that, as a whole, Wrest Park would teach him more than any other'.[1] The various layers of garden history are now to be well preserved by English Heritage. The present house of 1836 is on a different site from the seventeenth-century one shown on the Kip engraving (see Plate 45) for which the great gardens were originally made, and the grounds today incorporate the various gardens of the two great houses.

The key figure in the layout of the first gardens was Henry Grey, Lord Lucas, who was created Duke of Kent in 1710. He was the patron of the architects Archer, Leoni, Hawksmoor and Kent, but after his succession in 1702 gardening became his chief love. Whatever grandiose ideas he had for modernizing his largely Jacobean house were cut down to size when he suffered in the aftermath of the South Sea Bubble in the 1720s, but his garden works continued until his death in 1740. The great feature of the gardens was Thomas Archer's domed baroque pavilion, which stood, not like Archer's building at Chatsworth above the great cascade, but at the head of the calm waters of the half-a-mile long tree-lined canal. The Duchess of Chandos saw the pavilion being built in 1710. Having walked along the 'very long and hansome' terrace in front of the house she describes the new Duke of Kent's gardens:

> You goe into a very noble garden: ye Parterre is very large and ends with high trees

80 (right). The Chinese pavilion, built by Marchioness Grey in 1761, has recently been restored by English Heritage.

which meet at Top and are cut so as to make so many Arches; and to run up the bodys of the Trees are planted Honeysuckles and Sweet Brire. From the middle walk of the Parterre you look upon a very fine Canall at the end of which is the foundation laying of a very fine Sumer House. [she then enters a wilderness with] a green walk which brings you back to the Terras Walk before the House; about the middle of the walk you go into a piece of ground prettily divided with water for wilde Fowle: and at the end of the walk from the Terras is a Flower Garden divided by a Pallisade from Courts to feed tame Fowle and Pheasants in.[2]

The Duke of Kent was succeeded in 1740 by his seventeen-year-old granddaughter, the Marchioness Grey, who married Philip Yorke, later to become Earl of Hardwicke. She and her husband set out in the 1740s on a number of tours of country houses, including Stowe, Studley Royal, Wroxton, and Warwick with a view to noting garden improvements.[3] It was not until the late 1750s that they decided to extend their gardens at Wrest and to call in Capability Brown to give professional assistance. The inscription on a memorial column the marchioness erected when these improvements were completed shows how she in no way considered his work as superseding but rather continuing that of her grandfather, whose memory she revered: 'These gardens were begun in the year 1706 by the Duke of Kent, who continued to beautify them until the year 1740; the work was again carried on by Philip Earl of Hardwicke, and Jemima, Marchioness de Grey, with the professional assistance of Lancelot Brown, Esq., 1758–60'.

Walpole visiting in 1771 deplored the duke's old-fashioned gardens and regretted that Brown was not allowed to make a clean sweep:

79 (left). Thomas Archer's baroque domed pavilion still stands at the end of a tree-lined canal.

The Gardens were fine and very ugly in the old-fashioned manner with high hedges and canals, at the End of the principal one of which is a frightful Temple designed by Mr Archer the Groomporter. Mr Brown has much corrected this garden and built a hermitage and cold bath in a bold good taste. In two quarters of the wood, the Duke erected in his lifetime two monuments to the memory of himself and his first Duchess.[4]

Thomas Pennant in 1782 was also of the opinion that 'the pleasure grounds have, since their first creation, been corrected by Brown', but did not take Walpole's view of the pavilion, obelisks and other buildings which although in 'the taste of the age before' he felt graced their part of the grounds.[5]

When formal gardening was to make its revival at the end of the nineteenth century Alicia Amherst was relieved to find that the grounds of Wrest were not a typical Brown landscape and that 'in spite of passing through his hands they have retained much of their original charm'.[6] The subtlety of this joining of two different styles of gardening whereby the great canal and Archer's pavilion remained as the central axis but the other encircling canals and planting were naturalized is described by the marchioness in August 1760 when Brown's work was nearing completion:

The design for laying the waters together round the garden is finished. The waters behind the bowling-green have been joined this year, and one end turned through

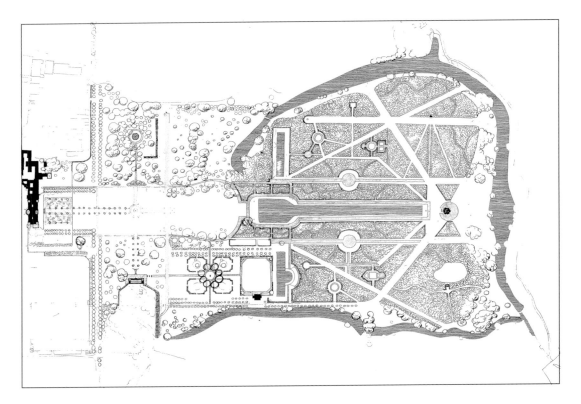

81. The master plan for restoration drawn up by Land Use Consultants and based on the several stages of development. This will take many years to carry out.

the little additional piece of grove into the ditch that came from the mineral spring, the other carried to meet the serpentine. The serpentine in the same manner joins to the brook at the lower end of the garden, and from that brook is now really a fine piece of water, one undivided large stream made out of the different canals on the Cain Hill side as far as the upper end of the old mill-pond. The parterre too has been opened this year by taking away the berceaus as far down as the evergreens, which had let in the view to the windows of the house and to the terrace of all the lawn, the trees on the hill and the water with a large bridge over it.[7]

One of the marchioness's additions to the garden was a Chinese pavilion in 1761, shortly after the publication of William Chambers's *Designs of Chinese buildings*. She and her husband had already seen and admired Chinese buildings at Stowe, Studley Royal, Wroxton and their brother-in-law's Shugborough on their tours. The pavilion was more substantial than those at Wroxton and Studley and survived until the 1950s; it has now been restored by English Heritage. There was apparently further work requiring Brown's 'magic wand' as in 1769 the marchioness was writing to a friend:

> Mr Brown has been leading me such a fairy circle and his magic wand has raised such landscapes to the eye, not visionary, for they were all there, but his touch has brought them out with the same effect as a painter's pencil upon canvas, that after having hobbled over rough ground to points that I had never seen before for two hours, I return half tired and half foot-sore and must really break off.[8]

The 'wretched low bad house', as Walpole called it, was demolished in 1833, and a new one built some distance to the north. Formal gardens with extensive terracing and balancing parterres were made on the south of the new house which extended to the site of the old one and these, like the house, were French-influenced. The 2nd Earl de Grey made frequent visits to Paris and studied French books for his new house: 'One book called Architecture Française was most valuable, it was a collection of prints from all such works by many masters it was my textbook till my works were completed many years later'.[9] It seems he chose a design from Blondel's *Maisons de plaisance* for his house and was indebted to Le Blond, the pupil of Le Nôtre, for the inspiration of his *parterres de broderie*. Cecilia Ridley, a Bedfordshire neighbour visiting in 1839 was very much aware how much the earl had been in charge of the works: 'He draws the patterns for all the ceilings and ornaments of every description and then overlooks the execution of all his orders, so that he must look upon it all as his child—and a most promising one it is'.[10]

Archer's pavilion at the end of the long canal is now half a mile away but is still on axis with the nineteenth-century house and seen across the now simplified parterre with its four lead statues. The three stages of Wrest's garden history have blended together harmoniously without losing sight of the original character of the early eighteenth-century layout. Jemima, Marchioness Grey, had always insisted that it should be her grandfather's layout that should be the basis for any subsequent improvements, and it is to be hoped that she would not be disappointed by the present programme of gradual restoration that the visitor can follow over the next ten to twenty years.

5

EIGHTEENTH-CENTURY GARDENS

82. The artificial ruins at Shugborough 'one of the finest improvements in England', painted by Nicholas Dall, 1775. (Shugborough House, courtesy of the Earl of Lichfield and Staffordshire County Council)

The eighteenth century produced the new phenomenon known as the 'English' garden throughout Europe. C. C. L. Hirschfeld, Professor of Fine Art at Kiel, after extensive tours of Europe, wrote in his five-volume review of garden history, *Theorie der Gartenkunst*, in 1779 that 'at last there arose a new taste in gardens—the English'.[1] The English-style landscaped garden was in its infancy when the early editions of John Macky and Daniel Defoe's Tours were published. Macky claimed that his *Journey through England* in 1714 was the first English systematic tour guide.[2] It was published in French as *Le guide d'Angleterre* in 1744, Macky having complained that the usual French guides were by people who had never visited England but took extracts from Camden and natural histories of counties, which were the only topographical books then available.

Defoe was, like Macky, a Government spy and had a way of uncovering information, not necessarily accurate. Perhaps the first modern journalist, his popular Tour went into nine editions between 1724 and 1778, revised by successive editors, including Samuel Richardson, during which time the accounts of gardens had to be amended as taste changed. His 1724 edition had nothing but praise for Hampton Court but a critical note about its formality crept into the later editions. Macky, who died in 1726, saw Lord Burlington's gardens at Chiswick well advanced and Defoe's Tours cover the transitional stage of the English landscaped garden, when the ideas of Charles Bridgeman, royal gardener in 1728, held sway. Although still adhering to regularity, Horace Walpole could detect, in retrospect, that Bridgeman had 'many detached thoughts, that strongly indicate the dawn of modern taste'.[3]

Sir Thomas Robinson, an improver who was taking a keen interest in gardens in his country house visiting, seems to catch the moment in 1734 when the Bridgeman-type gardens were to be replaced by the real landscaped gardens that according to Walpole came into being when William Kent 'leaped the fence, and saw that all nature was a garden'. Robinson wrote to his father-in-law, the Earl of Carlisle, who was busy with his own improvements at Castle Howard, about the 'new taste in gardening just arisen'. 'Mr Kent's notion of gardening' he explains, is to 'lay them out, and work without level or line . . . when finished, it has the appearance of beautiful nature, and without being told, one would imagine art had no part in the finishing'. He continues: 'the celebrated gardens of Claremont, Chiswick and Stowe are now full of labourers, to modernise the expensive works finished in them, even since every one's memory'.[4]

The famous Whig Kit-Kat Club was a veritable hotbed of eighteenth-century gardening ideas. The club's 'Teeming-Noddles', who plotted not only politics but parks and gardens, included Addison, Vanbrugh and many owners of important gardens in the process of improvement: Lord Cobham of Stowe; the Duke of Newcastle of Claremont; the Earl of Lincoln of Oatlands, and John Dormer of Rousham. Some had time on their hands at the end of the Marlborough Wars and others were out of political office. Aislabie had to retire to Studley Royal when disgraced by the South Sea Bubble. 'Chiefs out of War and Statesmen out of Place', as Pope put it, were then happy to 'hang their old trophies o'er the Garden Gate'.[5] They all had time to travel and see each other's improvements.

Joseph Addison was undoubtedly a great influence on landlords who were in the throes

83. William Kent's drawing of Pope's influential garden. It shows the Shell temple and the view through the arched opening to the river, which is being studied with a landscape mirror. (British Museum, London)

84. Lord Burlington was the chief arbiter of eighteenth-century taste. His portrait, 1717–19, attributed to Jonathan Richardson, shows the Bagnio, one of the garden buildings he designed at Chiswick. (National Portrait Gallery, London)

of enclosure and agricultural improvement. 'But why may not a whole Estate be thrown into a kind of Garden?' he asked in his influential *Spectator* essays.[6] The idea of integrating parks and rural scenery gave rise to forest gardening and the concept of the *ferme ornée*. It was Stephen Switzer who, in his *Ichnographia rustica*, showed how Addison's ideas could be put into practice. Estate gardening, involving husbandry and aesthetic planning, took over the English countryside. Voltaire in 1726 was most impressed by the progressive, agriculturally-minded country gentlemen he met, comparing them favourably with French nobles, and Montesquieu was so taken with the vast areas of green grass in English gardens that he returned to La Brède in 1731 to improve his park and told an English visitor that he was applying 'the taste of your own country here in order to improve my estate in the English way'.[7] Much later the Danish visitor, Steen Eiler Rasmussen, looking back on the phenomenon, concluded that 'the English garden is not designed, it is planted in the country, it grows' and he could see that what passed for 'an English garden' on the Continent was often a travesty of the real thing, as it lacked the essential ingredient of the English countryside.[8]

Washington Irving in his *Sketch Book* of 1820 wrote that 'the taste of the English in the cultivation of land, and in what is called landscape gardening, is unrivalled. They have studied Nature intently, and discover an exquisite sense of her beautiful forms and harmonious combinations. Those charms, which in other countries she lavishes in wild solitudes, are here assembled round the haunts of domestic life'.[9] The literature read and quoted by visitors to landscaped gardens from home and abroad showed that it was Addison, Thomson and Pope who were seen to be their inspiration; Addison because he linked estate gardening with classical ideas of beauty and utility; Thomson for extolling prospect gardening in *The Seasons*; Pope for his nature poetry in 'Windsor Forest', with its lawns and glades, varying greens and opening and retiring shades, and for introducing into his own famous Thames-side garden the poetic elements which made gardening into 'practical poetry'.[10] His plea to 'consult the Genius of the Place' became a rallying cry for sensitive landscape improvers.

The Grand Tour with the first sight of Palladian villas and the actual 'classic ground' of the mythological subjects painted by Claude and Poussin had a profound effect on young noblemen, like Lord Burlington, who had inherited estates and were forming art collections. Landscaped gardens were ideal places in which to erect classical temples as a deliberate device to promote spiritual qualities as in a sacred landscape. The Society of Dilettanti was formed in 1732 for the cultural élite who had travelled in Italy and wished to promote a feeling for antiquity at home. They sponsored 'Athenian' Stuart and Nicholas Revett in the publication of *The antiquities of Athens* and by their measured drawings classical park buildings, such as those erected for two founder members, Thomas Anson at Shugborough and Lord Harcourt at Nuneham, gained authenticity.

For both these dilettanti landscapes it had been necessary to move villages from the park and in the case of Nuneham to destroy the old church to accommodate Stuart's classical temple. It was on account of such actions brought about by 'pressure of contiguous pride' that Oliver Goldsmith condemned landscape gardening and lamented that the 'country blooms a garden and a grave'. In the preface to *The Deserted Village* he stated that the poem was the result of four or five years investigations on 'country excursions' and asks that it should be taken at its face value and not as pastoral imagery. It could take many years, however, to clear a park of habitation when the landlord had to wait for leases to expire and few late eighteenth-century visitors to landscaped gardens would have had any idea of the implication of Goldsmith's accusation and that under the Capability Brown lake or the smooth lawns on which they were standing might lie a once 'smiling long-frequented village'.[11] On a visit to Castle Howard the Duke of Rutland was surprised to find in the hall an old map which showed the old village of Hinderskelfe 'where the house now stands, and divers small inclosures, where now a beautiful park and pleasure grounds are spread'.[12] The villagers would have been rehoused, however, and it was Goldsmith's portrayal of heartless evictions in *The Deserted Village* that confused his readers, and many like Jeremy Bentham exclaimed that there were no such villages in England and assumed that the incident must have taken place in the poet's Ireland, where such evictions were all too common.

The mid-century saw the growth of professional landscaping led by Lancelot Brown. This was a new stage in the development of the English garden, rather different in concept from the early gardens of the amateurs at Studley Royal, Painshill or Stourhead with their individual themes and different influences. Thomas Whately, whose *Observations on modern gardening* in 1770 proved so influential for foreign travellers, reflects the systematized ideas of Brown's pure landscape where 'water, wood and ground' in beautiful forms are the materials of his profession. What looks like the first travelling scholarship was awarded in Sweden to Fredrik Magnus Piper to study English-style gardens and Whately's book, which had been translated into French and German, was his guide. Thomas Jefferson on a three-week tour of English gardens with John Adams in 1786 made his itinerary from the *Observations*. 'I always walked over the gardens with Whately's book in my hand, examined with attention the particular spots he described, found them so characterized by him as to be easily recognized and saw with wonder that his fine imagination had never been able to seduce him from the truth'.[13] The study tour proved invaluable for his Monticello improvements.

Whately objects that whereas garden buildings had been intended for shelter, retirement or parties, they had increasingly become mere eye-catching features. The appreciation of less embellished scenes, in the Brown manner, is reflected in the tourists' comments at the end of the century. Richard Warner, a picturesque traveller, found the numerous buildings at Studley 'satiate and disgust'; Frederick Montagu scoffed at the 'ridiculous temples' of Stowe';[14] John Wesley objected to heathen temples especially those, as at Stourhead, with nude gods in them, and Mrs Lybbe Powys, having climbed over 200 steps up Alfred's Tower at Stourhead, lamented that there was no place to sit down.[15]

There was universal praise for the way Brown had apparently waved a magician's wand and produced artificial water features as at Blenheim or Bowood. His plantations had not as yet matured but eighteenth-century tourists were prepared to look at them with the 'prophetic eye of taste' as William Pitt called it. Today's visitors see Brown's landscapes in what Walpole envisaged at Petworth as 'venerable maturity'. Stowe became a public school in 1927 and in *Mistress Masham's repose* one of its housemasters, T. H. White of the Arthurian legends, describes the experience of looking out on to the mature landscape of the Grecian Valley stretching before him just 'as Capability Brown had always intended that it should'.

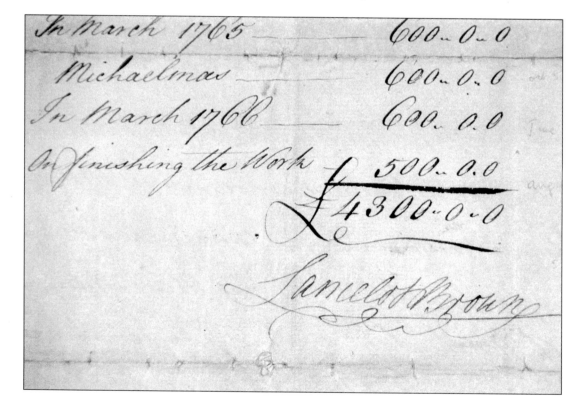

85. Lancelot Brown's signature on a letter in the Bowood archives. Brown was always known as Capability Brown because of his tendency to tell estate owners that their land had 'capabilities'. (Courtesy of the Trustees of the Bowood Estate)

BLENHEIM PALACE
WOODSTOCK, OXFORDSHIRE

'Breath-taking' is the adjective most frequently used by visitors to Blenheim when they enter from Woodstock through the triumphal arch and Vanbrugh's monumental palace, set in Brown's finest landscape, bursts upon their astonished eyes. Vanbrugh, of course, would never have known this landscape, which was Capability Brown's contribution to his splendid baroque palace, built by a grateful nation to commemorate the Duke of Marlborough's great victory at Blenheim in 1704. Vanbrugh planned a grand baroque progress to the palace to give the sense of homage that Defoe describes when on his tour in 1724, two years after the duke's death, he saw the still unfinished palace: 'Nor can any nation in Europe show the like munificence to any general, no nor the greatest in the world'.[1]

Defoe, like Macky, approached the palace through the Grand Avenue, said by Bobart to have been planted in the formation of the Battle of Blenheim.[2] Once the palace was finished Vanbrugh's ceremonial approach was seldom put to use as a carriage entry as other approaches from Woodstock and the Oxford road were more convenient. Today's pedestrian visitors, who are prepared to walk the extra two miles, can enter through the Ditchley gate and walk down the Grand Avenue, observing, like the antiquarian Stukeley, Grims Ditch and Akeman Street crossing it, Rosamund's Well and the site of Woodstock palace; they will then enjoy the intended baroque experience of seeing the palace with its square towers, colonnades and striking ornaments on the roof like distant Marlborough trophies come gradually nearer.[3] Vanbrugh's bridge, which is so picturesquely featured in Brown's landscape, is seen from the Grand Avenue approach to look like a causeway to a great citadel.

Vanbrugh was the ideal architect to have been entrusted with the nation's commission to build a home for a hero on a grand scale to rival Versailles. First and foremost he was a dramatist and stage manager with a truly theatrical outlook. He had also been a soldier before as Swift quipped:

> *Van's genius, without thought or lecture,*
> *is hugely turn'd to architecture.*[4]

'Van' was a leading light of the Kit-Kat Club, where he met the Duke of Marlborough, who had been most impressed with the model of Castle Howard made for the Earl of Carlisle, a fellow Kit-Kat member, in 1699. Addison, another Kit-Kat, was soon praising 'Van's' triumphal architecture at Blenheim: 'Behold the glorious pile ascending, Columns swelling, arches bending'.[5] Vanbrugh had used his playwright's feeling for the dramatic presentation of a play or opera when siting Blenheim. He chose a plateau at the southern end of Woodstock Park above a steep-sided valley in which ran the little brook, the Glyme; this he would cross by a truly heroic-scale bridge. On his plans this was called *Pons Blenheimensis* to recall the conquering Roman legions who had marched along Akeman Street in the park. The other piece of dramatic scenery planned to be seen from the palace would have been the evocative

86. J.M.W. Turner: *Blenheim House and Park – Oxford*, *c*.1832. The breath-taking picturesque view planned by Capability Brown for the visitor entering from the Woodstock gate. (Birmingham City Museums and Art Gallery)

remains of Woodstock manor to the east of the bridge. Vanbrugh's predilection for ruins was well known to the Kit-Kat Club, but few then agreed with him that 'they move more lively and pleasing Reflections (than History without their Aid can do)' and certainly the Duchess of Marlborough would not hear of marring Blenheim's triumphal landscape by preserving ruins. Finally Vanbrugh pleaded in a published paper in 1709 that the whole history of the royal hunting park and manor and the association of Rosamund's Bower, of which the duchess did not approve, should be considered. The ruins would, he said, 'make One of the Most Agreable Objects that the best of Landskip Painters can invent'.[6] His plea was unsuccessful and a stone plaque now marks the site of demolished Woodstock manor.

Vanbrugh's monumental bridge was not seen to advantage when first erected and visitors had been united in condemning the trickle of water under it. After the duke's death and Vanbrugh's dismissal the duchess called in Colonel Armstrong, a military engineer, in 1719, to construct a canal, a cascade and circular basin. Sarah was triumphant: 'Sir John would never have thought of this cascade, which will be the finest and largest ever made, and the water constantly will flow from it without any trouble'.[7] But in 1735 John Dodd could not help

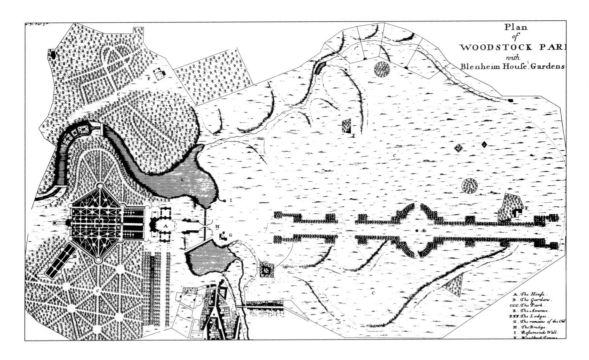

Plan
of
WOODSTOCK PAR[
with
Blenheim Houſe.Gardens

A . The Houſe .
B . The Gardens .
CCC . The Park .
X . The Avenue .
III . The Lodges .
G . The remains of the Old
H . The Bridge .
I . Roſamonds Well .
K . Woodſtock Tow .

87 (left). Plan in Colen
Campbell's *Vitruvius Britannicus*,
1725, of the grand avenue
approach and Henry Wise's
military garden layout. This was
described by Thomas Salmon in
1740 and not removed by
Brown until the 1760s.

'laughing to think that this prodigious large Bridge [whose arch is 101 foot wide] was first built
and then a monstrous Sume of money expended to fetch water to run under it, which is but
very scanty, and in no proportion to the Bridge. . . . Who can admire the Largeness and
magnificence of the House and not deplore the absence of Beauty and Taste from this place'.[8]
A late critic of the 'dreadfully out of proportion' bridge in 1761, three years before Brown
waved his wand on the waters, was Count Kielmansegge, who recalled Voltaire's opinion of
Blenheim: 'Que c'était une grosse masse de pierre, sans agré'ment et sans goût'.[9] Perhaps it
would not be out of place to recall, however, that Prince Pückler-Muskau thought that, *pace*
Voltaire, the architecture of Blenheim was in 'bad French taste', anyhow.[10]

Thomas Salmon visiting in 1740, when the Duchess of Marlborough was alive, gives a
detailed account of the splendour of the gardens laid out by Queen Anne's gardener, Henry
Wise, as the original accompaniment to the palace:

> The gardens consist of 70 acres of Ground, which are encompassed by a Stone Wall,
> and laid out in Form of an Hexagon, having a round Bastion at each Angle, of 200 ft
> diameter: There is, in this Garden, a Wilderness of a vast extent, with Vistos cut
> through it; the Trees whereof must have been very large when they were planted; for
> it already appears almost a full grown wood. The grand Gravel Walk, which runs
> from the house Southward to the farther End of the Garden is 2200 ft long; and
> there is another, which crosses it in the Middle, 1850 ft in Length. Noble Terrasses,
> from whence we have an extensive View of the Country, run from Bastion to
> Bastion; which in a fortified Town, would have been denominated in Curtains.

88 (right). View of the palace
as originally intended by
Vanbrugh from a baroque
approach.

There are also beautiful green walks, planted with Evergreens, Summer-houses,
Alcoves, Fountains, and everything that can render the Place agreeable.[11]

It must have required a considerable work-force to remove these bastions and terraces before
converting them into great lawns in the improvements of the 1760s. Brown retained the
Grand Avenue with its heroic approach and left much of the mediaeval park with its ancient
pollarded trees almost untouched thus giving the 'pleasing reflections' on the origin of
Woodstock Park for which Vanbrugh had pleaded.

Thomas Whately writing of Brown's great achievement shortly after his work had been
completed aptly described how the great architectural features 'which before were dispersed
are now by the interest of each in a relation which is common to all, collected into one
illustrious scene'.[12] When the lake filled the valley tourists were ecstatic: 'the most superb
piece of water, in which art has any share, in this kingdom' and, 'one of the most enchanting
views that imagination can conceive', enthused the Reverend Stebbing Shaw.[13] William
Gilpin, who was usually critical of landscaping and of artificial lakes in particular went so far as
to say that 'the banks of the Wye scarce exhibit more romantic scenes, than are here displayed
in the level plains of Oxfordshire'.[14]

The Reverend William Mavor, whose Woodstock rectory had these scenes displayed
before the windows, attempted to do justice to it all for visitors in ten editions of his
Description of Blenheim, including one in French. Throughout the revisions he had seen a
change in attitude to Vanbrugh's genius, which he modestly hoped his guides had gone some
way to promote. The change was more likely the result of the remarks of Reynolds and
Uvedale Price, who hailed Vanbrugh as an innovator of the Picturesque. Reynolds in his
Discourses delivered to the students of the Royal Academy recognized that 'in the buildings of
Vanbrugh, who was a poet as well as an architect, there is a greater display of imagination than
we shall find perhaps in any other . . . he perfectly understood in his art what is the most
difficult in ours, the conduct of the background, by which the design and invention is set off to
the greatest advantage'.[15] In his *Essays on the Picturesque* Price described the magic moment of
seeing Vanbrugh's picturesque palace which Turner was later to capture: 'Whoever catches
that view towards the close of evening, when the sun strikes the golden balls and pours his
beams through the open parts, gilding every rich and brilliant ornament will think he sees
some enchanted palace'.[16] Reynolds, Price and Turner were of course seeing Vanbrugh's
palace, as the visitor does today, in Capability Brown's romantic landscape composition.

Changes on such a huge estate were inevitable in the nineteenth century and in 1827
Prince Pückler-Muskau wrote that 'one cannot help admiring the grandeur of Brown's genius
and conceptions, as one wanders through these gardens: he is the Shakespeare of gardening',
but already a new possessor was misunderstanding these conceptions and 'in a miserable taste;
transforming the rich draperies that Brown had thrown around Nature, into a harlequin
jacket of little clumps and belts. A large portion of the old pleasure ground is thus destroyed; as
the old gardener almost with tears in his eyes remarked to me'.[17] Loudon had seen Blenheim
several times before on his 1833 tour he recorded his disappointment in the state of its upkeep,
especially the lake which was 'quite green with aquatic weeds'.[18] More agriculture had been

introduced into the park and the Grand Avenue, left by Brown, was deformalized at this time. It was only reinstated in 1900 by the 9th Duke, who was the restorer of Blenheim as we see it today.

The avenue was a victim of elm disease in the 1960s, but has once more been replanted, this time with limes.[19] The 9th Duke wanted some of the original formality restored near the palace and granite setts were laid to replace Brown's lawns in the Great Court. The French landscape architect Achille Duchêne designed a garden on the east front with patterned beds of scroll broderies and arabesques recalling Wise's parterre. He later created a water parterre for the west front. Sir Sacheverell Sitwell encouraged the duke to go further and restore the Great Parterre to the south, but this was beyond resources. Sitwell, who so greatly admired Brown's work at Blenheim, 'the one great argument of the landscape gardener. There is nothing finer in Europe, in its way this is one of the wonders of the 18th century', saw Duchêne's work, finished in 1929, as complementary in excellence both to Brown's masterpiece and to the concepts of Vanbrugh and Henry Wise: 'This is probably the most successful work of the formal gardener done in our time, and being conceived on the original lines is really in scale with the whole gigantic planning'.[20]

89. The water parterre on the west front by the French landscape architect Achille Duchêne.

CASTLE HOWARD
near MALTON, NORTH YORKSHIRE

On the evening of 12 August 1772 Horace Walpole wrote a letter from York to his friend
George Selwyn, describing his day's excursion, which had been to Castle Howard:

> I never was so agreeably astonished in my days, as with the first vision of the whole
> place . . . nobody . . . had informed me that I should at one view see a palace, a
> town, a fortified city, temples in high places, woods worthy of being each a
> metropolis of the Druids, vales connected to hills by other woods, the noblest lawn
> in the world fenced by half the horizon, and a mausoleum that would tempt one to
> be buried alive—In short, in short, I have seen gigantic places before, but never a
> sublime one. [1]

Castle Howard's grandeur is still astonishing tourists over 200 years on. As the lane from
Welburn turns into the immense axial approach, today's visitor to Castle Howard enters one
of the greatest baroque layouts of the early eighteenth century, and one of the best survivors of
that age today. In contrast to Blenheim, the original grandiose drive remains: it runs straight
over the rising and falling ground towards the distant obelisk, the ornate archways under
which it passes successfully heightening the sense of entering a vast, private domain.

While the names of Vanbrugh and Hawksmoor are strongly associated with the
designing of Castle Howard, it seems that the guiding hand was always Carlisle's. He inherited
the family seat, Hinderskelfe Castle, in 1693 at the age of twenty-three. It had been rebuilt by
his grandfather the 1st Earl, but still stood between the church and main street in the village of

90. The Mausoleum at Castle
Howard, designed by Nicholas
Hawksmoor as the terminal
point to the view from the
house.

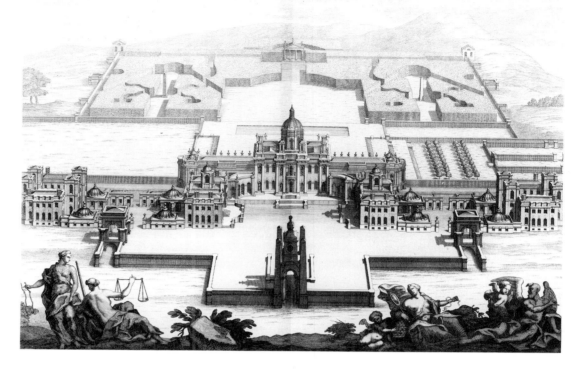

91. Castle Howard as depicted in Colen Campbell's *Vitruvius Britannicus*, 1725, showing Vanbrugh's formal wilderness to the south.

Hinderskelfe. In 1694 it burnt down, and Carlisle began seeking designs for a new building. In 1699 John Vanbrugh made drawings for Carlisle, undercut his rival, William Talman, and secured the contract. Building work began in the following year.

Vanbrugh's scheme involved destroying the old village and creating a princely setting for the new palace. His patron's confidence no doubt grew from discussions with other fellow Kit-Kats. Thus, although the framework of his garden was axial, and the parterre and wilderness depicted in *Vitruvius Britannicus* were strictly symmetrical, he was innovative from the first in preserving the adjacent Wray Wood as semi-natural woodland. Rather than cutting a star of avenues through it, as George London (Talman's partner) had suggested, he wound informal walks through it, punctuated by waterworks and statuary. It has been suggested that he employed Stephen Switzer to advise on the woodland, and Switzer certainly commends Wray Wood in *Ichnographia rustica*. It seems quite possible that he had Wray Wood in mind when he described the laying-out of a wood, in which 'the natural Gardener . . . has made his Design submit to Nature, and not Nature to his Design':

> The Inside of his Wood is fill'd with Hares, Pheasants, the Statues of Rural and Sylvan Deities all cut out in Wood, while he contrives likewise that living Hares and Pheasants shall abound . . . . He is often surpriz'd with little Gardens, with Caves, little natural Cascades and Grotts of Water, with Pieces of Grotesque Painting, Seats, and Arbors of Honeysuckle and Jessamine, and, in short, with all the Varieties that Nature and Art can furnish him with.[2]

Punctuated by statues, water features, an amphitheatre and summerhouses, it must have been a marvellous place. The Duke of Rutland described Castle Howard in 1796. He wrote lyrically about Wray Wood's 'mantling umbrage', and tells how, so intricate were its winding paths, that even Lord and Lady Carlisle once became lost in the 'mossy labyrinth' during an evening

92. An estate plan of Castle Howard, 1727, showing Wray Wood, the wilderness, the parterre and the irregular grass terrace. The Temple of the Four Winds, completed in 1728, has been inked in at a slightly later date. (Castle Howard, courtesy the Hon. Simon Howard)

walk.[3] It avoided being claustrophobic by the use of 'openings . . . that as Mr Pope expresses it "Calls in the Country catches opening Glades" in the most agreable Manner that can be imagin'd'.[4] Accounts throughout the nineteenth century grew more melancholy about the wood's decay, and it was finally clear-felled during the war. The oaks and beeches that were subsequently planted are now enlivened by the exotic trees and shrubs planted by Mr James Russell, the present Arboreta Curator. Lumps and bumps may indicate the site of original water features, while of the architectural incidents one gnarled pyramidal plinth of rusticated stone is all that remains in place. The Apollo on a plinth carved with woods, ruins and streams which now stands at the end of the Lime Avenue, came from Wray Wood and was part of the early eighteenth-century ornamentation there.

Apart from the house itself, the first area of concern for Vanbrugh was its immediate environs and its approaches: he had built the walled kitchen garden with its grotesque Satyr Gate by 1705; the obelisk inscribed to the memory of the Duke of Marlborough in 1714; the Pyramid Gate in 1719 (to which wings were added later in the century to house visitors); and of course the extraordinary park wall, castellated and buttressed, and adorned with no less than eleven sham castle towers. Still, by 1725 the place evidently had the appearance of a building site: 'the Court yards and garden rough and neglected—several fine new statues, Urns gilts, high pillars in the spot of ground designed for a garden'.[5]

Defoe quoted the earl as sometimes saying 'that Noblemen should only design and begin great Palaces, and leave Posterity to finish them gradually'.[6] Around 1724–5 Carlisle turned

Vanbrugh's attention away from the unfinished house towards the area of the park to the east. Skirting Wray Wood, and following the line of the old village street, they designed an irregular grass terrace, at the end of which Vanbrugh's Temple of the Four Winds was erected. Its building was only finished in 1728, two years after Vanbrugh's death, when his assistant Hawksmoor took over as the earl's architectural adviser. Carlisle's principle of leaving posterity to finish his works seems to have extended to these structures. Lady Margaret Hay visiting in 1745 remarked of the Temple, 'exceeding pritty . . . the floor not finish'd', and of the Mausoleum, 'Magnificent . . . not quite finished'.[7]

It was Hawksmoor who built the Mausoleum as the terminal point in the landscape, as well as the Temple of Venus on the eastern angle of Wray Wood. He also built the obelisk-adorned Carrmire Gate over the drive, and the Pyramid. Given that Vanbrugh had already decorated the parterre with 'a small plantation of young obelisks',[8] there seems to have been an excess of pyramids, evidently Carlisle's particular fancy. In 1729 Hawksmoor was writing

93. A romantic view of the Castle Howard landscape in a painting by Hendrik de Cort, exhibited at the Royal Academy, 1800. (Castle Howard, courtesy the Hon. Simon Howard)

94. The landscape composition at Castle Howard: foreground, middleground and background all carefully designed.

to him to convey the opinion of his son and heir: 'Lord Morpeth wishes your Lordship would be pleased to make some other Ornaments in ye park of a different form from ye pyramide, his lordship thinking there are enough already'.[9] The bridge over the serpentine 'New River' does not actually belong to Carlisle's landscape, for although he created the serpentine, the bridge was built in 1744, six years after his death.

The woods remained safe from censure but the style of the landscape went out of fashion later in the eighteenth century. Arthur Young criticized most of the buildings as 'heavy and clumsy', and even the Mausoleum 'is far enough from being free from these objections . . . the bridge is heavy, and even ugly . . . . I should not, however, forget to remark, that the inn, although deficient enough in beauty, is an excellent one'.[10] Prince Pückler-Muskau thought the layout had 'something to the last degree melancholy, stiff and desolate'. He also found it crowded: 'Obelisks and pyramids are as thick as hops, and every view ends with one, as a staring termination. One pyramid, is however, of use, for it is an inn'.[11]

In the twentieth century Castle Howard's sublimity and its poetic qualities have been rediscovered. Sacheverell Sitwell wrote of 'the poetry' of Castle Howard 'as a domain, with its trees and waters': the Mausoleum, with its 'high dome and the drum of columns as we catch sight of them from far away, through the trees or across the landscaped waters . . . is one of the poetical beauties of the Kingdom'.[12] And for Christopher Hussey, 'Sublime is still the descriptive word for the whole great scenic creation. Walpole used the word in the sense freshly given to it by Burke for the sensation produced by vastness, and by powerful forms producing the illusion of infinity, which we can still experience here'.[13]

CHISWICK HOUSE
HOUNSLOW, LONDON

95. The map of Chiswick by John Rocque, 1736. It is bordered by Lord Burlington's temples and pavilions.

Chiswick was a great contrast after the baroque of Blenheim and Castle Howard. This was now frowned upon by the followers of Shaftesbury, whose writings had promoted the concept of the Man of Taste. 'I assure you Chiswick has been to me the finest thing this glorious sun has shined on', wrote Alexander Pope in 1732.[1] Richard Boyle, 3rd Earl of Burlington, had by

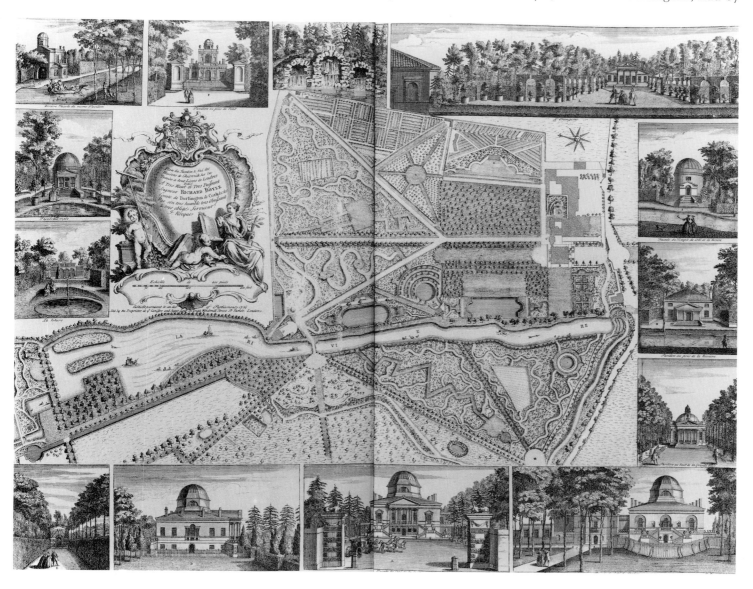

then made Chiswick into a great cultural centre near London and was hailed as the 'Apollo of the Arts' and arbiter of architectural taste. He was the leader of the Palladian Revival, and his Chiswick Villa, which he began in 1725, surpassed 'every thing of its kind in England, if not in Europe', according to Defoe's Tour.[2] The entrance to the house had flanking statues of Burlington's mentors Palladio and Inigo Jones. Pope, in his 'Epistle to Lord Burlington' in 1734, saluted the pioneering work in Chiswick Villa and its grounds and enquired admiringly, 'Who builds like Boyle?'[3]

Richard Boyle had succeeded to the Burlington title and estates in 1704 when he was ten and had made the obligatory Grand Tour from 1714–15. On his return he was obsessed by two books just published, Leoni's translation of the *Four books of architecture* by Palladio and *Vitruvius Britannicus*, containing drawings of English buildings inspired by Roman models, by Colen Campbell, the architect who was improving Burlington House in London. The young Burlington was determined to return to Italy to study Palladian architecture, which he did in 1719, but before this he tried his hand at designing a garden building for the grounds of his Jacobean house at Chiswick. He was obviously very proud of his work as it figures in the background of his portrait painted at the time, and it was very influential. The Duchess of Marlborough, after her husband's death, thought she would have a 'Bagnio' at Rosamund's Well, 'something like those temples which they talk of which are at my Lord Burlington's country house'.[4]

Campbell, who probably gave a guiding hand with the design, wrote in his third volume of *Vitruvius Britannicus* that 'the new Casina in the gardens of Chiswick was the first essay of his Lordship's happy invention'. His Lordship's invention covered the grounds as well as the

96. Engraving after P. A. Rysbrack, *c.*1729, of the orange tree garden at Chiswick.

97. One of a set of paintings by Rysbrack of Chiswick, *c*.1729–30. This one illustrates how 'every walk terminates with some little building'. (Trustees of the Chatsworth Settlement)

garden buildings. As early as 1716 Pope, who was living nearby in Chiswick, saw improvements, and after he had been entertained by Burlington, who was patron of Handel, wrote, 'his gardens are delightfull, his musick ravishing'.[5] Writing in 1724, also before the villa was built, Macky wrote of the gardens which still related to the Jacobean house and how they provided a setting for Burlington's architectural essays and were the 'effect of his Lordship's own genius, and singular fine taste':

> Every walk terminates with some little Building, one with a Heathen Temple, for instance the Pantheon, another a little villa, where my Lord often dines instead of his House, and which is capable of receiving a tolerably large Family; another walk terminates with a Portico, in imitation of Covent Garden Church.[6]

The Rocque map of 1736 as commissioned by Burlington shows how the temples and pavilions dominate the Chiswick layout in which the villa might be said to be the largest and most elegant garden building. The gardens as shown can be seen, from contemporary accounts, to be from Burlington's first stage and include the *patte d'oie* with its three vistas each terminating in a building, the Ionic temple and obelisk in a circular pond, the canal and the terrace, which gave a view of the adjacent country and of the boats on the Thames at high tide.

When he returned from his second Grand Tour in 1719, Burlington entered into a partnership with William Kent, who immediately became his protégé. They had both been captivated by Italian villas and classical gardens and in the 1730s the versatile Kent embarked on a career of landscape gardening in the natural style which was to earn him the title of 'Father of Modern Gardening' from Walpole. His activity at Chiswick followed the completion of the villa adjacent to the old house in 1719, which necessitated a new orientation to the gardens; it included a spacious lawn to the south-west giving an open vista of his new natural-style lake, the exedra in which were statues said to have come from Hadrian's villa at Tivoli, and in 1738 the grotto cascade.

By the mid-century when ideas on naturalized landscape had progressed there were mixed feelings about the juxtaposition of the Kent irregular gardens and Burlington's formal *patte d'oie* and clipped hedges through which his buildings were seen. In 1746 the antiquarian John Loveday thought that there was 'great Taste shewed in the disposition of the Gardens, wherein is a fine serpentine river',[7] but Samuel Richardson, writing in the revised Defoe's Tour of 1742, while conceding that 'the Gardens are laid out in an elegant Taste' and that 'there is more Variety in this Garden, than can be found in any other of the same Size in England, or perhaps in Europe', was critical of the formality of Burlington's part, which conflicted with Kent's more natural style:

> On each Side the Serpentine River is a Grass walk, which follow the Turns of the River; an on the Right-hand of the River is a Building, which is the exact Model of the Portico of Covent Garden Church; and on the Left is a Wilderness, which is laid out in regular Walks, with clipp'd Hedges on each side, which is too mean for the other Parts of the garden; and it is much to be wondered his lordship should suffer them to remain in the present Form.[8]

The writer of the appendix to Whately's *Observations* in the 1801 edition saw the hand of Bridgeman in the 'phlegmatic' planting in Burlington's part of the garden which he compared unfavourably with 'the gentle unevenesses of Kent'.[9] William Gilpin, visiting in 1765, did not distinguish between Burlington and Kent but found Chiswick,

> laid out entirely in the old taste. You have a serpentine river, a terras, with clipped

98. Chiswick House: The Palladian villa was a great contrast to Vanbrugh's baroque houses.

99. Lord Burlington's Bagnio as seen in his portrait (Plate 84) and the formal canal are shown in this further painting by Rysbrack. (Trustees of the Chatsworth Settlement)

hedges, several strait walks terminating in obelisks, or buildings; and a great profusion of statues and urns, which give the lawn before the house the appearance of a statuary shop. Upon the whole however there is great plenty of wood and water which are capable of great improvements. The buildings in the garden are, as we might expect to find them, very beautiful.[10]

Count Kielmansegge, visiting in 1761, admired the villa, 'in the best taste', but was disappointed with the gardens.[11] Another visitor, Thomas Jefferson, in search of ideas to take back to America in 1786, was likewise not impressed with the garden which 'shews still too much of art'.[12]

At that time further landscaping was being planned by Burlington's grandson, the 5th Duke of Devonshire. Brown was dead and Samuel Lapidge who had been running his business was called on for the Chiswick improvements. Further layers were to be added to Chiswick and substantial alterations to the wilderness followed the demolition of the old Jacobean house in 1788. The 6th Duke added to the estate by acquiring the neighbouring house and making further alterations to the gardens with a 300 foot long conservatory as a communication between the two gardens 'making the prettiest effect possible', wrote Miss Berry in 1813.[13] In 1814 Lewis Kennedy, who had worked at the Empress Josephine's garden at Malmaison and was much influenced by French taste, introduced the formal flower gardens in front of the new conservatory. The empress, an ardent gardener who had managed to maintain her connection with the Lee and Kennedy nurseries of Hammersmith during the Napoleonic Wars, loved roses above all and her aim was to collect every species and variety then known.[14] Louis Simond, who visited Chiswick in 1815, admired Kennedy's new rose garden, which he said the gardener told him had '120 varieties of roses'.[15]

In 1822 the duke, who was keenly interested in horticulture, leased some of the former open field to the Horticultural Society and it was from there that Joseph Paxton was recruited to be head gardener at Chatsworth. Few changes took place at Chiswick after this time as gardening interest was transferred to Chatsworth. Today the grounds are a public open space administered as a local amenity by Hounslow Borough Council, who are co-operating with English Heritage to preserve the villa's historic setting. It is the different layers of garden history that disappointed or confused eighteenth-century visitors expecting to see pure landscaping which are of great interest and are being restored by English Heritage with the encouragement of the Friends of Chiswick.

CLAREMONT
ESHER, SURREY

Until 1975 Claremont Lake and Woods was a pleasant rather wild public park, with tangled woody slopes and a reed-infested lake overhung with evergreens. A ruinous pile of stones fenced off by the local authority crouched at one end of the lake. The eighteenth-century landscape seemed to be a matter for the history books and few visitors guessed at its survival in the undergrowth. Now restored, Claremont shows the garden tourist a fine example of a semi-formal garden, with its great turf amphitheatre and later irregular landscaping.

Claremont was one of the most famous gardens of the period. In 1708 John Vanbrugh had a house built for himself just over the hill, near the present mansion (now a school). But in 1711 he sold it to the eighteen-year-old Thomas Pelham-Hobbes, shortly to become Earl of Clare and Duke of Newcastle. The young peer employed Vanbrugh to extend the house, quadrupling it in size. Vanbrugh also produced designs for the surroundings: on the hill which gave the estate its name he built the belvedere, originally painted white, and he built a kitchen garden of heroic proportions with massive fortified walls.

In 1716 the earl purchased the 50 acres which now comprise Claremont Landscape

100. John Rocque's view of the
lake and amphitheatre at
Claremont, from his second
survey, published 1754.

101. The amphitheatre today,
as restored by the National
Trust.

Garden. He commissioned Charles Bridgeman to design a layout, and by 1725 there were serpentine paths winding up through woods from the house to the belvedere, a straight avenue along the spine of the hill to the bowling green and, most spectacular of all, the turf amphitheatre. This was built above a rather small circular basin of water: Switzer reckoned the amphitheatre a fine example, its 'prodigious Grandeur' marred only by the lack of room for an equally grand piece of water.[1] The result of Bridgeman and Vanbrugh's efforts was highly thought of at the time. In 1726 Pope built a 'Bridgmannick Theatre' at Twickenham,[2] and Colen Campbell in 1725 praised Claremont's 'singularly romantick' situation: 'from the high Tower [it] has a most prodigious fine Prospect of the *Thames* and the adjacent Villas'.[3] In the 1730s Newcastle, as he now was, employed William Kent at Claremont. As Sir Thomas Robinson described it, Claremont in 1734 was one of those celebrated gardens full of labourers already modernizing recently finished and expensive works.[4]

The labourers were working on a number of projects for Kent. They made an extension to the basin to create an irregular lake; they built a cascade; they removed Bridgeman's obelisk from the centre of the lake—although only as far as the nearby Home Farm where it still survives—and replaced it with the island on which they built a pavilion. The bastion Bridgeman had built beside the perimeter walk south of the lake was replaced by a ha-ha and several garden buildings were erected: a temple by the bowling green; a 'Thatched House' on the slopes south of the belvedere—the present little nineteenth-century thatched house is on its site; and a temple called the 'Nine Pin Alley' which stood above the amphitheatre at the head of a curving ride—three stone steps are all that remain of this building. Kent also introduced more winding walks along the hillside between the house and the amphitheatre, and softened the straight lines of the avenue to the bowling green. A drawing of *circa* 1750 shows the cascade turned into a grotto, though it is not clear whether this was Kent's initiative. The grotto resembles the one built by Joseph and Josiah Lane for Charles Hamilton at neighbouring Painshill, with its inner chambers similarly adorned with spars and stalactites.

Newcastle's career, in the thick of the wheeling and dealing of mid-eighteenth century politics, left less and less time for landscaping. There seems to have been little activity between Kent's work and Newcastle's death in 1768, when the estate was sold to the returning hero, Lord Clive.

By this date the style of the house was out of fashion and Clive commissioned a new design by Capability Brown. Apart from building the neo-Classical mansion, Brown must have worked on the landscape, even though no plans have been found. He certainly had the Portsmouth road, which ran close to the pleasure ground, re-routed—its line can still be distinguished to the south of the lake—and he seems to have been responsible for planting over the geometrical lines of the amphitheatre.

Claremont was featured by Thomas Whately in his *Observations on modern gardening*. Whately uses 'the walk to the cottage', presumably from the mansion to Kent's thatched house, as an example of the art of grouping and spacing trees. Here an area 'destitute of many advantages, and eminent for none . . . is yet the finest part of the garden', by virtue of the

102. John Rocque's drawing of the Bowling Green at Claremont from his first survey, published 1738. This view shows Vanbrugh's belvedere at the end of the formal layout on top of the ridge. (Victoria and Albert Museum, London)

grove planted along the side of the hill. This grove was not so much a wood as a succession of clumps:

> Each is full of groupes, sometimes no more than two trees, sometimes four or five, and now and then in larger clusters: an irregular waving line, issuing from some little croud, loses itself in the next; or a few scattered trees drop in a more distant succession from the one to the other. The intervals, winding here like a glade, and widening there into broader openings, differ in extent, in figure, and direction; but all the groupes, the lines, and the intervals, are collected together into large general clumps, each of which is at the same time both compact and free, identical and various. The whole is a place wherein to tarry with secure delight, or saunter with perpetual amusement.[5]

After Clive's death there was a succession of owners until 1816 when Claremont was purchased as a home for Princess Charlotte, daughter of George IV. A Gothic tea-house was built for her, but she died young in 1817 and her tea-house was turned into her mausoleum. Its foundations can still be seen at the top of the amphitheatre. G. F. Prosser in his *Illustrations of the county of Surrey* described how, 'passing onwards' from the mausoleum, 'through a finely varied succession of lawns and shrubberies, a circular lake, having a luxuriantly wooded islet

103. A view of the island and pavilion at Claremont, also showing the ha-ha, painted *c.*1742–5 by the Master of the Tumbled Chairs and another. (Private Collection)

in its centre, and a broad margin of turf, interspersed with trees is agreeably presented to view. The whole encompassed with lofty trees and plantations, forming an extensive and beautiful amphitheatre'.[6] The formal lines of the amphitheatre had by this date disappeared beneath the romantic hanging woods.

Charlotte's widower, Prince Leopold, stayed on at Claremont. In 1824 he had a conservatory built—Vanbrugh's belvedere already having been unsuccessfully tried in this role—and although it was demolished in the 1950s the terrace and iron balustrade with his monogram LL worked into it still survive, as do many of the camellias originally grown in the glasshouse.

J. C. Loudon visited several times between 1804 and 1834, when he wrote a long piece on Claremont in the *Gardener's Magazine*. The prince's gardener, Mr M'Intosh, was highly esteemed by Loudon, who typically pointed out the unsatisfactory nature of Vanbrugh's kitchen garden design, which featured an entry through the gardener's cottage. Of the pleasure garden he mentioned in particular 'a glade, rendered interesting from the circumstance of the Duke of Newcastle, when proprietor of this place, encouraging his servants to play at skittles there, himself sitting in an arbour, smoking his pipe, enjoying their sport.' Then, as the party descended towards the lake from the mausoleum, 'Mr M'Intosh pointed out to us several parts of the original plan of Brown, which he had restored: a mode of improvement highly to be commended'.[7] Loudon seems not to have guessed that the most spectacular of the garden's historic features was under his feet as he descended, but it sounds as though he would have approved of its clearance and recovery.

Claremont remained a royal residence throughout the nineteenth century. In the twentieth century the estate again passed through various hands, but in 1949 the National Trust acquired the pleasure grounds, and since 1975 has carried out an ambitious restoration programme. The hanging woods, many of whose trees were self-seeded birches, were cleared to reveal the lines of the amphitheatre still visible, which were then recut; the lake was dredged; the grotto and island pavilion restored; the avenue cleared and a programme of new planting begun. Future plans include the return of Bridgeman's obelisk, and the rebuilding of Kent's Nine Pin Alley building.

ADDISON'S WALK
MAGDALEN COLLEGE, OXFORD

Designed rural walks, an important factor in the appreciation of landscape, were first to be found in Oxford and Cambridge colleges. Those of Magdalen College, Oxford, later to be known as Addison's Walk after the famous alumnus who frequented them, are a remarkable legacy from mediaeval Oxford. The Magdalen Cherwell water meadows joining with the Christ Church Thames water meadows make a green girdle round that part of the city giving it the rural keeping of the days of Duns Scotus. At Magdalen Bridge the Cherwell branches into several streams and backwaters giving the college a large island meadow within its boundaries. The walks round it can clearly be seen on the Agas map of 1578 and in the Loggan map of 1675 as extended in the Civil War; the water walks were then banked up for defence purposes, which later formed a most unusual garden feature, 'the green natural cloister of our Academe'.

Institutional walks have a special character being designed as a respite from communal living and as a humanistic aid to contemplation through exercise. Only Magdalen College, built in 1458 on the extensive grounds of the former Hospital of St John the Baptist, outside the city walls and adjoining the countryside, could then offer real rural walks. Realizing that some members might see this as an opportunity for country sports, the founder had it built into his statutes that it was forbidden to keep 'A Harrier, or other Hound of any kind, or Ferrets, or a Sparrow-Hawk or any other Fowling Bird'. Thanks to William of Waynflete the Magdalen water meadows became a nature reserve for botanists and naturalists over the centuries.[1]

Joseph Addison, who entered the college in 1689 and held a fellowship until 1711, took particular pleasure in the water walks round the meadows and it was here that he took 'pains in forming his Imagination'. Addison was a disciple of John Locke of Christ Church and shared his enlightened views. Following Locke's *Essay on human understanding*, published in 1690, he sought to trace the source of aesthetic enjoyment in the same empirical way that Locke had

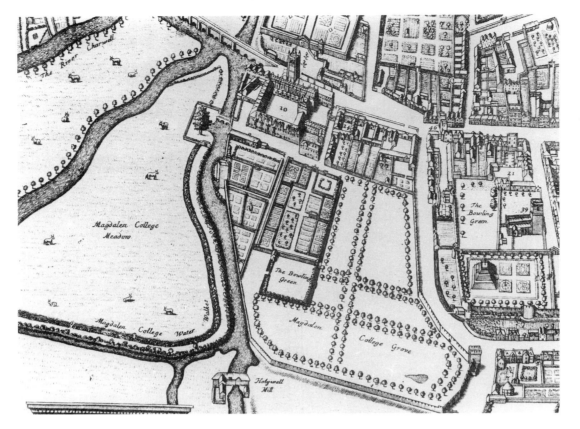

104. The Magdalen water walks from Loggan's *Oxonia illustrata*, 1675.

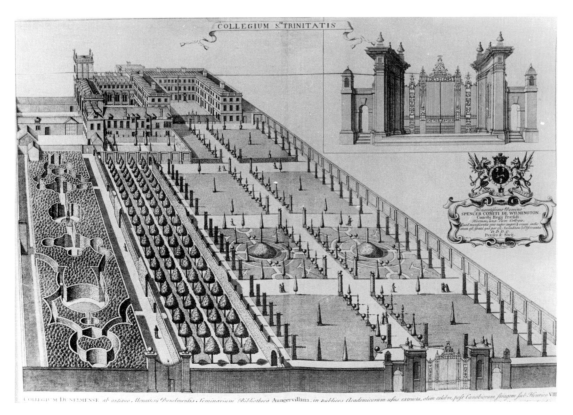

105. Trinity College from William Williams, *Oxonia depicta*, 1733, showing the type of topiaried Dutch garden that Addison abhorred.

investigated understanding. He considered the subject from many aspects, art, natural science, literature, architecture and gardens. The single essay he wrote at Oxford on 'The pleasures of the imagination' was expanded into a series for *The Spectator* in 1712.[2] These were extremely popular and seen in every coffee-house and gentleman's library, and in 1720 were translated into French.

The most influential passages concerning gardens, which are frequently quoted by garden tourists, occur in No. 414, *The Spectator* issue of 25 June 1712. In it Addison commends the appeal of the 'rough careless strokes of Nature' to the spectator's imagination rather than 'the nice Touches and embellishments of Art':

> The Beauties of the most stately Garden or Palace lie in a narrow Compass, the Imagination immediately runs them over and requires something else to gratify her; but in the wide Fields of Nature, the Sight wanders up and down without Confinement, and is fed with an infinite variety of Images, without any stint or Number. For this reason we always find the Poet in love with a Country-Life, where Nature appears in the greatest Perfection, and furnishes out all those Scenes that are most apt to delight the Imagination.

Artificial effects particularly condemned by Addison were the topiaried evergreens, which were everywhere to be seen and particularly in some Oxford college gardens, such as Trinity and St John's:

> Our Trees rise in Cones, Globes, and Pyramids. We see the Marks of the Scissars upon every Plant and Bush. I do not know whether I am singular in my Opinion, but, for my own part, I would rather look upon a Tree in all its Luxuriancy and Diffusion of Boughs and Branches, than when it is thus cut and trimmed into a Mathematical figure; and cannot but fancy that an Orchard in Flower looks infinitely more delightful, than all the little Labyrinths of the most finished Parterre.

Walks round the Magdalen and Christ Church meadows with their 'natural embroidery' were greatly to be preferred to formal gardens as a pleasure of the imagination. What pleasure could the imagination possibly derive from rigid clipped evergreens, abhorrent alike to man and birds, compared with 'Green Shadows of Trees, waving to and fro with the Wind and woodland walks where the season's variations could be enjoyed accompanied by shade, movement and the melody of birds'? Addison, calling himself 'Philander', describes his pleasure in the wooded Cherwell and Thames walks round the college meadows with his colleagues deep in academic discussion:

> Philander used every morning to take a walk in a neighbouring wood, that stood on the borders of the Thames. It was cut through by an abundance of beautiful allies, which terminating on the water, looked like so many painted views in perspective. The banks of the river and the thickness of the shades drew unto them all the birds of the country, that at Sun-Rising filled the wood with such a variety of notes, as made the prettiest confusion imaginable. . . . Philander had no sooner done talking, but he grew sensible of the heat himself, and immediately proposed to his friends the retiring to his lodgings and getting a useful shade over their heads.[3]

The Magdalen Walks have frequently been compared with the classic haunts of the Muses. The poet William Collins delighted in them, as did Gerard Manley Hopkins, and even Gibbon, who otherwise had not a good word to say for his college, fell under their spell when he had rooms in the New Building in the 1750s and found the 'adjacent walks, had they been frequented by Plato's disciples, might have been compared to the Attic shades on the banks of Ilissus'.[4]

107 (right). The rural walks along the Cherwell that gave rise to the 'pleasures of the imagination.'

Addison's beloved meadows and water walks were very nearly sacrificed for picturesque improvements when the college asked Repton to provide a landscape scheme in 1801. Repton pointed out the unique opportunities possessed by Magdalen and lamented that there had been 'no advantage taken of the adjacent Meadow, and trees or the River Charwell which flows through the premises. . . . Redundance of water is natural to the situation, it would surely be advisable to display this in one broad rather than in many narrow channels'.[5] Repton and Nash would have turned the college into a Gothic castle to be reflected in the new lake. Repton recognized that the meadow was 'sacred to Addison' and suggested in a very handsome Red Book that by way of compensation for the loss of his hallowed walk a temple named after Addison should be built on rising ground looking across his beloved meadow transformed into

106 (below). In his Red Book for Magdalen College Repton proposed to float a lake in the meadow 'sacred to Addison' and to build a temple dedicated to him by way of compensation.

a lake to the new picturesque palace. The scheme described by J. C. Buckler, a member of the college, as 'designs for the disfigurement of Magdalen College and the disposal of its pleasure grounds' was rejected.[6]

Addison was acclaimed in his lifetime by an Oxford admirer as the

Great Patron of our Isis groves,
Whom Brunswick honours and Britannia loves,

and since the nineteenth century part of the water walks has been named after him. Recently the wrought-iron gates from his house at Bilton, bearing his initials JA and those of his wife CW, have been placed in front of the stone seat on which he loved to sit in the wildest part of the water walks to muse on the 'pleasures of the imagination'.

RICHMOND AND THE VILLA LANDSCAPE
RICHMOND, SURREY

Richmond was hailed by eighteenth-century travellers as the Frascati of England for its delightful prospects of the Thames and the elegant villas scattered like classical retreats along the banks of the river. When Baron Waldstein visited Richmond by boat in 1600, however, it was to see the royal palace and not the view from Richmond Hill.[1] The palace, which had been built by Henry VII, stood between what is now Old Palace Lane and Water Lane. It had originally been called the palace of Sheen but was renamed after the king's ducal title of Richmond in Yorkshire. Charles I enclosed a large area adjoining East Sheen for a hunting park, which is still famous for its deer and is one of the greatest delights of suburban London. The palace was allowed to decay during the Commonwealth and was cleared away in William and Mary's reign.

The area was fashionable with the aristocracy, not only to take advantage of the delights of the park and a riverside setting, but because the river provided easy transport to London and royal Hampton Court. In the eighteenth century the idea of the Palladian villa as a classical retreat transformed the architectural scene. Many of the new villa residents had places at court but chose to retire to the delights of Richmond and Twickenham (the area to be called Twickenhamshire by Horace Walpole when he settled at Strawberry Hill in 1747) where they could enjoy more freedom for cultural pursuits and more reasonable hours than prevailed in London with its nightly assemblies, balls and card-playing. Lady Mary Wortley Montagu, who took up residence as a close neighbour of Pope in 1719, found she could pass her time 'in great indolence and sweetness' out of London in almost perpetual concerts with musicians lodged in Twickenham.[2] Poets, painters, actors, architects, gardeners and musicians met together in the villas along the river and had the freedom of the residents' gardens, libraries and harpsichords.

108. Aquatint by Joseph Farington in Boydell's *History of the river Thames*, 1794. The cult of idealizing landscape began early here, 'where the silver Thames first rural grows'.

Mrs Henrietta Pye thought that 'my Villeggiature' opened new horizons for ladies who could not make Grand Tours, 'the only way we have of becoming at all acquainted with the Progress of the Arts. . . . Architecture seems their chief Delight: in which if anyone doubts their excelling, let him sail up the River and view their lovely Villas beautifying its Banks'.[3] Daniel Defoe, who had made many tours at home and abroad, had been able to set the beauties of Mrs Pye's 'little Kingdom situated on the Banks of the Thames' in a wider context when writing in his Tour in 1724:

> Nothing in the world can imitate it. . . . But I find none has spoken of what I call the distant Glory of all these Buildings. There is a Beauty of these things at a distance, taking them en Passant, and in Perspective, which few people value, and fewer understand; and yet here they are more truly great, than in all their private Beauties whatsoever. . . . The banks of the Sein are not thus adorned from Paris to Roan, or from Paris to the Loign above the city: the Danube can show nothing like it above and below Vienna, or the Po above and below Turin; the whole Country

109. Pope's villa, 1749, showing the exit of the subterranean grotto tunnel. The main garden (see Plate 83) was across the public highway.

here shines with a lustre not to be described. Take them in a remote view, the fine seats among the Trees as Jewels shine in a rich Coronet; in a near sight they are mere Pictures and paintings; at a distance they are all Nature, near hand all Art; but both in the extremest Beauty. In a word nothing can be more Beautiful; here is a plain and pleasant Country, a rich fertile soil, cultivated and enclosed to the utmost perfection of Husbandry, then bespangled with Villages; those Villages filled with these Houses, and the Houses surrounded with Gardens, Walks, Vistas, Avenues, representing all the Beauties of Building, and all the Pleasures of Planting. [4]

A few years later James Thomson, in *The Seasons*, similarly exclaimed: 'On every hand thy villas shine', and gave poetic expression to this 'stretching' landscape beauty from Richmond. The cult of idealizing landscape and the art of landscape gardening went hand in hand and was fostered at an early stage here where 'the silver Thames first rural grows'. It was small wonder that this cultural élite who had settled along the Thames favoured the new art of landscape gardening, especially when in 1719 Alexander Pope joined them in his Twickenham villa, which he called 'my Tusculum' in memory of Cicero's rural retreat outside Rome. 'Gardening is near a-kin to Philosophy' he maintained and his garden became his great delight when he moved to 'Twit'nam's Bowers'. [5]

Pope had, like Addison, been seen to make a plea for natural landscaping in his *Guardian* essay in 1714 by praising 'the amiable simplicity of unadorned nature'. Voltaire, who visited Pope in 1726, told a visitor to Ferney that he had made a garden 'in the english Taste. There says he is the Thames—and there is Richmond Hills . . . no french Gewgaws—All is Nature'. [6] After Pope's death his garden became a place of pilgrimage. In 1766 Richard

Stockton of Princeton went to view Pope's gardens and grotto taking with him 'a gentleman who draws well, to lay down the exact plan of the whole'. On his return he laid this out with the Highway from Philadelphia to New York standing in for the Thames.[7] In 1789 a Russian traveller, Karamzin, found his way to Pope's villa and lovingly broke off a twig of the willow 'beneath which the philosopher loved to think, the poet to dream'.[8] Pope's villa was destroyed in 1807 by an occupant who was inconvenienced by such persistent visitors, but happily the subterranean grotto survived and is now embedded in the convent opposite a pub called 'Pope's Grotto'.

Pope's advice had been eagerly sought on landscaping matters and soon after his arrival he had been summoned by Princess Caroline to a gardening conference at Richmond Lodge, where Charles Bridgeman was working.[9] The royal gardens at Richmond were joined in 1772 to the contiguous gardens at Kew containing Princess Augusta's botanic garden which later became the famous Kew Gardens with its well-known landmark, William Chambers's ten-storeyed Pagoda, built in 1761. William Gilpin's picturesque eye saw the Pagoda as 'a whimsical object, but has a very good effect'.[10] Chambers had astounded everybody with his *Designs of Chinese buildings* in 1757 when he was beginning to lay out Princess Augusta's gardens. Chambers's books were translated into French and the French persuaded themselves that the *jardin anglais* was, after all, a *jardin anglo-chinois*, an idea taken up by many foreign observers.

Pope is known to have given advice to his Twickenham neighbour, Henrietta Howard, later the Countess of Suffolk, at Marble Hill. She was the Mistress of the Robes to Queen

110. The royal gardens at Richmond were joined in 1772 to the contiguous gardens at Kew, where Chambers had erected his ten-storeyed pagoda in 1761 for Princess Augusta.

Caroline and, by what seems to amount to the queen's encouragement, was King George II's mistress even before his accession. Amateur architects and garden designers flocked to offer their services in 1724 when the Prince of Wales advanced her the money to build Marble Hill. Her friend and fellow courtier Lord Herbert, later to become the Earl of Pembroke, designed the little textbook Palladian villa for her with the help of Roger Morris. Swift advised on the wine cellar, while Pope was preoccupied with her garden with Bridgeman on hand for practical matters. Lord Bathurst sent lime trees from Cirencester Park and Lord Islay, who was one of the trustees appointed by the Prince of Wales to take care of her allowance, gave expert arboricultural advice and shared his gardener Daniel Crofts with her. Lord Islay, later Duke of Argyll, had a large nursery of recently-introduced trees and shrubs at his nearby seat at Whitton, and the huge black walnut tree, *Juglans nigra*, at Marble Hill, one of the largest in the country, is still from his planting.

111. Henrietta Howard's little textbook Palladian villa, 'as white as snow', was one of the cultural retreats along the Thames.

The many eighteenth-century prints of Marble Hill from the river show Pope's 'amiable simplicity' in the garden with grass terraces and arcs of trees probably planned by Bridgeman. As with Pope's river frontage garden nothing was allowed to detract from the Palladian view of the moving river scenery: the more formal gardens were behind the villas. Henrietta Howard had to keep within a strict budget and 'amiable simplicity' also suited her purse. Mrs Henrietta Pye wrote:

> It is most properly stiled Marble Hill, for such it resembles, in a fine green Lawn open to the River and adorned on each Side, by a beautiful Grove of Chestnut Trees, the House is as white as Snow, a small Building without Wings, but of most pleasing Appearance; the Garden is very pleasant; there is an Ally of flowering Shrubs which leads with an early Descent down to a very fine Grotto; there is also a smaller Grotto, from whence there is a fine View of Richmond Hill.[11]

There would have been no lack of grotto advice with Pope and a Pembroke of Wilton to hand. Pope's subterranean grotto provided camera obscura effects of the river and the smaller grotto at Marble Hill may have had similar devices.

A later friend and adviser was Horace Walpole who came to know the Countess of Suffolk in her retirement. Her first 'committee of taste' had been Palladians but now the Strawberry Hill gothicists persuaded her to convert one of her barns into 'a priory of St Hubert' in 1758. It was pulled down after her death in 1767 but was in best gothic taste with pinnacles, lantern and spire, and it hoodwinked at least one traveller, which would have pleased Walpole. Poor Count Kielmansegge wrote that 'while boating, we saw a country house, near which quite a new Gothic building with a tower stood. I took it for a church, but heard afterwards that it was a barn which had been built in that style to look better: just as if such a useful building could be disfiguring!'[12] Henrietta Howard's little Palladian villa 'as white as snow', now owned by English Heritage, certainly still makes a delightful Brenta-like sight along this stretch of the Thames, even though in its public park setting it is now incongruously surrounded by football pitches.

Artists found Richmond irresistible and William Combe's picturesque *History of the river Thames* devotes much space to this 'magnificent reach of the river'.[13] Louis Simond after extensive travels wrote in 1811 that 'after all we have seen in the course of this long tour, this latter view appears to us as beautiful as ever; quite perfect of the kind'[14] and Goethe's romantic friend, Pastor Moritz, was overcome by the view from Richmond Hill:

> It was evening, the sun was just shedding his last parting rays on the valley; but such an evening, and such a valley! O, it is impossible I should ever forget them. The Terrace at Richmond assuredly affords one of the finest prospects in the world. Whatever is charming in nature, or pleasing in art is to be seen here. Nothing I had ever seen is to be compared to it. My feelings, during the few, short, enraptured minutes that I stood there, it is impossible for any pen to describe. . . . In every point of view Richmond is assuredly one of the first situations in the world. Here it was that Thomson and Pope gleaned from nature all those beautiful passages, with which their inimitable writings abound.[15]

CIRENCESTER PARK
CIRENCESTER, GLOUCESTERSHIRE

The layout of the vast park at Cirencester is almost entirely the inspiration of Allen, 1st Lord Bathurst, who termed his domain a 'pretty little plain work in the Brobdingnag style'.[1] In 1787, twelve years after his death, Cirencester was visited by Viscount Torrington. He conceded that Bathurst 'did wonderful things here; but I cannot think with taste, as he adher'd to the formal stile of his youth'.[2] The formal lines at Cirencester are indeed the first characteristic which strikes the visitor even today. The immense and straight Broad Ride stretches nearly five and a half miles from the gates in the town towards the village of Sapperton. However within the formal framework there were informal garden areas, serpentine walks and rides, an irregular lake, Gothic follies, and the feature for which Cirencester was most famous in the eighteenth century, Oakley Wood. Subsequent management of the park has been conservative and as a result much of the original layout remains.

It was only after the death of Queen Anne in 1714, when the Tories, among whom he was a rising star, were swept from power, that Bathurst turned his attention to his Cirencester estate. Thirty years old when he became one of Pope's 'Statesmen out of Place', he was to live for another 61 years, during which time the layout of his park was one of his major concerns. He had the old Jacobean house rebuilt, extended the estate through purchases of land, and began to plant. He was a knowledgeable arboriculturist, and the layout owes much to his association with Stephen Switzer, in particular the latter's notion of 'Rural and extensive gardening'. If we are puzzled by the coexistence of formal and informal elements at Cirencester we need look no further than Switzer. In his book *Ichnographia rustica* of 1718, he promoted 'that extensive Way of Gard'ning . . . the *French* call *La Grand Manier*', but by 'rural' he meant a garden with features 'set off not by nice Art, but by the luxury of Nature'. In addition, following on from Addison, he urged landowners to aim at 'the Decoration and Embellishment of a whole Estate'.[3] Switzer worked for Bathurst, probably at Riskins, Bathurst's ornamental farm in Buckinghamshire, which exemplified this style and he also dedicated one of his books to Bathurst as 'the best of masters and best of friends'.[4]

The other influence was Alexander Pope. Pope first visited in the summer of 1718; in Oakley Wood a 'Silvan Bower' was reserved especially for him, and he soon became Bathurst's collaborator. Pope described that autumn thus: 'I write an hour or two every morning, then ride out a hunting upon the Downes, eat heartily, talk tender sentiments with Lord B. or draw Plans for Houses and Gardens, open Avenues, cut Glades, plant Firrs, contrive waterworks, all very fine and beautiful in our own imagination'.[5] From then until his death Pope spent a good deal of time at Cirencester, and he and Bathurst conferred regularly about the architecture and planting in the park.

The Broad Ride is not the kind of avenue Pope ridiculed in the *Epistle to Burlington*, in which 'Grove nods at grove, each Alley has a brother,/And half the platform just reflects the

112 (right). The Broad Ride, looking back towards Cirencester church, on which it is aligned.

113 (far right). A plan of Oakley Wood, published in Samuel Rudder's *New history of Gloucestershire*, 1779. The vignettes show Alfred's Hall in its eighteenth-century setting, complete with Bathurst's 'little baubling works around it'.

other'. As well as the variety within the formal frame, the sheer scale precludes this sort of paucity. Pope wrote enthusiastically of 'the noble Scenes, Openings, & Avenues of this immense Design', and of 'planting a whole Country with Clumps of Firs': 'No words, nor painting, nor poetry . . . can give the least Image proportionable to it'.[6] Above all, the trees themselves were a feature: 'rising Forests', as Pope called them, of beech, oak, elm, chestnut, that stretched, and still do stretch, 'from down to down' in great luxuriant waves of varying colour and texture.[7] Pope saw in Bathurst not the arrogance of a prince, but the care of a husbandman. His estate, with its 'rising Granaries and Temples . . . mingled Farms and Pyramids' proved Pope's dictum:

> *'Tis Use alone that sanctifies Expence,*
> *And Splendor borrows all her rays from Sense.*[8]

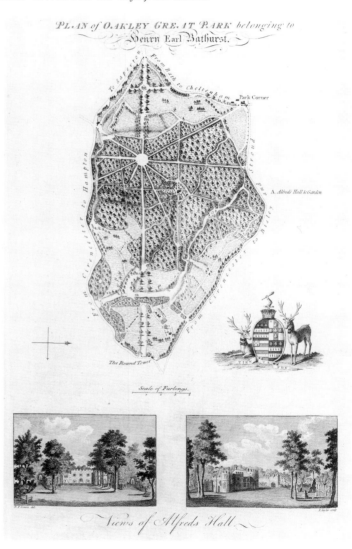

114. *The park at Cirencester*, painted by George Lambert (*c.*1730), showing the Broad Ride and Ivy Lodge, in a typical balance of formality and informality. (Cirencester House, by kind permission of the Earl Bathurst)

In addition to this planting Cirencester also had the appeal of scenes on a smaller scale. Bathurst designed the hexagon to be 'backed with wood, so that nothing can be seen but the three sides';[9] while Alfred's Hall, the Silvan Bower, the lake and the three Gothic farm buildings which now front the polo ground, were all incidents within what Pope called 'the Elysian Groves of *Cirencester*'.[10] Thus Oakley Wood was both a profitable investment by a skilled arboriculturist, and an 'enchanted Forest' of which Pope could write: 'I look upon myself as the Magician appropriated to the place, without whom no mortal can penetrate the Recesses of those sacred Shades'.[11]

Although the Broad Ride now reaches to the Cecily Hill gates in the town, the last mile eastward from Seven Rides was only created after Bathurst's death. When Samuel Rudder described the park in 1769, the Hexagon and Pope's Seat were approached by a 'serpentine walk . . . above a mile in length, finely arched and shaded by the plantation through which it passes'.[12] The immense vista would only have opened out after this more Arcadian and embowered landscape, where, as William Combe described it in the early 1790s, 'the flowering shrub dispenses its fragrance, and the laurel offers its verdure'.[13]

The lake, dug out by 1736, was one of the earliest irregular pieces of water in the history of English gardening. Rudder noted that by the cunning planting of 'clumps of trees to conceal the extremities of the lake', it has the appearance of 'part of a considerable river'. He was also impressed by the apparent boundlessness of the park: 'The eye is nowhere offended with the appearance of bare walls, nor can it judge of the extent of the park, as the country about it is taken into view, over fossees and concealed boundaries made for that purpose'. Either Rudder actually had in mind Pope's principle of surprising, varying and concealing the bounds, or Bathurst had successfully put Pope's principles into practice. A good example of such a fossee or ha-ha runs with the footpath across the axis from the house to Queen Anne's column.

In 1742 Cirencester was visited by the Reverend Jeremiah Milles, cousin of Bishop Pococke. He described it as 'a fine park, wch Ld Bathurst has adornd with several beautifull buildings'. He noted the Queen Anne monument, and the vistas and cross vistas. He also penetrated Oakley Wood and discovered Alfred's Hall in its plantation of yews:

> There is likewise a little old house situated in the thickest part of ye wood; to wch Ld
> Bathurst has given a very romantick appearance by building some walls in an
> irregular manner, & in a Gothick taste, in order to make it look like ye ruins of a
> castle. Ld Bathurst has a Pheasantry here, & sometimes dines & drinks here.[14]

Although not complete until 1734, it had been begun in 1721, and is probably the first ruin purpose-built as an ornament to a landscape. In 1733 Mrs Delany wrote with satisfaction to Swift that it had already been taken by an antiquarian for a genuine relic of King Arthur's time.[15] It seems to have been designed by Pope and Bathurst together. It was never inhabited

115. Alfred's Hall at the beginning of the century. Although it has since fallen into real ruin, recent initiatives offer strong hopes of the building being restored.

but was an occasional retreat; Rudder mentions a bowling green and 'many beautiful lawns and agreeable walks around it'. The walls Milles refers to may be those of Alfred's Hall itself or they may be the additional fragmentary 'ruins' Bathurst built nearby; in writing to Pope about the folly he made mention of the 'little baubling works around it'.[16]

Viscount Torrington objected to the lack of decorum in the folly: 'It is call'd Alfred's Cave (why I know not) and there is an intention of deceit by old dates; but why shou'd the outside be dirty, and in filthy nastiness? Gothic, and monastic buildings may be kept in taste; and yet as nice as a drawing room'.[17] But a later visitor, Barbara Jones, praised Pope and Bathurst for achieving here the genuine 'amorphous squalor of the Middle Ages'.[18] Alfred's Hall survives, to be found by adventurous tourists deep in Oakley Wood. This wonderful building is at present genuinely ruinous, but now there is hope that it will be restored to its proper mock-ruinous state.

As a result of Bathurst's longevity, and perhaps the grandeur of what he had achieved by the time of his death, Cirencester escaped 'naturalizing'. The estate remains in his family, and his descendants have continued Bathurst's custom of allowing free access to the park all year round.

ROUSHAM HOUSE
ROUSHAM, OXFORDSHIRE

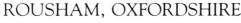

Rousham as it stands today is, as Christopher Hussey has said, 'the *locus classicus* for the study of Kent'.[1] It has no later additions and it is indeed fortunate that what Walpole called the 'most engaging' of his works, where garden and countryside are so perfectly integrated, should have been the one to survive virtually intact.[2] It has an unmistakable freshness of inspiration which was not lost on a recent 'glasnost' Russian art historian who in a summing-up of his tour of English landscaped gardens wrote: 'Most of all I was charmed with the impression of youth in Rousham; there I received the feeling of the spring of landscape style. The strangely simple Kent's invention gave the appreciation of strength, which promised the future glory of picturesque'.[3]

Kent's versatile talents as architect, painter, decorator, furniture designer and landscape gardener are all displayed in the house and garden at Rousham. Walpole may have seen Lord Burlington as the Apollo of the Arts and Kent his proper priest, but at Rousham, with General Dormer, Kent was an innovator and his landscape gardening owed little to Chiswick. Rousham had a most advantageous situation above a bend in the River Cherwell overlooking well-cultivated and wooded countryside. In 1677 Robert Plot described terraced walks, 'no less than five one under another, leading from the Garden above, down to the Riverside, having Steps at each End, and parted with Hedges of Codlings etc'.[4] Charles Bridgeman was involved in the laying-out of a new garden in an area to the north of these terraces, formerly

116. At Rousham the views out into the countryside are as important as those within the garden.

part of the warren, which John Gay found 'extremely improved' in 1726.[5] The garden consisted of a 'Bridgemannick' theatre, square ponds, cascades and fountains and a wilderness seen from a bastion viewing-point, which delighted Pope, who wrote to Martha Blount in 1728: 'I lay one night at Rousham, which is the prettiest place for water-falls, jetts, ponds inclosed with beautiful scenes of green and hanging wood that ever I saw'.[6] The five terraces had been made into a grass slope, as George Berkeley, who had a special reason for viewing the little tributary of the Thames with pleasure, wrote in 1734 to Henrietta Howard, whose second husband he was soon to become: 'I own a partiality for Rowsham. One advantage must be allowed it; there is at the bottom of a sloping hill . . . a most delightful stream, which runs from thence direct to Marble Hill'.[7]

The second phase of the landscaping was undertaken when General James Dormer, a veteran of Blenheim, inherited after his brother's death in 1737 and engaged Kent to naturalize the garden. Bridgeman's formal viewing-points and 'phlegmatic' planting were, as at Chiswick, to be changed.[8] Pope was a great friend of both Dormers, and Walpole, who much admired Rousham, felt that Pope's ideas for his Twickenham garden had been very influential on Kent and the general, who needed 'philisophic retirement'.[9] Dormer had been a member of the Kit-Kat Club and a friend of Addison, whose ideas that a whole estate should be 'thrown into a kind of garden' had also influenced the Rousham layout. The pleasure and profit motive of Virgilian husbandry particularly appealed to the Dormers, who were progressive farmers; agricultural as well as landscape improvements were carried out on their estate, increasing crop yields and improving stock raising.[10] Addison's idea that 'Fields of Corn make a pleasant prospect' was almost a necessity at Rousham as the Dormers did not own the land across the Cherwell and their views were by courtesy of neighbouring farmers. Oxfordshire, especially the region north of Oxford, was ideal for the new naturalistic garden art of creating living landscapes: its numerous streams, gently undulating terrain, wooded hills and cultivated valleys were reminiscent of the Campagna around Rome, so beloved by painters.

The general, who was concerned with every aspect of the garden, saw it as an ideal setting for his antique sculptures. A plan of Kent's intended garden was drawn up in 1738 by his gardener, John MacClary,[11] with annotations by the steward, William White, who conveyed it to General Dormer so that he could indicate where he wanted the statues to go.[12] The plan also shows where Kent wanted conifers and whether forest trees were to be planted in underwood or to show bare column-like stems, like stage sets. MacClary clearly had a great deal to do with the laying-out of the garden as a letter from him of 1750 shows.[13] By then the general had died and a cousin, Sir Clement Cottrell, George II's Master of Ceremonies, had inherited but seldom visited Rousham. Walpole could not imagine how the family could leave it all: 'Well, if I had such a house, such a library, so pretty a place, and so pretty a wife, I think I should let King George send to Herrenhausen for a Master of Ceremonies'.[14] The gardener was more contemptuous and began his long letter: 'Madam I'afraid my Master and all of you have forgot what a Place Rousham is, so I have sent you a description of it that it may not quite creep out of your Memorys'.

MacClary knew exactly how the general had instructed him to show Rousham to visitors, who entered by a special pedimented gate from the highway, designed by Kent. Doubtless he received rewarding tips from people like Mrs Delany, who found Rousham 'past my skill to describe; all I can say of it is that I never saw a garden which pleased me so well'.[15]

117. Van Nost's statue of Pan is one of many such statues which participate in the poetic scenes and were an important element in General Dormer's garden.

118. William Kent's drawing of the cascade in Venus Vale. This was the climax in the garden circuit. (Private Collection)

MacClary shows how the immediate impression must be from looking outwards to the countryside and how this was done by the placing of the general's prize Scheemakers' sculpture of a lion devouring a horse not in a niche but free-standing, to attract attention so that when the tourist approached his eye was led to the 'rural and chearful' scene beyond:

> When you walk out at the Hall Door . . . you walk forward to view the Lion nearer, when your eye drops upon a very fine Concave Slope, at the Bottom of which runs the Beautiful River Charvell . . . the prettiest view in the whole World . . . you see from hence five pretty Country Villages, and the Great Triumphant Arch in Aston Field, together with the naturial turnings of the Hills, to let that charming River downe to butify our Gardens, and what stops our Long view is a very pretty Corn Mill, Built in the Gothick manner but nothing sure can please the Eye like our Short View, their is fine Meadow, cut off from the garden only by the River Charvell wheron is all sorts of Cattle feeding, which looks the same as if they were feeding in the Garden, and through the middle of the meadow runs a great High Road, which goes from several Cities to several Cities, their you see Carriers Wagons,

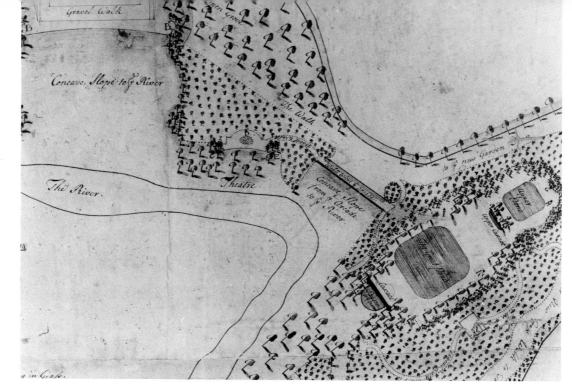

Gravel Walk

Concave Slope to ye River

The River.

Theatre

119 (left). Venus Vale: It seemed to Walpole that Pope's influence was apparent in its feeling of 'practical poetry'.

120 (right). Detail from the steward's plan drawn up so that the general could approve the positions for the statues. The circuit shown by Kent is not the one usually taken today.

Gentlemen's Equipages, Women riding, Men walking, and sometimes twenty Droves of Cattle goes by in a Day, then you see Hayford Bridge . . . and Turn about you see a good old House uninhabited.

All the general's statues on the perimeter walk looked outwards across the river to Kent's eyecatcher on the hill and his Gothic mill. MacClary goes on to describe the *ferme ornée* perimeter walk with the first seat being placed to view Kent's gothicized house across the ha-ha and grazed field. The inner garden was screened by evergreen walks enlivened with flowery underplantings, delightfully described as 'deferant sorts of Flowers, peeping through the deferant sorts of Evergreens, here you think the Laurel produces a Rose, the Holly a Syringa, the Yew a Lilac, and the sweet Honeysuckle is peeping out from under every Leafe, in short they are so mixt together, that youd think every Leafe of the Evergreens, produced one flower or a nother'. Venus Vale is the climax of Kent's surprises when, after the 'roundabout' walk, the visitor sees the cascades and fountains and the frolics of fauns and satyrs participating in the enchanted scene. 'Sure no tongue can express the Beautyfull view that presents itself to your eye'. This is the part of the garden Walpole felt owed most to Pope and ideas of 'practical poetry'.[16, 17] William Burgh said that Kent had been greatly influenced by 'reading the picturesque descriptions of Spenser', whose *Faerie Queene* he illustrated.[18]

Later foreign visitors studying English gardens seem to have passed Rousham by, even when visiting nearby Stowe and Blenheim. This is almost certainly because Thomas Whately, for some reason, omitted it from his book. Every book on garden history now devotes much space to Rousham and certainly landscape architects from all over the world come to see it. A Polish professor interested in restoring English gardens looked out from General Dormer's purposefully placed lion and horse statue and exclaimed, 'but we never realized that what was outside the garden was as important as what was within'. *Le jardin anglais* was seen as a jumble of serpentine paths and whimsical ornamental buildings from pattern books; it needed the message of Rousham to appreciate that the essential ingredient was the idealized English countryside.

STUDLEY ROYAL
near RIPON, YORKSHIRE

Studley Royal is still rated as one of the scenic 'Wonders of the North', just as it was by many eighteenth-century travellers who visited the Aislabies' creation near Ripon. Situated in beautiful Skelldale it opened up new possibilities for exploiting natural scenery in landscape gardening, far more romantic than the Addison-inspired rural gardening, which was more appropriate in the tamer south. '*Une vallée enchantée*', exclaimed a French visitor in 1751.[1] The wild scenery was, however, tamed and humanized by what Richard Sulivan in his Tour called 'a beautiful assemblage' of buildings and objects, 'most elegantly diversified' temples, rotundas, a banqueting house, statuary, pavilions, canal, towers, cascades, bridges and lodges, all seen through 'artless vistos'.[2]

121. One of the paintings of Studley Royal attributed to Balthazar Nebot. Fountains Abbey was shown to visitors through an 'artless visto' even before it was acquired by the Aislabies in 1768. (Private Collection)

John Aislabie, a friend of Vanbrugh and Burlington, began building a new Palladian house at Studley after the old one was destroyed by fire in 1716. Work on his famous water-garden began in earnest after his precipitated retirement to his Yorkshire estate when the South Sea Bubble burst in 1720 and he as Chancellor of the Exchequer was discredited. In 1723 he wrote to Colonel Grahme of Levens, a long-standing political exile and garden-maker, that he was now 'an outlaw myself and surrounded by impenetrable obscurity'.[3] John Aislabie worked unceasingly on his gardens at Studley Royal and his son William extended the layout and added further embellishments after his death in 1742.

Every estate owner who was contemplating improvements visited Studley Royal. Philip Yorke and his wife, Jemima, who were laying-out Wrest Park, took note of the siting of buildings in which they were particularly interested and in the contrast of elegance and wildness everywhere to be seen. They visited in 1744, shortly after John Aislabie's death, and Philip Yorke observed in his journal:

> Spent 6 hours in riding over Mr Aislabie's park at Studley. The natural beauties of this place are superior to anything of the kind I ever saw, and improved with great taste both by the late and the present owner. The extent of the whole is 710 acres, of which about 150 are reckoned into the garden, and the river Scheld, which runs through the ground, covers (as they told us) 23 of them. It is impossible from a single survey, however well conducted, to conceive oneself or give a stranger an adequate idea of Studley. Imagine rocks covered with wood, sometimes perpendicularly steep and craggy, at others descending in slopes to beautiful lawns and parterres, water thrown into 20 different shapes—a canal, a basin, a lake, a purling stream, now gliding gently through the plain, now foaming and tumbling in a cascade down 8 or 10 steps. In one place it is finely turned through the middle arch of a rough stone bridge. The buildings are elegant and well suited to the ground they stand upon. The temple of Venus is at the head of a canal in the midst of a thick wood; that of Hercules on another spot not less delightful. A Gothick tower overlooks the park and gardens from the summit of a rock. Mr Aislabie designs to erect a Chinese house of a pyramidical form, with a gallery encircling every story, upon the point of a ridge which encloses on each hand a valley finely wooded and washed by a rivulet. One side is formed into a number of small terraces interspersed with rock, which makes a Chinese landscape. You have besides several agreeable views of Ripon, the adjacent country, and Fountains Abbey; and what seems almost peculiar to Studley is that the same object, taken at a different point of view, is surprisingly diversified and has all the grace of novelty.[4]

Lady Margaret Hay, who visited Studley the following year, saw 'a Chinese House now building in the Park',[5] but the Yorkes saw Studley Royal as 'a Chinese landscape' even before the Chinese pavilion appeared on the scene. A painting (Plate 122) attributed to Balthazar Nebot shows the rocky scenery of the 'Chinese landscape' the Yorkes admired, with the Chinese pavilion now perched on the top of the hill. The idea of natural scenery, especially of rocks, mountains, trees and water, being embellished by pavilions would have seemed to the

122. Another of the series of paintings of Studley Royal by Balthazar Nebot (see also frontispiece). This one shows buildings and rocky scenery in what the Yorkes saw as 'a Chinese landscape'. The Chinese building on the hill was added in 1745.

Aislabies and the Yorkes particularly Chinese. Missionaries were bringing home stories of the imperial hunting parks at Jehol and Yuan Ming Yuan with pleasure pavilions set on crags by water, and the walk through Skelldale with its temples and towers would have looked to them like a Chinese scroll being unwound.

Lord Burlington had acquired one of Matteo Ripa's albums of drawings of the emperor's hunting park at Jehol when he visited London in 1724, and these became well known to his set, but if Chiswick offered little hope for scenic Chinese landscaping, even if Burlington had wished, Studley Royal was ideal. Another Chinese trait which Yorke found new and 'almost peculiar to Studley' was the way the buildings had reciprocal functions and as well as embellishing the scenery and providing retreats for contemplation and dreams of immortality were themselves viewing-points for other scenes. Vanbrugh had achieved this with his Temple of the Winds at Castle Howard but at Studley there are endlessly changing vistas. The banqueting house is the best example of Aislabie's subtle control of vistas, which are now being painstakingly restored. Framed by trees it is glimpsed from the bridge between the fishing lodges at the head of the canal. It was said that the Aislabies frequently took meals in the banqueting hall and from the level lawn in front of it there are three separate vistas across the park; one of them with views on several levels focused on the statue of Neptune in the Moon Pond, the Temple of Piety and a column on the brow of the hill.

The most magnificent of all the eye-catching buildings was ruined Fountains Abbey, which was not actually acquired until 1768. It had from the beginning been used as the culmination of the surprise vistas even before it came into the Aislabies' possession. The Yorkes saw it as making 'a very venerable magnificent appearance' and commiserated with William Aislabie that the Roman Catholic gentleman who owned it would not part with it. The antiquarian Bray in his Tour, performed in 1777 after the abbey had been landscaped into the garden, saw it as 'one of the most picturesque and beautiful objects that any seat in

England can command'.[6] William Gilpin, however, in his *Tour of the Lakes*, published in 1786, was full of criticism: 'What a lovely scene might a person of pure taste have made at Studley, with one tenth of the expence, which hath been laid out in deforming it. . . . On the whole it is hard to say, whether nature has done more to embellish the scenes of Studley or art to deform them'.[7] Louis Simond, the French-American, who travelled with Gilpin in his pocket, disliked the idea of the Skell being trapped into 'old-fashioned square ponds, in very bad taste'.[8] The Duke of Rutland, although a devotee of Gilpin, approved of Studley Royal, and was 'by no means determined to subscribe to the justice of his censure'.[9]

Gilpin's picturesque curate, Richard Warner, however, having arrived at the destined viewing-point for the abbey, disapprovingly wrote in his own *Tour through the northern counties* that 'for a moment we were imposed upon, by the surprise arising from such a magnificent object bursting upon the view unexpectedly; but as soon as judgement resumed its office, all pleasing emotions were destroyed, by the senseless incongruity and unnatural association in the scene before us', and his picturesque eye also frowned on 'all the artificial ornaments' which 'satiate and disgust, instead of affording pleasure'.[10] John Byng, Viscount Torrington, in his 1792 Tour to the north, also voiced the general disapproval for the proliferation of unsuitable buildings in landscaped gardens, particularly 'the paltry Gothic temple with sash'd windows' from which to get the first view of the 'noble remains' of the abbey.[11] The romantic Prince Pückler-Muskau on a visit in 1829 was delighted by the natural beauty of Studley

123. William Alexander: Watercolour of an imperial Chinese landscape with picturesque buildings sited on hilly, rocky scenery. (Victoria and Albert Museum, London)

124. Moon Pond at Studley Royal. The contrast of elegance and wildness delighted visitors.

Royal, which he agreed, however, would be better for some pruning of Aislabie's garden buildings:

> Leaving the abbey, in half an hour you reach a beautiful and finely kept pleasure-ground, which is rendered peculiarly delightful by its diversity of hill and vale, noble trees, and well-placed clumps; though rather encumbered with a multitude of old-fashioned summer-houses, temples and worthless leaden statues. In one of these temples, dedicated to the Gods of antiquity, stands a bust of—Nero!. But these slight defects might easily be removed, while such a combination of natural beauty can rarely be met with. At the end of the deer-park stands the house of the proprietress, an elderly single lady of large fortune. I met her in the garden, and was invited by her to luncheon, which I gladly accepted, as my long walk had made me very hungry.[12]

The twentieth century, in Christopher Hussey's words, sees Studley Royal as 'one of the most spectacular scenic compositions in England',[13] and today's visitors can take refreshment, by courtesy of the National Trust, as they enter by the lake. Before it was acquired by the National Trust Studley Royal had been saved from dereliction in 1966 when West Riding County Council bought the estate and it was painstakingly researched by the deputy county architect, Mr W. Walker. At the time it was said that 'restoration will take a number of years. But that is appropriate. The Aislabies' was not an instant world but one in which there was a respectable pause for anticipation between the conception of a project and its realisation'.[14]

STOWE
near BUCKINGHAM, BUCKS

Of all the great landscaped gardens none was more frequently visited or cited than Stowe. It is an indication of its popularity that Stowe was the subject of the first guidebook for garden tourists. Bridgeman, Vanbrugh, Kent and Brown were all employed on this grandiose layout and ensured that Stowe was in the vanguard of gardening taste throughout the eighteenth century.

The house we now see is a modified version of a design by Robert Adam and was built in the 1770s. It incorporates the late seventeenth-century mansion visited by Celia Fiennes in about 1694. Early in the eighteenth century, Sir Richard Temple, later made Viscount Cobham, employed Vanbrugh to make additions to the house and Charles Bridgeman to design a suitable garden. Bridgeman's layout, expanding southwards, was irregular but bounded largely by straight ha-has. He built a large octagonal pond, a formal canal and plantations with both straight avenues and asymmetrical winding paths—'cross walks [that] end in vistos, arches and statues, and private ones cut thro' groves', as an early visitor, Lord Perceval, described them.[1] Bridgeman's perspective drawing of *circa* 1720 shows this early stage of the design. Vanbrugh ornamented the grounds with several buildings, including the 60 foot high pyramid, but only the Rotunda and the Lake Pavilions now survive. The Rotunda, which was aligned on three different avenues, originally contained a gilded copy of the Venus de' Medici, and was designed to stand at the western end of the canal. This was the centrepiece of the 'Garden of Venus'. At the other end of the canal, according to Jeremiah Milles who visited in 1735, was 'a statue of Q Caroline by four fluted Ionick pillars with their entablature, on each side are three statues of shepherds and shepherdesses, dancing'. The Lake Pavilions adorned the octagonal lake (in which Vanbrugh also built an obelisk-fountain), and were, Milles wrote, painted 'al Fresco with two storys out of Pastor fido'.[2] At this stage, evidently, Stowe was a light-hearted pleasure garden.

In 1724 Lord Perceval wrote to Daniel Dering that the garden 'is now almost finished', and summed up the character of Bridgeman's first phase succinctly: 'Nothing is more irregular in the whole, nothing is more regular in the parts'. He continued: 'What adds to the bewty of this garden is, that it is not bounded by walls, but by a Ha-Hah, which leaves you the sight of a bewtiful woody country'.[3]

Between 1727 and 1732 Home Park was brought into the garden, nearly doubling its size. Bridgeman added the Eleven Acre Lake with its straight edges meeting at irregular angles and also, perhaps responding to the new ideas of Stephen Switzer, left most of the ground as pasture surrounded by straight paths. On the southern edge William Kent designed the first of his buildings for Stowe, the 'Persian Pavillion', now known as the Temple of Venus, and the hermitage. The garden as it was when Bridgeman left is depicted in the drawings of Jacques Rigaud, published in 1746 but made, according to George Vertue, in 1733. It was the garden

125. Charles Bridgeman's perspective drawing of Stowe, c.1720. (Bodleian Library, Oxford)

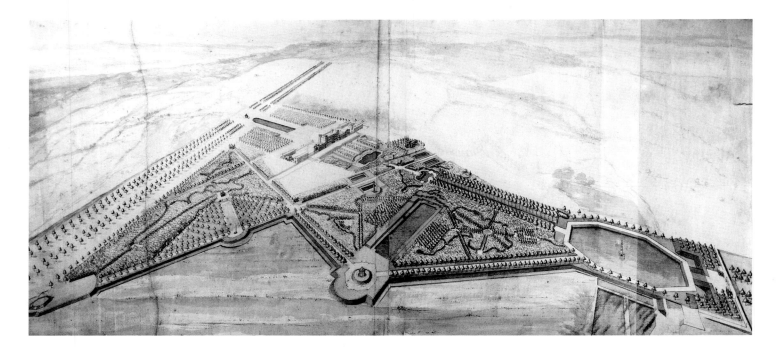

at this stage of its development that was the 'Work to wonder at' which Pope held up as exemplary in the *Epistle to Burlington*.

By 1734 Cobham had re-routed the approach and was thus able to bring into the garden land east of the main axis. He had also quarrelled with the prime minister over the Excise Bill in 1733 and, although a Whig, had gone into opposition. With Lord Lyttelton and George Grenville he formed an independent Whig group, known as the 'boy patriots', and Stowe became a centre for their opposition alignment with the Tories. Although Walpole's fall brought Cobham back into active political life, in 1742 he resigned his commission from the army, objecting to the use of British troops to support Hanoverian interests in Europe. In 1744 James Thomson added a description of Stowe to *The Seasons*, in which he praised its 'Elysian vales', but expressed disappointment at Cobham's retirement:

> *What pity, COBHAM! thou thy verdant Files*
> *Of order'd trees shouldst here inglorious range,*
> *Instead of Squadrons flaming o'er the Field.*[4]

Cobham's political exile certainly affected the tone of the garden. In the newly acquired area a very different type of layout was created. The Elysian Fields are small-scale, literary and allusive in character. William Kent designed the buildings, but it was Cobham who introduced the element of political satire into the garden. Unlike Bridgeman's luxurious layout with its temples of Bacchus and Sleep and its Garden of Venus, the Elysian Fields were ornamented with the moralizing temples of Ancient and Modern Virtue (the latter symbolically ruinous). A grotto was built and the river re-named the Styx. The eight busts of the British Worthies had previously stood on the circuit round Home Park, but were brought over here, and eight more added to complete this 'very elegant Piece of Satyr' as Gilpin termed it.[5]

However the moral element did not preclude the picturesque. As Philip Southcote

remarked, 'Lord Cobham began in the Bridgeman taste: 'tis the Elysian Fields that is the painting part of his gardens',[6] and the Elysian Fields were not wholly serious. In the plantation between the river Styx and the south vista stood one of the oddest of the vanished follies, described by Milles as 'a little square room irregularly built wth ye doors made uneven & little windows. It is call'd ye witch house ye inside is painted wth odd representations of witches by one Thomas Ferrand a servant of Ld Cobhams'.[7]

In the early 1740s the area east of the Elysian Fields was developed, ornamented with buildings by James Gibbs. Gibbs had been involved sporadically at Stowe since 1726: his Boycott Pavilions date from 1730. He was now recalled, and built the Temple of Friendship, the Queen's Temple (now the school music room), and possibly also the column erected in 1749 to the memory of Lord Cobham. This area is crowned by his most unusual building at Stowe, the red ironstone Gothic Temple, his only Gothic building, of 1741–4. The Saxon deities which used to stand in a glade in the plantation north of Home Park were moved into the temple and it shared the Whig iconography of 'Liberty' which dominates the Elysian Fields. It not only survives but has been refurbished by the Landmark Trust and can be rented for holidays.

Capability Brown, head gardener from 1741, probably helped Cobham in designing this area. He certainly had a hand in the final piece of the garden laid out in Cobham's time, the Grecian Valley, the softly contoured, 'naturally' planted vale that bends away north-east of the house. Apart from the Temple of Concord and Victory at its head, this area was left devoid of temples and is clearly part of the new landscaping movement of which Brown was the inspiration.

Stowe was the first garden to be the subject of a tourist guide. Guides to the art collections of houses like Wilton had been produced earlier, and in 1732, a poem, Gilbert West's *Stowe, the gardens of the Right Honourable Richard Viscount Cobham* had been published. This was, however, a celebration rather than a guide, taking the reader on a circuit round the garden, praising its features and expanding on its themes. It was not addressed to tourists: where later guides begin at the public entrance, West starts on the steps of the house. In 1744 however, Benton Seeley's *Description of the gardens of Lord Viscount Cobham at Stow* appeared, and this was designed to show tourists round the ornamental layout. The garden quickly became a publishers' battleground, as a rival to Seeley, George Bickham, competed in this evidently quite lucrative trade. But Bickham's *Beauties of Stow* (1750) was cobbled together without even the benefit of a visit to the garden and he was finally routed by Seeley when the latter in 1759 included a tour of the principal rooms of the house in his now comprehensive guide.

Seeley's map of 1759 shows the seventeenth-century kitchen garden still in its original position close to the house; an unusual survival when kitchen gardens were being moved to

127. The Temple of British Worthies in the Elysian Fields at Stowe.

128. James Gibbs' Gothic Temple at Stowe, depicted in its romantic early nineteenth-century setting by J.C. Nattes in one of a series of views, 1805–7. (Buckinghamshire County Museum)

less prominent parts of the estate. Cobham evidently had some feeling for the old formal elements. Below the south front he retained 'a Parterre wch is clos'd on each side by trees, cut in Arcades, under wch stand gilt vases, & Bay trees alternately'.[8] The map also shows the garden with its new pieces of land, with the lines of the Bridgeman lakes and walks made irregular, the canal filled in, and the avenues reduced to the faintest of outlines. Cobham had died in 1749 and Brown left in 1751, so much of this was work carried out under Cobham's successor, Richard Grenville, Earl Temple. In 1765 the triumphal arch was erected on the southern horizon, while the remodelling of the house was completed between 1772 and 1774.

The Swedish artist, Fredrik Magnus Piper, on his travelling scholarship to study English gardens, visited Stowe in the 1770s and voiced a common criticism of the number of buildings in the park:

> This park includes an [un?]usual number of ornamental structures, of a scale, size and variety that reveal a desire to win fame by outdoing every other place in respect of expense and numbers, but which through just this attempt has lost much of the simple *champêtre* appearance, and the romantic and picturesque character, that one notices with so much delight at Stourton [Stourhead] as I have described.[9]

The Prince de Ligne cited Stowe as an example of 'Templo-mania' and commented, 'my lord Temple has been too much led astray by his name'.[10] But the highly ornamented and rather bare appearance of the gardens in Rigaud's time was now being changed by the growing trees as well as Temple's less formal style. Mrs Lybbe Powys visited Stowe in 1775 and described the natural improvements effected by the growth of the plantations:

> The buildings used, I know, to be thought too numerous, but in such an extent I do not even think that, and the fine plantations now grown up to obscure them properly, must add infinitely to many picturesque views of porticos, temples, &c., which when originally were expos'd at once, with perhaps three or four more seen from the same point, must have had a very different and crowded effect.[11]

John Wesley, visiting in 1779, found much to censure: 'Buildings, called Temples' often upset him, but those at Stowe in particular he found 'most miserable': 'Vanbrugh's' (presumably the Temple of Bacchus which was demolished early this century) he thought 'an ugly, clumsy lump, hardly fit for a gentleman's stable'. The statues he considered 'coarse', and, a common complaint—of Gilpin at the Leasowes or of Louis Simond at most places—he commented on the dirtiness of the water in the ponds. Despite his sermonizing, and his vituperative tone, his response highlights the change in garden ideas since the 1730s, when he writes:

> It is a childish affectation to call things here by Greek or Latin names, as Styx, and the Elysian Fields. It was ominous for my Lord to entertain himself and his noble company in a grotto on the bank of the Styx; that is on the brink of hell. The river on which it stands is a black, filthy puddle, exactly resembling a common sewer.[12]

129. Jacques Rigaud's view (c.1733) from Kent's Temple of Venus: 'A work to wonder at'.

Temple died in that year and the completion of his schemes was overseen by George Grenville, 1st Marquis of Buckingham. The finished article is beautifully illustrated in the

collection of drawings made by John Claude Nattes in 1805–9. They show thickly umbrageous and romantic scenes, clumps of maturing trees and softly contoured slopes. Their mood is reflected in the account by Baron van Spaen van Biljoen in 1791. The alder plantation below the Elysian Fields, for example, 'offers a deep retreat, wreathed in shade and impenetrable to even the brightest shaft of sunlight. . . . Pines and ancient gnarled elms, dead tree-trunks wreathed in ivy, the stillness of the water, everything in this deep solitude encourages meditation and inspires melancholy'.[13] The moral element has been lost in the picturesque shades.

By the time Pückler-Muskau visited Stowe its interest was almost antiquarian: 'The grounds were laid out long ago; and though in many respects beautiful, and remarkable for fine lofty trees, are so overloaded with temples and buildings of all sorts, that the greatest possible improvement would be the pulling down ten or a dozen of them'.[14]

The marquis had spared little expense, but the family fortunes declined quickly in the nineteenth century. J. C. Loudon wrote in 1831 that he was 'sorry to learn that these gardens are not being kept up as they used to be; the number of hands being yearly lessened'.[15]

In 1848 bankruptcy was declared and much of the family property was sold. The house and grounds were finally sold in 1923 and became the home of the newly-established Stowe School. In 1986 a trust was set up with the aim of restoring the 32 surviving garden buildings to their appearance in 1800, and very recently (1989) the National Trust has agreed to take charge of the whole landscape which had been painstakingly maintained by the school since 1923.

SHUGBOROUGH
near STAFFORD, STAFFORDSHIRE

'I must hasten to describe a Place I never heard of before last night and yet in my opinion Deserves to be accounted one of the finest Improvements in England. I mean Mr Ansons Lord Ansons Brothers at Shockborough'.[1] So wrote the Irish landowner, John Parnell in 1769. Parnell was on his second trip to England, making notes for his own estate improvements. At Shugborough he was viewing the results of Thomas Anson's determined efforts for over forty years, which had replaced a riverside village with its fields, roads, mills and cottages with an extensive ornamental landscape. By the early nineteenth century the process was complete

132. The Chinese House at Shugborough. When John Parnell saw it in 1769 its exterior was painted blue and white 'with Indian Birds Mandarins &c.'

133. 'Athenian' Stuart's Tower of the Winds at Shugborough, 1765. The lake in which it stood was destroyed by the flood of 1795. The temple was originally only accessible by a bridge.

and the present National Trust property still shows the garden tourist much of his achievement.

In 1720 Thomas Anson inherited the manor of Shugborough, which his great-grandfather had bought only a hundred years earlier. Anson was a traveller and a scholar, and a founder-member of the Society of Dilettanti. His brother was Admiral George Anson, who completed his famous and highly profitable circumnavigation of the world in 1744. Admiral Anson was married to Elizabeth Yorke, sister of Philip Yorke who had inherited Wrest Park through his wife Jemima, Marchioness Grey. The Yorkes were in the vanguard of informed taste and with the admiral's money helped Thomas Anson in his plans for Shugborough.

When he inherited the manor Anson was just another freeholder in Shugborough, but around 1730 he began acquiring freeholds, leases and copyholds from other villagers. There is evidence that the village's traditional economy was faltering and this obviously put Anson in a strong position when pressing to acquire properties.[2] The process was finally completed when the last copyhold tenement in the village, that of Widow Sayer, passed into the Anson estate in 1802. All the same the acquisitions did not always happen quickly enough: the Lanthorn of Demosthenes, standing as a signal of the park's extent, was erected by Anson on land he did not own, and much of the landscaped ground which Parnell saw Anson occupied solely as a squatter. He also engrossed large tracts of Cannock Chase over which he had no legal rights and by 1769 he had put up an obelisk on the Chase, 'which gives his Improvements a most Extensive appearance'.[3] This obelisk blew down in the early nineteenth century. Once he had acquired and demolished their cottages, Anson re-housed the villagers and the cottagers who had lived on the Chase in model cottages of his own. Those at Shugborough must be among the first such dwellings, having been built by the time of Parnell's visit.

In 1748 Philip Yorke visited Shugborough with his wife and described in his travel journal the ground near the house, 'disposed in the manner of a ferme ornee';[4] presumably much of this was the recent remains of real farmland. The marchioness described the site as 'a little green spot, the Trent winding along one side of it, and a canal round two others; in the canal a Chinese house and a Chinese boat, extremely pretty'.[5] The canal to which she refers was the remnant of the old manor house moat, in which the Chinese house had been built on an island reached by two Chinese wooden bridges. It was, according to Thomas Pennant, 'a true pattern of the architecture of that nation . . . not a mongrel invention of *British* carpenters'.[6] Parnell described its exterior as painted blue and white, 'with Indian Birds Mandarins &c', while inside were chinoiserie objects, pictures, vases, lacquer-work 'which can only be Excelld by the View of Wood & Water and Dress'd ground from the front of the Building and above all the Great Extent of Hill you have in your Eye Reclaimd and spotted with great clumps of firr and single trees in a fine taste.' The finely made rococo chinoiserie ceiling is now to be seen in the Verandah Room in the main house. Parnell especially admired the planting around the Chinese house: 'there are abundance of fine Larch which are justly Placed as being Indian trees'.[7]

The multi-talented Thomas Wright was evidently at Shugborough between 1748 and

134. A plate from Stuart and Revett's *Antiquities of Athens*, 1762, depicting the Choragic Monument of Lysicrates, which Stuart recreated in the landscape at Shugborough as the Lanthorn of Demosthenes. It can be seen between the pagoda and the Tower of the Winds in Plate 135 above.

135. Shugborough from the east by Nicholas Dall, c.1769. This view shows the heterogeneous mixture of buildings collected together in the rococo landscape. (Shugborough House, courtesy of the Earl of Lichfield and Staffordshire County Council)

1749, making the domed pavilions for the house, and the Shepherd's Monument. Scheemakers' marble relief of Poussin's famous image, *Et in Arcadia ego*, was framed by Wright in rustic stonework: 'Athenian' Stuart later added the columns and entablature. The motto was a popular one—Shenstone found 'the *idea* of it so very pleasing . . . that I had no peace till I had used the inscription on one side of Miss Dolman's urn'[8]—the element of delicious melancholy it introduced into the pleasure of gardens was much appreciated by eighteenth-century Arcadians. The artificial ruins (see Plate 82), now considerably diminished, may have been founded on a real ruin: Lady Anson writes in September 1749 of 'some little additions to the Ruin [that] have a very pretty effect'.[9] The Cat's Monument, erected in memory of Thomas Anson's Persian cat, 'Kouli-Kan', seems to date from this period too.

By 1752 Anson had erected a pagoda. This was part of the improvements round the lake, which he had formed from the old village mill pond. The lake was the centre of the ornamental landscape and by 1769 it was an elaborate affair of fragile rococo artifice. It was dotted with 'a multitude of Islands' and there were 'Clumps of flowering shrubs by the water side'.[10] At the bottom was a cascade and a covered colonnade which Parnell termed a Palladian bridge. Below the cascade was a second smaller lake with the pagoda at the far end. At the top of the lake and actually in the water, 'Athenian' Stuart's Tower of the Winds was built in 1765. All but the last were swept away when the great flood of 1795 tore through the watercourses. The outline of the lake can still be discerned, stretching from the Tower of the Winds towards the end of the car park.

Stuart had designed the triumphal arch for Shugborough some time before the end of 1761, but his brief expanded when Thomas Anson found himself suddenly enriched by his brother's death in 1762. Stuart and Nicholas Revett had published the first volume of *The antiquities of Athens* in that year. This was a sumptuous scholarly record of an expedition which had been promoted by the Society of Dilettanti. At Shugborough Anson gave Stuart the chance to reconstruct the only two buildings he and Revett had managed to record in full detail: the Choragic Monument of Lysicrates and the Horologium of Andronicos Cyrrhestes reappearing in Staffordshire as the Lanthorn of Demosthenes and the Tower of the Winds.

Stuart's other buildings for Thomas Anson were the Doric Temple and the orangery, now demolished, which housed many of Anson's statues among the plants. Statuary was also dotted around the walks and with the ruins had the effect for Parnell of making the garden 'look like an old Roman Villa as I conceive did not the Rich meads on the other side of the River coverd with cattle bring back the English farm to mind'.[11]

Thomas Anson died in 1772 and the estate was inherited by his nephew, George Adams, who subsequently took the Anson name and on his death in 1789 passed it on to his son Thomas. This Thomas Anson, made a viscount in 1806, employed Samuel Wyatt to remodel the house, to build lodges and to build Shugborough Park Farm near the site of the upper lake—a tame farm once the real farms had been dismantled. The viscount's father-in-law was 'Coke of Norfolk', and Holkham's agricultural improvements must have spurred him on. The Tower of the Winds was now made into a dairy and the farm replaced the rococo lake in the prospect from the house. A new channel for the river Sow was dug at this time, creating an island, and the last of the old moat by the house was removed. Land purchases and road diversions continued and by 1825 the park had assumed its present shape.

The last major planting was undertaken in the 1870s, and in 1890 the process of expansion finally went into reverse when the 2nd Earl sold some land in Stafford Wood and some on the Satnall Hills for a pumping station and reservoir. In the Second World War a prisoner-of-war camp was established in the park and many trees felled in the process. Large tracts of parkland were also taken into cultivation by the Land Army. In 1960, on the death of the 4th Earl, the estate was bequeathed to the National Trust. In the house fifteen watercolours by Moses Griffiths, Pennant's draughtsman, and five oils by Nicholas Dall show the garden in its heyday in the 1770s.

THE LEASOWES
HALESOWEN, WEST MIDLANDS

Few gardens have had both such fame and such a short life as the Leasowes. William Shenstone's 'Arcadian farm' grew, flowered and faded within about 30 years.[1] By the time Goldsmith saw it ten years after Shenstone's death the only picture it presented was one of 'sublunary vicissitude'. Yet for a few years in the mid-eighteenth century it was one of the four or five most visited and often cited gardens in England. The principles of 'landskip-gardening'—a phrase that Shenstone seems to have coined—which it embodied were deeply influential.[2] Around the Halesowen golf course much of his layout can still be traced.

William Shenstone was born in 1714, the son of a moderately prosperous farmer. He was sent to Oxford, and studied desultorily for a career in medicine. But, as his father had died young, Shenstone inherited the family estate when he came of age. He left Oxford without a

136. Tourists at the Leasowes enjoying the scene in Virgil's Grove. Engraving after Thomas Smith of Derby, 1748.

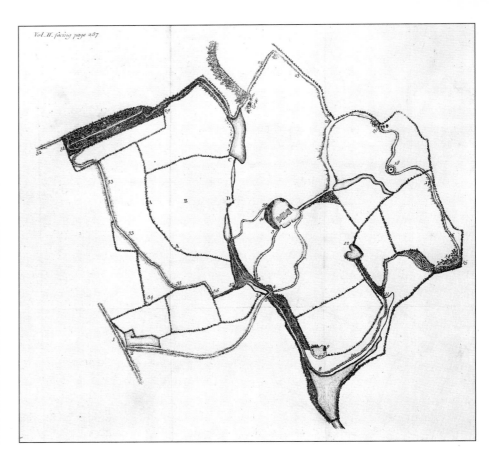

An Inscription in my Grove . June y. 1st
or Fairy-Spell 1749.

Here in cool grott, or fringed Cell,
We rural Fauns & Fairies dwell;
Tho' rarely seen by mortal Eye,
When y. pale Moon ascending high.
Darts thro yon Limes her orient Beam;
We frisk it near this crystal stream.

Then fear to spoil these favour'd Bowrs!
Nor wound y: Shrubs, nor crop y: Flow'rs!
So may your Path with sweets abound!
So may your Couch w.th Rest be crown'd!
But ill-betide. or Nymph or Swain.
That dares our hallow'd Haunts profane

Oberon.

Vol. II. facing page 287

137 (above left). One of William Shenstone's evocative 'incantations' for his garden. (Wellesley College Library, Massachusetts)

138 (above right). The circuit round the Leasowes as illustrated for Dodsley's 'Description of the Leasowes'.

degree and returned to Halesowen. Here he first stayed with his mother's family, visiting or entertaining his friends from Oxford and in 1737 publishing his first volume of poems. By 1739 he was living at the Leasowes, initially boarding with his tenant. He divided his time between the country, London and Bath, but by 1745 the Leasowes had become his permanent residence, and from this date he rarely travelled and began to concentrate on his farm. His improvements were a continuous, unfinishable work, circumscribed by his comparative poverty on a mere £300 a year and inspired by the Arcadian vision of the pastoral poetry he read and imitated:

> . . . And DAMON dreamt he saw the fawns,
> And nymphs, distinctly, skim the lawns;
> Now trac'd amid the trees, and then,
> Lost in the circling shades again. . . .
>   Thus glow'd his breast by fancy warm'd:
> And thus the fairy landskip charm'd . . .[3]

Shenstone termed his estate a *ferme ornée*, but once he took it over the farm was disastrously hampered by his indifference to efficiency and profit. J. C. Loudon featured the Leasowes in his *Encyclopaedia of gardening*, and his account concluded that 'root-houses, seats, urns and inscriptions were too frequent for the whole to be classed with a common, or even an improved or ornamented, English farm. It was, in fact, intended as an emblematical scene, in which constant allusion was made to pastoral poetry'.[4]

By 1746 Shenstone was evidently very busy, for his neighbours at Hagley Hall, the

Lytteltons, started bringing visitors to see the improvements. In 1746 his fellow-poet James Thomson was brought over, much to Shenstone's pleasure, and made jokes about the hills being 'the bubbies of Nature'.[5] At about this time Shenstone was working on what remained his most admired creation, 'Virgil's Grove'. Here, in the narrow cleft north of the house, he laboriously collected together the meagre natural streams and created a series of cascades which descended between 'mossy banks, enamelled with primroses, and variety of wild wood flowers', beneath a one-arched bridge into a small lake.[6] The walk through Virgil's Grove can still be followed today.

Shenstone continued, in Samuel Johnson's elegantly grudging phrase, 'to point his prospects, to diversify his surface, to entangle his walks, and to wind his waters',[7] but it was not until 1749 that he actually began to link his scattered scenes together. The circuit walk he made was celebrated in the 'Description of the Leasowes' published by Robert Dodsley in Shenstone's posthumous *Works in verse and prose*. Both Joseph Spence and Thomas Hull wrote detailed accounts of the Leasowes,[8] but the published 'Description' reached a wide audience, many of whom never visited the actual garden. The Scottish tourist, Hugh Miller, described a forlorn pilgrimage to the Leasowes in 1857, but wrote of how enchanting he found the 'Description' as a youth:

> I could never form from it any idea of the place as a whole: the imagery seemed broken up into detached slips, like the imagery of a magic lantern; but then nothing could be finer than the insulated slips; and my mind was filled with gorgeous pictures, all fresh and bright, of 'sloping groves,' 'tufted knolls,' 'wooded valleys,' 'sequestered lakes,' and 'noisy rivulets'.[9]

It is indeed written in an enticing style: 'umbrageous' paths 'wind downward' into glades,

139. A watercolour view of the Leasowes by Shenstone himself. It vividly conveys the farm-like atmosphere of the garden. (Wellesley College Library, Massachusetts)

groves and bowers, where you are 'over-arched', 'over-shadowed' and 'inclosed'. The passive eye is 'caught', 'led', 'conducted' and 'thrown' in a kind of seduction by scenery, while the landscape rises, falls, swells, slides and rolls around you. Peopled by the nymphs of Shenstone's pastoral imagination, continually conjured up by the inscriptions he painted on deal boards and attached to seats, trees and alcoves, the landscape's erotic element was clearly part of Shenstone's design.

The Arcadian fantasy which Shenstone invoked via his inscriptions and verses rested more or less uneasily with the real scene. Richard Graves satirized this in *Columella*, an

140. The Leasowes today: a view across the lake towards the house. Dudley Borough Council has embarked on a restoration programme, which it is hoped will see this most influential of eighteenth-century gardens brought back to something like its original appearance.

affectionately mocking portrait of Shenstone, in which the rural recluse, leading his visitors round his garden, is met by his man Peter, with the news that the heifers 'were got into the young plantation at the bottom of *Aaron's Well*': '"Aaron's Well! you blockhead," says Columella, "Arno's Vale, you mean." "Nay, nay," quoth Peter, "I know the right name of it is Tadpole Bottom . . . Aaron's Well, or Arno's Vale, or something, I suppose there's no great difference"'.[10]

Dodsley also employed the kind of picturesque viewing made popular by Gilpin 30 years later. He presents the layout as a series of 'scenes', 'landskips', 'pictures' and even 'sketches'. So, for example, early in the circuit the reader is led past the Ruined Priory which stood by the lake, but, we are warned, it 'is not meant for an object here'.[11] The pictures depended on the visitor following the circuit path precisely, and the Lytteltons piqued Shenstone when they brought visitors in at the wrong end of Virgil's Grove. When Thomas Jefferson visited in 1786 he approached with Dodsley's account and map in hand and treated the garden almost like a picture gallery: 'The landscape at number eighteen, and prospect at thirty-two, are fine'.[12]

Most visitors after Shenstone's death commented on the sad appearance of the garden: it suffered from a rapid succession of owners, and by Loudon's time, 1831, was in 'a state of indescribable neglect and ruin'.[13] Louis Simond in 1812 found it a 'damp and forlorn place'. His guide was 'a poor, old, sickly-looking man, whose uncombed hair was full of feathers'.[14] Gilpin poured scorn on the inscriptions inviting Naiads 'to bathe their beauteous limbs in *crystal* pools, which stood before the eye, impregnated with all the filth which generates from stagnation'.[15] Goldsmith wrote eloquently on the garden's demise: with mournful relish he describes the new owner, Mr Truepenny, cutting down the gloomy walks and making 'vistos upon the stables and hog-sties';[16] while John Parnell wrote indignantly, 'what has Captain *Turpenny* of Birmingham and Powell of Liverpool or any other trafficking West Indian slave master to do with urns, inscriptions, mottoes, shady recesses dedicated to poets, muses, etc. etc.?'[17]

The water so painstakingly collected to form the cascades and pools soon returned to its natural sluggishness and the seats and inscriptions dedicated to friends and poets were gone within a few years of the poet's death. Nothing remains of the buildings, which were always modest constructions. The most substantial, the Ruined Priory, which was built out of remains from Halesowen abbey and within which Shenstone contrived to create a dwelling he could rent out, survived intact into the 1930s, but its remains have now also been cleared away.

But the garden's future is brightening. Much of the circuit walk can still be followed: the original paths can often be discerned as shallow depressions, like ghostly images, following a gentler gradient near the modern tracks. The Priory Pool survives much as in Shenstone's day, as does a good deal of the woodland, and because the layout was always a perimeter circuit the golf course's presence in the central areas is not as intrusive as it might have been in other ornamental landscapes. The local authority has carried out much work already, creating a 'Shenstone Walk', and has recently initiated a full landscape survey. There is now the prospect of restoration for this most influential of historic gardens.

PAINSHILL
near COBHAM, SURREY

Painshill's name recurs continually in the records of eighteenth-century tourists and garden theorists, but before the 1970s the park was widely thought to have more or less disappeared. Then a campaign by local people with a mysterious jungle behind their back gardens began and culminated in 1980 when 160 acres of the old park were bought by Elmbridge Borough Council. Now, ten years on, one of the most ambitious restorations ever attempted is nearing completion and the garden tourist can again experience 'the fairy-land of Paine's Hill'.[1]

In 1738 Charles Hamilton, youngest son of the 6th Duke of Abercorn, purchased 125 acres of poor farmland near Cobham in Surrey. Defoe reports how, to make the ground fertile, he burnt off the heath and planted turnips which he fed to sheep who in turn manured the ground. He was a keen plantsman and within ten years had, according to Horace Walpole, 'made a fine place out of a most cursed hill'.[2]

Hamilton never commanded the kind of wealth which lay behind gardens like Stowe or Stourhead. He held a succession of minor posts in the household of the Prince of Wales and in the civil service, and on his estate he tried a number of business ventures. He took great trouble over his vineyard, which produced a champagne which was drunk at court, and

141. A view of the vineyard and Ruined Abbey at Painshill by George Barret and Sawrey Gilpin, mid 1770s. (Private Collection)

142. A general view of Painshill from the Gothic Temple, page from William Gilpin's sketchbook, 1772. (By courtesy of Mrs George Benson)

behind the Ruined Abbey was a tile-works. But these never made very much money. The funds he poured into the estate were largely borrowed, and it was pressing creditors who eventually forced him to sell up in 1773.

Painshill is characterized by a succession of distinct, evocative 'scenes'—the word Thomas Whately used in describing Painshill—of widely differing moods. The Irishman, William Robertson, reported that 'Mr Hamilton studied painting for the express purpose of improving this place'.[3] It is noticeable that most contemporary accounts describe the same route via the same scenes: the visitor was led past these 'several landskips' by Hamilton or his well-versed gardener.[4]

By 1761 Hamilton had begun building, for in August of that year Walpole went to Painshill 'to see the Gothic building and the Roman ruin'. He caustically dismissed the Gothic Temple—'an unmeaning edifice. . . . The Goths never built summer-houses or temples in a garden'—and quibbled pedantically with the Mausoleum.[5] However, Walpole admired intensely the hanging woods at the western end of the lake, which he described as 'an alpine scene': 'All is great and foreign and rude; the walks seem not designed, but cut through the wood of pines; and the style of the whole is so grand, and conducted with so serious an air of wild and uncultivated extent, that when you look down on this seeming forest, you are amazed to find it contain a very few acres'.[6]

In 1763 Painshill was visited by John Parnell. His journal of this first tour, which includes advice to garden tourists, contains a detailed account of Painshill. The gardener took Parnell round the circuit: up Wood Hill to the Gothic temple, down around the lake (which at this date did not have its eastern arm), past the partially-built grotto, the Mausoleum, the water-wheel and out to the hermitage, then back via the Gothic tower, the Doric temple and the Turkish tent. He admired the cascade where the water was fed into the lake: 'This has a very pretty effect joined with the awful appearance of the wood'. Of the latter he wrote, 'the forest trees seem . . . to grow with their roots each in the tops of another like a Wicklow Mountain'. The hermitage was found deep in 'a wood of different firs and acacia etc.', and was 'formed to the front with the trunks of fir trees with their bark on, their branches making natural Gothic windows'. From the top of the Gothic tower, Parnell wrote: 'It is inconceivable how beautiful Mr Hamilton's grounds appear, all spotted with pavilions, clumps of evergreens or forest trees'.[7]

This opinion contrasts sharply with that of William Gilpin, who visited Painshill two years later. Gilpin climbed up to the Gothic temple, which he thought 'a disagreeable object', and considered the scene Hamilton had made there. He thought the view was 'hurt by too many clumps upon the lawn'. The five-arched bridge, which Hamilton had built at the far end of the lake, and the Turkish tent, were 'glaring objects; and but spots in ye. view'. From the tent, the view was marred by the lawn 'too much patched by clumps; & ye eye is disagreeably caught by white seats, & bridges, & ye. grotto'. Gilpin did commend the 'natural and

romantic landscape' around the cascade, the walk up to the tower, and the Temple of Bacchus, but he poured scorn on the grotto—'a whimsical & little object . . . trifling & unnatural'—which Hamilton had just completed at a considerable cost.[8] The brand-new grotto probably did look a little raw in the landscape, but it may have been the blatant artificiality of the structure which offended this devotee if not of nature, at least of natural appearances. Gilpin was evidently more impressed than his rather grumpy notes suggest, for he returned in 1772 and made a series of sketches of the park (see Plate 142).

The grotto must have been a fantastic place. Built by the mysterious Wiltshire grotto-makers, Joseph and Josiah Lane of Tisbury (who were also responsible for Fonthill, Bowood and Oatlands), it was extraordinarily elaborate, with water and light effects as well as its highly ornate decoration of tufa, spar and fossils. F. M. Piper drew a plan, and wrote a precise description on his visit in 1779. Arthur Young visited Painshill on his southern tour (1768), and classed it as a model of the Beautiful, in contrast to the Sublime at Piercefield. He too was evidently enchanted by the grotto—'an incrustation of fossils; and spar hanging every where like isicles'—and he also admired the Mausoleum for its 'exceeding good taste, in decay'.

Young's only complaint was at 'the contradiction of emotions' he suffered with the 'dark and gloomy' ruin succeeding the 'elegant and agreeable' lakeside walk,[9] and this question, of

143 (far left). Painshill today: the grotto and the Gothic Temple. The restoration of Painshill is perhaps the most ambitious and best-known of such projects.

144 (left). The restored vista from the Gothic Temple, now once more bursting upon the tourist's eye after the walk along Wood Hill.

145 (right). A view from the Turkish tent over the lake and grotto at Painshill, attributed to George Barret the Elder, painted before 1773. (Private Collection)

how successfully Hamilton avoided a Disneyland effect of incongruity in all these juxtaposed scenes, is one which may well strike the modern visitor. John Parnell suggested that he did avoid such a pitfall through skilful planting of the various areas. Thus the hermitage and the Gothic tower stood among 'Scots fir, larch, cedar and pines mixed with birch', which 'has really the air of a wild forest'; while the Doric temple stood on a lawn 'dressed and clumped with flowering shrubs, sweet trees and flowers, like the Elysian Plains'.[10]

After Hamilton's enforced departure in 1773 the estate went through a succession of hands. The future American president, John Adams, visiting the park in 1786 remarked: 'It belongs to Mr. Hopkins, who rides by it, but never stops. The owners of these enchanting seats are very indifferent to their Beauties'.[11] Painshill remained a tourist attraction well into the nineteenth century—in 1837 Moule's *English counties delineated* reported that 'all the original features which contributed to its celebrity are still preserved'[12] and a *Country Life* article of 1904 depicts an apparently secure and tranquil Edwardian estate.

By the 1930s however the park was becoming overgrown, and after the war, when the house and grounds were requisitioned by the Canadian army, a new owner broke up the estate and sold it off in lots. A pig farm was established in the park, the lake became clogged with fallen trees and silt, and the garden buildings were left to decay in the spreading undergrowth. But Hamilton's design had not been significantly altered by subsequent owners and the Painshill Park Trust is bringing back to shape one of the eighteenth century's greatest gardens.

STOURHEAD
STOURTON, WILTSHIRE

Stourhead's lake and garden are now an icon of the eighteenth century's picturesque vision of English landscape, but the garden's progress towards this status began early. It is hard to find any dissent at all from the reaction voiced by John Parnell in 1769, when, 'not twenty Paces from the Inne door', he caught his first sight of 'the most delightful Scene almost I ever beheld'.[1]

In 1741 Henry Hoare II returned from the Grand Tour to inherit the estate which his father had bought from Lord Stourton at the beginning of the century. Henry Hoare I had commissioned Colen Campbell to design a new house in the latest Palladian style but had done little to the grounds. The family fortunes had been founded in the late seventeenth century and Hoare continued the business, acting as banker to such eminent improvers as Carlisle and Burlington. For the first two years there is no evidence of substantial works on the ornamental landscape; it seems to have been after the death of his young wife in 1743 that he turned to landscape gardening.

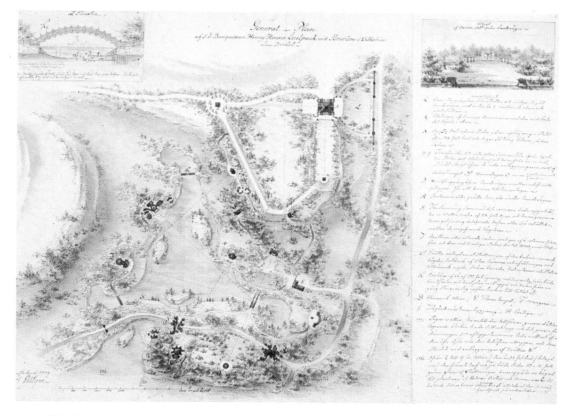

146. Plan of Stourhead, drawn by the Swedish garden tourist, Fredrik Magnus Piper, 1779. (Kungl. Akademien für de Fria Konsterna, Stockholm).

The landscape was in the main created between 1745 (the building of the Temple of Flora) and 1765 (the Temple of Apollo). Three largely bare valleys met near the village and down one of them, known as Six Wells Bottom, ran a chain of ponds: two larger ponds lay in the basin below the house. The lake, the centrepiece of the improvements, was not created out of the two ponds until about 1754, when Bishop Pococke refers to the dam 'which is making at great expense',[2] although it seems to have figured in Hoare's plans since at least 1744, when his architect at Stourhead, Henry Flitcroft, was discussing it in their correspondence. The design of the garden was based on a circuit walk, which began on the south lawn of the house, led to the southern end of the Fir Walk, down to the lake, where a steeply arched wooden bridge led over to the grotto, then round the present walk to the village. It was only with the garden's growing popularity with tourists, and the consequent use of the village entrance, that the present circuit was established.

Along the scarp west of the house Hoare had laid out the straight walk as early as 1734, planted not only with 'stately Scotch firs', but also, according to F. M. Piper who visited in 1778, 'beeches, cedars and American silverpines'.[3] The obelisk was built in 1746 at the end of an axial drive from the house, and to terminate the Fir Walk. In the angle of the two avenues was a meadow bounded by a ha-ha, reserved for sheep or, in Parnell's day, for 'Pett cattle'.[4] Parnell compared the Fir Walk to the hill-top walk at Claremont, which he thought not 'so well contrasted with a natural walk before you enter it'.[5] The firs were cut down in the early nineteenth century by Richard Colt Hoare, Henry's grandson, who reported that the outline of the woods surrounding the lake was 'much improvd by taking down all the fir trees, so aptly called by Mr Price "spears and daggers"'.[6] The original effect, however, has now been recreated by the National Trust.

The lake was crossed below the Fir Walk by a single-arched wooden bridge, taken from Palladio. Parnell called it the 'geometrical Bridge', and it certainly approached the semicircular. Mrs Lybbe Powys, visiting in 1776, wrote in her diary that she found 'the idea of going over a kind of ladder only is frightful', and that some of her party could not bring themselves to venture it.[7] However, the Reverend Richard Warner advised the tourist in his *Excursions from Bath* of 1801, that once over the lake you 'reach classic ground, and dropping all modern acquaintance, associate for a time, only with the gods and heroes of antiquity'.[8] The grottoes (early visitors distinguished between the caves of the nymph and of the river god) were much admired: F. M. Piper made a detailed plan during his visit. Their appearance is virtually unchanged today, both within and in the approach, with its darkening laurels and yews. The temperature still drops as the visitor approaches, and an authentic eighteenth-century frisson can still be felt.

The Pantheon was widely considered the best of Flitcroft and Hoare's buildings. Warner, for example, waxed lyrical about his first view of it: the lake's 'tranquil majesty', and the temple, 'embosomed on all sides in wooded elevations, rising amphitheatrically around it'.[9] Horace Walpole admired the statues which Hoare displayed here, especially Rysbrack's Hercules: 'the head taken from the Farnese, and the body composed from the best formed parts of a noted Boxer's, who practiced before Figg's amphitheatre was suppressed'.[10]

The view from here was one of Hoare's most carefully composed landscapes. Writing to his daughter in 1762, when the stone bridge was being built, he enthused, 'when you stand at the Pantheon the water will be seen thro' the arches and it will look as if the river came down

147. Stourhead in 1790: a view by S.H. Grimm (British Library, London)

148. Flitcroft's Temple of Apollo, built in 1765.

thro the village and that this was the village bridge for publick use. The view of the bridge, village and church all-together will be a charm[in]g Gasp[ar] picture at the end of that water'.[11] Parnell noted that the effect of the village in the view was to help make the landscape appear a 'Beautifull Spott of existing country not a mere visionary scene'. From here too you saw a statue which Hoare placed in the rocky niche below the Temple of Flora, 'Neptune in his carr with Sea Horses Just as coming out of his cave & Launching into the Deep'.[12]

On from the Pantheon most visitors were impressed by the grottified arch over the road. In Hoare's time it was evidently more substantial: John Wesley called it the castle-grotto,[13] and Parnell described it as 'a sort of Ruind castle . . . grass growing &c Extremly Romantickly in Every Interstice of this whimsical Building'.[14] The path led to a hermitage, built of moss-plastered oak stumps, 'whose upturned roots form four pointed vaults'.[15] Charles Hamilton of Painshill advised Hoare on the design of the hermitage, but all that remains of it now is the inner recess, the 'Druid's cell', on the right of the present zigzag.

In Hoare's day the Temple of Apollo stood on an open slope of turf stretching to the lakeside. Not every visitor liked its rather peculiar shape: Parnell decided it was 'not Beautifull in proportion to its cost', the dome 'Rather Heavy & the Indented Entablature over the colonade unmeaning'.[16]

Mrs Lybbe Powys remarked how, 'In general these edifices are so alike at all gardens', adding 'the seats and buildings here put one greatly in mind of Stowe'.[17] A more vehement objector to the classical buildings and images was John Wesley. He thought Stourhead the best garden he had seen in England, enjoying above all the 'lovely grottoes', but his description ends abruptly: 'Others were delighted with the temples, but I was not'. He considered the statues of heathen gods 'images of devils', and, he burst out, 'I defy all mankind to reconcile statues with nudities, either to common sense or common decency'.[18]

Although the predominance of the classical style now seems part of the garden's character, in Hoare's time there was no such orthodoxy. No sooner had Jonas Hanway in 1757 praised 'this delicious abode' because it possessed 'no Chinese works, no monsters of imagination',[19] than Hoare began to introduce such monsters. The eastern slopes were dotted with a Gothic greenhouse ('false Gothic', Walpole sniffed), a Venetian seat, a Chinese alcove and a Turkish tent. In fact, as early as 1754, Pococke reports, Hoare was planning differently styled buildings on the islands in the lake 'one of which is to be a Mosque with a Minaret'.[20] It was the serious-minded antiquarian Richard Colt Hoare who created the present character by demolishing these heterogeneous structures in the 1790s, 'as not according with the Three Grecian Temples'.[21]

Finally, it is worth noting that for many of the eighteenth-century visitors the culmination of the landscape pleasures was the great terrace ride out from near the obelisk to Alfred's Tower. This can still be traced on foot, but it was designed to be ridden. Richard Warner thought it the 'grandest feature', running 'along the *dorsum* of a high hill for three or four miles, over a carpet of velvet turf'.[22] John Parnell had found that the gardens round the lake 'tho so Beautifull were Rather too Confined', but his desire for grandeur was fulfilled on this great drive, which reminded him of Cirencester.[23]

In the woods below the Tower the drive led to the eccentric little building called the

149. View from the outer circuit ride at Stourhead, looking down Six Wells Bottom towards the lake.

Convent, which has recently been restored as a private house. It was decorated with little figures of nuns of different orders in niches round the room, while the upper room was occupied by a couple who bred wild turkeys in the wood. Passing the Convent the drive wound back to Stourton along the valley. The scale of this circuit is vast: Parnell refers to 'Mr Hoares magnificent manner of Enjoying . . . the Beauties of the Country',[24] and it needs to be appreciated to set the Arcadian landscape around the lake in perspective. A fine view of these woods, with the tower and the Convent can be caught from the footpath that runs past the cascade and round the end of the south-west arm of the lake.

Despite the large amount of nineteenth-century planting the overall scene has changed little since Hoare's death in 1785. During Colt Hoare's time the firs were felled, but have now been replanted; the slope below the Temple of Apollo was planted; the most whimsical buildings were demolished although the grottified boathouse near the Temple of Flora was added; and the rhododendrons, which obscure the edges of the lake but attract many modern garden tourists, were added. Planting continued up to the early twentieth century and included many newly introduced exotics. For a few years at the end of the nineteenth century the house was abandoned by the Hoares, but the 6th Baronet and his wife lived there from 1894 until 1946, when, their only son having died in the First World War, they bequeathed it to the National Trust.

GOLDNEY HALL
CLIFTON, BRISTOL

At Goldney Hall in Clifton, on the hill high above Bristol, the modern tourist can visit one of the best-preserved eighteenth-century grottoes in England. As Mrs Delany wrote in 1756 to her friend Mrs Dewes describing her visit to the grotto 'you and I heard so much about last year': 'it is one of the few things that answers expectation'.[1]

Thomas Goldney III, who built the grotto, was, like his father before him, a merchant and a banker. He inherited the house and grounds at Clifton on his father's death in 1731 and augmented the estate with additional plots of land during the 1730s and 1740s. He was a Quaker, but this did not prevent him trading lucratively in guns when the Spanish war was declared. Mrs Delany reported that Goldney was 'reckoned a great humourist and a niggard', but whatever his character, on the hilltop in Clifton he created the garden which became one of the marvels of the west country tour—'a minor *Stow* on *Clifton*'s crown'[2]—and which survives largely unchanged today.

The family had lived at Clifton since 1705, and Goldney inherited a modest formal garden in what seems to have been the William and Mary style. In 1735 John Kelsall, a fellow Quaker, recorded in his diary: 'to Thos Goldneys at Clifton, went thro' his Gardens &c. wch are very fine with Walks, Greens, Water-works, Summer-Houses &c. there were many

Lemons and Orange Trees with fruit on them'.[3] In 1736 Goldney turned his serious attention to the garden: he began to keep a Garden Book recording the plantings and works, and the next year saw the start of his first and most famous work, the grotto.

Goldney evidently prolonged the pleasure of creating the grotto, for it was another 27 years before he finally declared it complete. The brick shell of tunnel and chamber, however, were finished in 1739: the date and his initials can be traced in shells under the skylight nearest the tunnel. The lavish ornamentation was begun before the grotto's structure was finished. The Duchess of Northumberland was overwhelmed by 'the Variety there is of Shells Fossils Oars Sparres Petrifactions &c', and affirmed that 'most of [them] were placed here by Mr Gouldney himself'.[4] In 1749 the grotto was described by the geologist Alexander Catcott as comprising '3 rooms, parted by pillars, that on the left hand finished with regard to the Shell-work . . . is designed for a basin of Water, which is to fall from out of an urn of a Sea-God'. The middle room was 'nearly finis[he]d. A Gloomy den in which there is to lye a Lion, presents itself first, the Lion not yet made'. 'From this Grotto', he continued, 'you pass thro a long entry thro which there comes a constant gale, at the end of this you have a fine prospect of the River Avon, a vast valley lying between Dundry Hills and Lye down'.[5] That 'gale' was shut out later by a door with a *trompe-l'oeil* painting of steps leading up into a wooded garden, 'the most perfect deception I ever saw', according to one visitor.[6]

Mrs Delany was delighted with the grotto on her visit in 1756, although it was 'not much more than half-finished'. It was 'much the finest thing of the kind I ever saw,' although, she adds, 'I could not but grudge at the shells *sacrificed there*, and exposed to the ruin of damp and time, that would have preserved their beauty for ages in a cabinet!'[7] Mrs Delany could not have guessed at the painstaking concern of posterity, which would see the grotto restored to its pristine glory.

Arthur Young, who had a soft spot for rococo excess, devoted two and a half pages to the grotto in his *Tour through the southern counties* of 1768. He entered it through the 'dark arched passage of brick' under the terrace, 'which has much the air of an approach to a wine-vault'. Of

150 (left). Goldney's bastions and rotunda as they appeared in 1788, sketch by the Swiss topographical artist, S.H. Grimm. (British Library, London)

151 (right). A view to the grotto along the line of yew trees: 'rather formal but not ugly'.

the lion in its den, he remarked, 'Pleasing objects are generally wished for in a sequestered grot; but the owner of this is more pleased with those of terror'. Goldney's lion and lioness certainly were unusual by eighteenth-century standards; as Young said, the grotto was 'curious in materials and taste'. Young could not reconcile himself to Goldney's overt taste for artifice: the regular pillars, albeit encrusted with Bristol diamonds, and the figures of Neptune, for instance, seemed out of place in a grotto, which unpredictably he termed 'an imitation of nature'. Still, he had great admiration for the 'fine shells, fossils, corals, spar &c. &c. &c. all in greater plenty, and better of their sort, than in any grotto I have seen'.[8]

The grotto was always the chief attraction, as it is today, but in the rest of the garden, Goldney took spectacular advantage of the site's position. The terrace, which was built up over the grotto tunnel, was designed to command extensive prospects, not only of the country outside the city, but also of the port and its busy shipping, where Goldney could actually see his wealth accruing. The garden's design was and still is quite regular, with its yew avenue, parallel canal and terrace at right angles. The Duchess of Northumberland described its appearance on entering from the house as 'rather formal but not ugly on each hand is a small fountain wth Leaden figures in wch are Gold & Silver Fish'. The terrace, she wrote, 'is a stupendous Work ye View is extensive very fine over the Downs the Wells the Fields Dundry Tower Cooks folly Towns Villages &c &c terminated at one End by the City of Bristol & at the other by fine Hills cover'd with vast Woods'.[9]

Below the terrace to the west, Goldney built the bastion, a mock fortification, which from the river must have stood out dramatically. His neighbour and fellow-merchant, Thomas Farr, adorned similar bastions below Blaise Castle with wooden cannon, but there is no evidence that Goldney, despite his trade in real guns, did the same. At the angle between terrace and bastion, the rotunda was erected in 1757. The sketch by Samuel Hieronymous

152. Thomas Goldney's Gothic prospect tower, which also served to pump water up for the grotto, whose entrance can be seen on the right.

153. The interior of the grotto at Goldney: 'the finest thing of the kind', according to one eighteenth-century visitor.

Grimm shows it with its original colonnade, removed some time in the nineteenth century.

The canal was built in 1758–9. The American, Samuel Curwen, described it as 'abounding in gold and silver fish' and supplied from a lofty fountain. The present fountain is Victorian, and there were alterations to the head of the water made in the nineteenth century, so any fountain or cascade of Goldney's no longer exists. It was fed, as was the cascade in the grotto, with water from the 'Fire Engine', a steam-powered pump which was housed in the basement of the Gothic prospect tower, built in 1764.

Goldney died unmarried in 1768 at the age of 72. He seems to have been entirely responsible for the planning at every stage of the grotto and garden. With the growing popularity of the nearby Hotwells, his garden became a major tourist attraction. Shiercliff's *Bristol and Hotwell guide* of 1793 devotes a page to an enticing description of the grotto and gardens. The grotto as described is almost unchanged today, although Shiercliff did spot 'several gold and silver fish' in the basin at the foot of the cascade. The view from 'one of the finest terrace walks in *England*' is commended, and the gardens generally, he writes, 'are extensive, kept in excellent order, and although in the old taste, are much admired'. The formality of the canal was augmented by grass plats on either side, and 'avenues decorated with statues, and bordered with lofty trees, whose verdure affords a cool refreshing shade in the most sultry season of the year'.[10]

The estate remained in the Goldney family until 1864 when it was bought by Lewis Fry of the prominent local Quaker family. He employed Alfred Waterhouse to make major alterations to the house and he also continued to open the garden during the summer. During the first half of the twentieth century the house remained a family home, but in 1956 it was sold to the university and became a hall of residence. In 1985 the grotto underwent a complete restoration by Diana Reynell and Simon Verity.

STOKE PARK
STOKE GIFFORD, AVON

'I went to see Stoke, Lord Bottetorts, from Bristol in 2 miles we came to Stapleton, and in a nother mile to Stoke; to be reckon'd among the finest things in England'.[1] So Bishop Pococke began one of his most detailed accounts of a landscaped garden. The garden in question, Stoke Park, was one of the principal attractions on the western tour in the eighteenth and early nineteenth centuries: a Bristol guidebook of 1815 affirmed that the 'spacious Woods, Temples, and Monuments . . . may justly be stiled a terrestrial Paradise'.[2]

Stoke Park was the masterpiece of Thomas Wright, 'the Wizard of Durham', one of the most engaging figures in the history of gardening. Mathematician, gardener, architect and astronomer, his publications range from the sumptuous pattern-books, *Arbours and Grottos*, to *An original theory or new hypothesis of the universe*. At Stoke he was given a free hand over an unusually long period, more than 30 years, working first for Norborne Berkeley, created Lord Botetourt, and after Berkeley's death, for his sister the Dowager 4th Duchess of Beaufort.

Berkeley, described by one disapproving historian as 'a semi-fraudulent and bankrupt peer of winning manners',[3] seems to have been a cultivated and amiable patron. His commonplace books are full of quotations from favourite poets like Pope and Prior, with notes and verses of his own. William Shenstone mentions Berkeley as one of his visitors at the Leasowes: he recited a poem for Shenstone in the root house there, an occasion which Shenstone later recalled with affection.[4] Berkeley and Wright toured the country inspecting

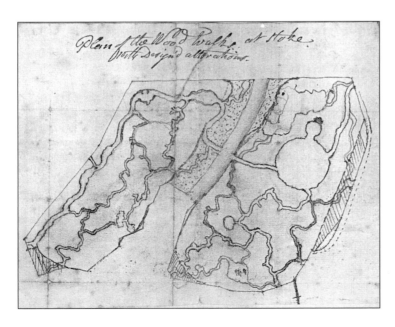

156 (above). *Stoke Park*, a painting by John Wootton of the 1740s, showing the spectacular landscape on which Wright was invited to work. The old irregular house was virtually encased in Wright's new design. (Badminton House, courtesy of His Grace the Duke of Beaufort)

154 (far left). Thomas Wright's 'Plan of the Wood Walks at Stoke with Design'd alterations', showing the green *cabinets* in the woods which were such a feature of this layout. (Badminton muniments, Gloucester Record Office)

155 (left). Drawing from one of Wright's sketchbooks, 'View of Stoke from the Verge near the Lodge'. Wright took great pains over every aspect of this layout. (Victoria and Albert Museum, London)

gardens on at least one occasion in the 1750s, and Berkeley's letters to his sister refer warmly to 'Mr. Wright'. On his death Berkeley left Wright an annuity which was apparently 'the chief support in his retirement',[5] and it is clear that Wright was considered a friend rather than an employee. He even had his own apartment at Stoke where he stayed most summers until very near his death in 1786.

When he arrived at Stoke in 1749 Wright was presented with a virtually blank canvas of agricultural land and game woods, plus dramatic contours and wide prospects. The natural advantages were spectacular and Wright remodelled the gabled sixteenth-century house to take full advantage of this situation. He had the slopes below and to either side planted up to render the house picturesque, 'bosom'd high in tufted trees'. From within, the rooms in his octagonal bays commanded wide views. Lady Anson who visited in 1755 thought she had never seen such a 'more than semi-circle of Prospect'; surpassing 'the richest as well as greatest Views I ever saw'.[6]

Lady Anson's visit was early in Stoke's development; Wright and Berkeley's creation at its height is described by Pococke on his visit at the end of fifteen years of work by owner and designer. Having inspected the terrace and the orangery, designed by Sir James Thornhill, Pococke set off to the west. He followed a circuit walk and arrived first at 'a wood with winding Walks, at the enterance [of which] is a kind of Tomb on a basement . . . erected to the honour of the late 4th Duke of Beaufort who was married to Lord Bottetort's sister, with the inscription "Fraterni Dignus Amoris"'. From here he went on to 'an Oblisk on an Eminence . . . it is on a pedestal adorn'd with rustic work, the top is crown'd with a Gilt Star'. The obelisk was another memorial, this time to Berkeley's niece, Elizabeth Somerset. Having read the inscription, Pococke climbed back into the wood to an Ionic rotunda, then over into one of the two top woods, 'in which are winding Walks, and some lawns with single trees in them, and seats in proper places'. Finally he was led round the perimeter of the hills 'to a brow on which is built a Model of the Monument to the Horatii at Albano with four round Obelisks on an arch'd building, adorn'd with a pediment every way: In the Freize round the four sides is this inscription "Memoriae Virtutis Heroicae SPQR"'.

The layout described by Pococke was a classical and elegiac landscape, an '*Epic* space' as it was termed in a topographical poem of 1767.[7] Wright has normally been considered chiefly as a builder of whimsical and slightly frivolous follies, but Stoke belies this. He did however erect one such folly, 'Bladud's Cell', deep in one of the higher woods. This was a moss-encrusted hermitage or root house, considered by the Duchess of Northumberland 'the prettiest of its kind I ever saw'.[8]

Another visitor was George Mason, who in his *Essay on design in gardening* praised Stoke as an example of Wright's art. He commented not on the buildings but the planting: 'Stoke gave me more than any thing I had seen an idea of what might be done by the internal arrangement of a wood. Some old pollards clad with ivy were made admirable use of. One of these sylvan spinnies was decorated with roses in the very manner which is advised in the fourth book of the *English garden*'.[9] Wright's drawings show the woods laid out as a series of irregular *cabinets* connected by twisting paths: the rotunda for example stood in a 'Saloon of Oaks'.[10] The paths wound up and down the slopes with the help of stone steps. The woods contained gardens planted with shrubs and exotics, and they were also enlivened with water—the stone tunnel to what seems to have been a cascade still survives, decorated with fossil-bearing lias limestone; and between the top woods Wright built a subterranean passage with ornamental entrances which is also still in existence. While the pleasure grounds stretched around the rim of the Purdown ridge, a large lake was excavated in the basin of the hills, known as Duchess Pond, and this parkland area was planted with clumps.

157. Stoke Park as it is today. It was only recently thought to be beyond rescue, but there are now hopes that this park will be restored to its former glory.

158. Thomas Wright's memorial to the 4th Duke of Beaufort, recently restored by the Avon Gardens Trust.

John Wesley visited Stoke in 1764 on one of his many whirlwind tours of the west country. No mean judge of earthly beauties, he wrote of the hour he spent in 'Lord B's gardens, or more properly woods':

> They are small to the late Duke of Kent's in Bedfordshire [Wrest Park], and therefore, not capable of so much variety; but, for the size, it is not possible for anything of the kind to be more agreeable; and the situation, on top of a high hill, in one of the fruitfullest counties in England, gives them an advantage which even Stow Gardens have not.[11]

In 1764 Berkeley was writing to a friend, 'Stoke improves every day, am already obliged to clear away plants that were sowed in the year 50—am become a workman myself and so pleased with the profession as to lament nights and Sundays'.[12] But four years later he was forced by his financial difficulties to leave Stoke and take up the post of governor of Virginia. He died of a fever only two years later, unmarried, and Stoke passed to his sister, the Dowager Duchess of Beaufort. She continued to seek Wright's advice: he designed new plantations and structures—a lodge and a Gothic gateway are recorded in the estate papers—and oversaw much of the work personally.

Throughout the nineteenth century the house was used by the Beauforts as a dower house. In the twentieth century its fortunes declined: it was sold and became a home for the mentally handicapped, then a National Health Service hospital. The grounds were neglected, although farming continued almost to the present, and the woods, overrun with self-seeded trees and undergrowth, decayed. Many of the parkland trees and clumps were felled during the First World War. In 1968 the M32 was built along the park's eastern boundary and the lake was drained amid much local protest. But now the tide has turned. Research is revealing how much of the landscape seen by Pococke survives: the terrace and orangery, the shrubberies to the east, the Beaufort memorial, and the obelisk, as well as the tunnels and the outlines of all the main plantations. Recent archaeological investigations have located the sites and foundations of Bladud's Cell, and the demolished rotunda and Horatii monument. A committee has been set up pledged to the park's restoration, and the Avon Gardens Trust has rebuilt the Beaufort memorial. Stoke Park restored is now an exciting prospect in the mind's eye.

WROXTON ABBEY
BANBURY, OXFORDSHIRE

The gardens at Wroxton are a rare survival of rococo landscaping by the amateur architect Sanderson Miller in the 1740s and, although most of his ephemeral buildings shown on the contemporary plan have disappeared, the layout, incorporating an older one, is still discernible today. The ponds belonged to the original Augustinian priory, which when dissolved was bought by Thomas Pope, Henry VIII's Treasurer of the Court of Augmentation. He founded Trinity College, Oxford, and endowed it from priory lands, reserving the right to lease the old abbey house for his descendants. By marriage Wroxton came to the North family, who lived there until 1932, when it reverted to Trinity College. It was sold to the Fairleigh Dickinson University in 1964. The most famous tenant of Wroxton was the Lord North who, as prime minister, is chiefly remembered for the foreign policy that led to the American Revolution. It is ironic that his home has now been bought by an American university.

A new house had been built on the site in 1618 with a modest accompanying layout of parlour garden, orchards and grass plots. The improvements made by Sir Francis North, Lord Guilford, in the 1680s were approved by Celia Fiennes: 'there was a part new built all the new fashion way, which was designed for the present Lord Guilford and his lady, the gardens are very good the outhouses and stables handsome'.[1] These alterations were made by Lord Guilford's brother, the architect and scientist, Roger North, who supervised Wroxton after his brother's death in 1685, while guardian to his heir.[2] A friend of Evelyn, he was also interested in gardening and the making of ornamental fishponds. In his *Discourse on fishponds* in 1713 he said that 'pondheads must be made large and firm for then you have not only a more secure bank, but a more beautiful walk', and his pondhead walk, incorporated into the Miller scheme, can clearly be seen on the Booth plan.

Thomas Salmon visiting in 1748 saw Wroxton as, 'a good old House, built after the taste of our Forefathers, secured on every Side by Hills or Groves from tempests, and consequently wants the Prospects that modern seats enjoy; however, this is not without its Beauties; for here are most extensive Walks cut through the Groves, fine Slopes, and noble Pieces of Water, which render it a charming retirement'.[3] As Salmon observed, Wroxton's low-lying situation precluded views of the Oxfordshire countryside such as could be enjoyed at Rousham or Blenheim, but advantage had been taken of the surrounding slopes and of the old water-courses.

Wroxton had two styles of landscaping imposed within 20 years, but in different parts of the garden so that both phases of improvements can still be seen. Just before his death in 1729 Francis North consulted Henry Wise, the last of the formal gardeners, about a grandiose scheme for Wroxton. This was undertaken by Tilleman Bobart, the son of Jacob Bobart of the Oxford Botanic Garden. Wise and Bobart had worked together at Blenheim, Canons Ashby

159 (above right). The cascade at Wroxton from the east by S.H. Grimm. (British Library, London)

160 (right). The cascade was restored by Paul Edwards for the Fairleigh Dickinson University.

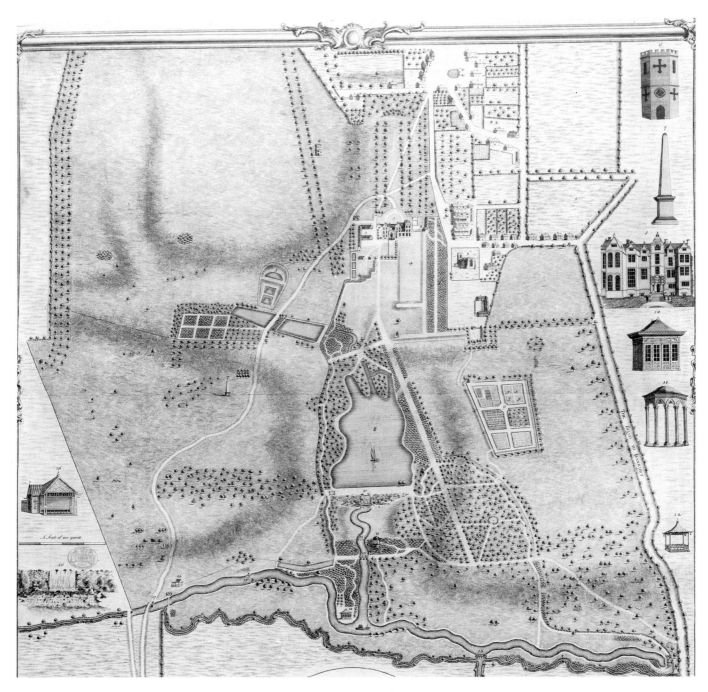

and Hampton Court. The works for Lord North included an octagonal basin and a canal 240 foot long and 40 foot wide, the earth from which was used to bank up the great terrace and walking slopes where the great terrace joined the Cross Walk.[4]

The second stage of the landscaping was undertaken by Sanderson Miller for Francis North, Lord Guilford, between 1737 and 1751, when Bobart's formal layout, including the canal, was grassed over. Today the terraces have the appearance of linear earthworks overlooking a vast expanse of lawn; the old bowling green has been retained. Francis North was Gentleman of the Bedchamber to Frederick Prince of Wales, who had Chinese

161. Plan of Wroxton, c.1750, by Francis Booth, showing the formal gardens near the house and Miller's rococo landscape beyond the terrace. The vignettes depict Miller's buildings. (British Library, London)

enthusiasms, and had around him a number of courtiers interested in natural landscaping, including his Secretary, Lord Lyttelton and Charles Hamilton. An obelisk commemorates the visit of the Prince of Wales in 1739, when attending the Banbury races. Miller erected a Gothic eye-catcher at Drayton, similar to that erected by Kent at Rousham. The Yorkes took it all in, particularly the Chinese elements, on their tour visit in 1748, when Sanderson Miller's landscaping of the area lying below the Cross Walk was complete:

> The garden is 70 acres and finely diversified with wood and water, and has from the irregularity of the ground many natural beauties which are well improved. There is an irregular piece of water or lake of 7 acres, surrounded with high trees, which ends in a cascade (it only plays occasionally) and falls 20ft perpendicular; and there is to be a small temple built on the mount against it. A grove of fine old oaks of 12 acres upon the side of the hill is kept rough with paths cut through it that carry you both to the lake and down the hill, at the bottom of which a serpentine river runs through the meadows. It seems to issue (we were told) from a rustic arch higher up in the garden and a little below this grove it parts into two small streams and upon the banks between them stands a very pretty Chinese summerhouse. At the end of this river is another Chinese lodge which is lived in, and a court with an old wall before it, behind it an open seat which fronts a little natural cascade. The green fields which surround these and the fine trees among them are one great beauty of the place, and in them is a pigeon-house like a Gothic tower, which has a very pretty effect. The parterre before the house rises in several small slopes, is bordered with wood on each side, and open to a large meadow at the end.[5]

It was Miller's rococo valley landscaping, rather than the gardens round the Jacobean house, that appealed to most travellers. In his diary entry for 1748 John Loveday enthused about his improvements: 'The gardens have the approbation of all judges, consisting of a piece of water admirably shaded with trees, of a Cascade, of a serpentine River etc. much of it made out of a bog'.[6] It was the rococo buildings, set in intimate naturalized settings which gave the garden its character. Mrs Delany sketched them with delight in 1740 and in 1772 said of Blenheim, 'I don't find with all its surprizes, improvements and Grandeur stands in any manner of competition with Wroxton'.[7]

Richard Pococke in 1756 saw the Temple on the Mount, which was only talked about when Philip Yorke visited, and admired its ingenious screens:

> But this place is more to be admired without doors . . . descended to a serpentine river, which is supplied from the large pieces of water and going up by it we came to the Gothic open rotondo of Mr Miller's design, in which he has practis'd curtains, that by turning screws let down so as to afford shelter which ever way you please. This commands a most delightful view of the head that supports the great body of water I have mentioned covered with shrubs, and a cascade falls down 20ft from it and forms a serpentine river which runs by the Chinese summer house; and there is another stream and small cascade to the left, which leads to a Chinese seat at a gate of this fine place that leads to Banbury.[8]

162. Mrs Delany's sketch of the Chinese house (14 on the Booth plan, Plate 161). The building was visited by the Yorkes, who had a similar one put up at Wrest (see Plate 80). (National Gallery of Ireland)

Arthur Young also admired Miller's work where 'from a Gothic temple, on a knole of land that rises in the valley, the water view is double and very pleasing'.[9] The architect of the Chinese buildings, one of which Mrs Delany sketched in 1740, is unknown. Her Chinese house (the term Chinese and Indian were interchangeable at this time), where favoured travellers were given 'cold meat and ice cream',[10] can be seen on the Booth plan in the bend of the river. According to Walpole, who spent 'a delightful day at Wroxton' in 1753, this was a very early example of the Chinese taste, of which he as the arch Gothicist disapproved and claimed that he could not be content until 'every pagoda took the veil':[11]

> This scene consists of a beautiful lake entirely shut in with wood: the head falls into a fine cascade, and that into a serpentine river, over which is a little Gothic seat like a round temple, lifted up by a shaggy mount . . . . There are several paltry Chinese buildings and bridges which have the merit or demerit of being the progenitors of a very numerous race all over the kingdom; at least they were of the very first.[12]

Walpole disapproved of the overall treatment of the surroundings of the house, however much he admired Miller's rococo scene. By the mid-century there were ideas of total landscape embracing house and environs in the Brown way. As Wroxton was not changed with the new fashion it remains an interesting example of the rococo style; the cascade, Gothic tower and icehouse have been restored, but it may be some time before an essential Chinese building is reinstated.

CASTLE HILL
near SOUTH MOLTON, DEVON

163. The hermitage at Castle Hill: a 'mote-confabricated cell'. James Fortescue's *Essays* were illustrated throughout with engravings of the garden buildings at Castle Hill.

Castle Hill is like a shy cousin to Stowe. Like Stowe its development spans the eighteenth century so that we now see a landscaped garden within the framework of an earlier more rigid design. Like Stowe it received great attention during the 1730s owing to its owner going into political opposition, and like Stowe it was ornamented with a multitude of garden buildings in a variety of styles. Much of the landscape survives, but it is comparatively unknown, tucked away on a shelf beneath a hill, deep in the Devon countryside. However, it was not always so little known: on his visit in 1764, Bishop Pococke stated that Castle Hill 'is allow'd to be one of the most beautiful places in England'.[1]

In the first half of the eighteenth century a formal garden was laid out around the new house of Hugh, 1st Lord Fortescue, Earl of Clinton. He was a friend of the 'Gardening Lords'. Indeed, Pococke wrote of Fortescue that it was 'He, Lord Pembroke, Lord Burlington, and Lord Cobham . . . who brought into England, taste in buildings and laying out of ground'. The architect Roger Morris was ordered to work on the house 'as my Lord Burlington or Lord Herbert [Pembroke] shall direct'.[2]

After 1733, when he resigned his Lord Lieutenancy and his position as Lord of the Bedchamber to the Prince of Wales, Fortescue devoted more of his time to laying-out his garden. He also spent a good deal of time on mysterious missions to France and the garden was in the grand manner of formal grass terraces, rows and avenues of clipped trees, a large geometrically shaped lake before the house, vistas—the main one leading to the triumphal arch still dominant in the landscape—and cross-vistas. But dotted around the park were a variety of more informal or informally placed garden buildings. As at Stowe there was a triumphal arch modelled on the Arch of Constantine and a copy of the Pyramid of Cestius. A new church for Filleigh was built in the latest Gothic style and carefully placed to act as an eye-catcher, and the 'Castle' itself was built, on the hill above the house. This contained a room, ornamented with old panelling and furniture, from which to enjoy the view. Further west there was another building also designed as an eye-catcher, 'the British Spaw', where there was a cold bath, 'esteem'd very good for the Gout'.[3] This still exists although it is now a private residence.

Along the river west of the house the Satyr's Temple and the Sibyl's Cave were both built by 1752, as was probably the cascade, and these were therefore part of the 1st Lord Fortescue's layout. Pococke admired the masonry in the grotto: 'so well executed that the joints of the mortar appear like veins in the solid rock'. The present owner, Lady Margaret Fortescue, has restored both these features, as well as, with her sister, the Triumphal Arch. Of the Cave, the Reverend James Fortescue wrote in a very bad poem of 1759:

> *Cave within cave, all crystal-deck'd; spar rocks,*
> *And glitt'ring stones, and variegated gems*
> *Mingle their pointed beams, reflecting round*
> *A tremulous gloom; while, from above,*
> *Descends the solemn, awe-creating light*
> *For abstract meditation meet . . .*[4]

Standing in the cave, with these words in mind, today's tourist may begin to understand that quality of self-induced poetic intensity which characterized much of the eighteenth-century approach to gardens.

Also dating from pre-1752, a Chinese temple, which stood on the site of the present statue of Pan, survived within living memory. A fairly substantial hermitage was likewise built at this time: an engraving of it was made to illustrate Fortescue's poem—he referred to it as 'the mote-confabricated cell'—and recently its site has been discovered. Pococke describes it as being approached by a 'winding way; it is coverd inside and out with wood of different Colours which resemble Trees; in the middle room is an Altar in a nich, made of the root of a

164. Painting of Castle Hill by J. Lange, 1741. This and its pair were photographed for *Country Life* before being destroyed by fire in 1934.

165. The pair to Plate 164 above.

tree, with a crucifix on it; On one side is the Kitchen, on the other the bedroom, with all the proper apparatus; and beyond the house is the Hermit's Garden'.

In 1751 Hugh Fortescue died unmarried and was succeeded by his half-brother Matthew, who became the 2nd Lord Fortescue. Between 1751 and 1785 the new owner redesigned much of the park as an informal English landscape. His correspondence with his steward Mr Hilliard bears witness to a close collaboration; the lord only too often deferring to the steward's acute awareness of design principles: 'without any compliment to you you enter so thoroughly into the true spirit and beauty of the place that I really suspect myself of being in the wrong whenever I differ in the least from your plans'.[5] They argued (Fortescue had to insist on a classical temple where Hilliard had set his heart on 'parts of an abbey ruin'); they debated; they trusted each other's judgement, and decisions obviously evolved rather than being dictated by any authority.

Between them Fortescue and Hilliard redesigned the garden. It seems likely that it was they who had the formal lake reshaped, although there is some confusion here. Of the two views by Lange both *circa* 1741, alas now destroyed by fire, one shows the formal cruciform lake, the other, apparently, an informal serpentine. Perhaps Hugh Fortescue was already pondering a new design and had the artist illustrate it in anticipation of its being built. The formal planting was broken up and new structures were erected, the largest of which was an imposing building on the hill east of the arch, the classical Holwell Temple. This still acts as a feature, although it is now a ruin after a fire in the last century. Matthew's sister, Lucy, became the wife of Lord Lyttelton of Hagley, celebrated in the poems of Thomson and Shenstone, and Lyttelton certainly visited Castle Hill (James Fortescue refers to Lyttelton's seat in the beech woods above the Sibyl's Cave), although there is no record of any professional advice being taken by the Fortescues and their steward.

In 1764 Pococke stated categorically that Castle Hill 'is the work of the late Lord Clinton', but he also noted the present lord's contribution, in particular, 'Upon a hill to the south East of . . . [the Pyramid] some scatter'd houses a sort of Village and the appearance of a Church'. This was 'Sham Town', a collection of ornamental cottages, one of which was adorned with two sides of a Gothic tower. This mock church fell down in the 1940s, but 'Sham Town', in which the appearance of a village was a picturesque feature, makes an ironic comparison with the general trend of eighteenth-century landscaping in which, as at Castle Howard, Chatsworth or Nuneham, real villages were destroyed for being unsightly.

Interestingly, the road itself was a picturesque feature in Pococke's view: 'the high road goes as through these improvements and the people are seen passing in several parts, which has a very pretty Effect'. The effect would have been very different if, as proposed in 1979, the road had been turned into dual carriageway as part of the North Devon Link Road.

166. The Satyr's Temple and the 'Ugly Bridge' today. The Sibyl's Cave is to the right of the stream.

167. John Wootton: *View of Castle Hill*, c.1735–40. The rotunda on the brow of the hill seems never to have been built, and its position is now occupied by the Gothic Castle which gives the house its name. (Castle Hill, courtesy of Lady Margaret Fortescue)

William Gilpin thought Fortescue had made the mistake of 'over-building his improvements. From one stand we counted eight or nine buildings'. Rather unsympathetically he criticized him for failing to give the landscape 'the air of nature'. Gilpin did admire the castle, but thought that 'little more . . . in the way of building, would have been necessary. This lofty castle might be object sufficient from almost every part of his improvements'.[6]

Matthew Fortescue died in 1785 and the garden we see today is substantially as he left it. Woods have grown up and remedied the rawness that bothered Gilpin. Nineteenth-century additions include the Sunset Temple and the Shrubbery Temple. Some buildings described by Pococke have disappeared without trace—a temple of Venus for example—others have fallen down, and planting has obscured parts of the designed views, but the place remains very much the same—bursting, in the words of a twentieth-century tourist, Christopher Hussey, 'entire upon the eye like one of Kip's "views of seats" . . . a prodigious string of golden-hued buildings, crowned here and there by little domes . . . against a background of lofty trees'.[7]

WARWICK CASTLE
WARWICK, WARWICKSHIRE

Warwick, according to Sir Walter Scott, is 'the noblest sight in England'. Unlike Kenilworth, it is not a ruin and has a long history. Prince Pückler-Muskau, the arch Romantic and disciple of Goethe, was overwhelmed when he visited it on his tour of Regency England and saw it rising up across the Avon 'like a vision of the Middle Ages':

> By Heaven—only now am I filled with true and immeasurable enthusiasm. What I have earlier described was smiling Nature combined with everything that art and money could bestow upon it. I left [Woburn] well pleased and although I have seen things like it before—indeed possessed them myself—not without admiration. But what I have seen today was more than this; it was an enchanted spot, enveloped in the most charming robe of poetry, surrounded with all the majesty of history, the sight of which still fills me with delightful astonishment . . . . Even from a distance

168. Aerial view of Warwick Castle showing the overgrown Mount and Marnock's hexagonal parterre in front of the Orangery, which has been maintained unchanged since it was laid out in 1869.

you can already glimpse the dark stone mass over the ancient cedars of Lebanon, chestnuts, pines and plane trees, rising perpendicularly out of the rocks on the banks of the Avon more than 200ft above the water level.[1]

Elihu Burritt, then American consular agent, visiting in the 1860s, also found Warwick 'impressive and venerable' and admired the cedars of Lebanon, trees which he had never seen before:

> England and all who speak its language owe the successive inheritors of this great living pile of buildings more than they have ever acknowledged. For it is really the only baronial castle that has survived the destruction or decay of all the other monuments of the feudal ages of the same order. We should not know what they were in their day and generation were it not for this. . . . Thus Warwick represents to us in its living being and form of today the hundreds of castles that were planted over the island in the first century after the Conquest.[2]

169. Canaletto: *Warwick Castle*, c.1748, showing the Mount with its cockleshell paths enabling the visitor 'to come to the top without payn'. (Paul Mellon Collection, Virginia, U.S.A.)

Sir Sacheverell Sitwell gives the modern view of its spell:

> The view of Warwick Castle from the bridge below it across the Avon has a
> sempiternal Englishness, as typical of England as the view of the Bay of Naples is of
> Italy. Warwick Castle is of the same antiquity as Windsor or the Tower of London.
> And the knowledge that Shakespeare, who was born by the same river Avon, must
> often have set eyes on Warwick cannot fail to give sanctity to its battlemented
> walls.[3]

The prince, the American consul, and Sir Sacheverell saw Warwick in its picturesque
eighteenth-century landscaped setting, but seventeenth-century travellers recorded their
admiration of the old formal gardens, laid out by Sir Fulke Greville, later Baron Brooke, to
whom as Chancellor of the Exchequer James I had granted Warwick Castle. Greville was at
the court of Elizabeth with Philip Sidney, a lifelong friend, and to Warwick he brought his
own 'Arcadia'. Making his 'Iter Boreale' from Oxford, James I's chaplain, Richard Corbett,
shortly to become Dean of Christ Church, visited Warwick in 1619, soon after Fulke Greville
had made his gardens. He particularly admired the feature of the Mount, recalling Leland's
description of how the visitor was able by means of a path 'writhen about in degrees like
turnings in cockleshelles to come to the top without payn':[4]

> It seems nor Art nor Force can intercept it,
> As if a Lover built, a Souldier kept it.
> Up to the Tower, though it be steepe and high,
> Wee do not climbe but walke; and though the eye
> Seems to be weary, yet our feet are still
> In the same Posture cozen'd up the hill:
> And thus the workemans Art deceaves our sence,
> Making these Rounds of Pleasure a Defence.[5]

Lieutenant Hammond, visiting in 1634, found Warwick a 'second Eden':

> And although this pleasant high Place, may seem tiresome to ascend, yet it is so
> finely and artificially contrived, with winding walks, that no man can be weary at all,
> to march up to the top; and the whole hill, and declining brow is so planted, and
> furnished with Beech, Birch, and severall sorts of Plum-trees, as it is most delightfull,
> and exceeding pleasant to ascend. By this large, and pleasant peece of ground, which
> is adorn'd with all kind, of delightfull and shady walkes, and Arbors, pleasant
> Groves, and wildernesses, fruitfull Trees, delicious Bowers, odiferous Herbes, and
> fragrant Flowers, betweene the River and the high, rocky Foundation of the Castle.[6]

The Mount is clearly seen in Canaletto's painting of Warwick from the Avon, just when it was
being planted with shrubs by Capability Brown, who was called to the castle in 1749 and
worked there for a decade to improve the old-fashioned gardens, so much admired by Corbett
and Hammond. Francis, Lord Brooke, later 1st Earl of Warwick, was one of Brown's first
patrons and in 1751 Horace Walpole, the apologist of landscape gardening, appeared
unacquainted with his work, as in a letter to George Montagu he referred to him as 'one
Brown'. Describing Warwick Castle as 'enchanting', he wrote:

The view pleased me more than I can express; the river Avon tumbles down a
cascade at the foot of it. It is well laid out by one Brown who has set up on a few
ideas of Kent and Mr Southcote. One sees what the prevalence of taste does; little
Brooke who would have chuckled to have been born in an age of clipt hedges and
cockle-shell avenues, has submitted to let his garden and park be natural.[7]

In place of the formal gardens Walpole saw the smooth naturalized riverside slopes with groups
of trees in a beautiful Brown landscape, but Brown's work at Warwick was to be modified in
the 1770s to accord with the new earl's picturesque taste. The Picturesque did not supersede
naturalizing until the 1790s, after the publication of Gilpin's Tours and Uvedale Price's *Essay
on the Picturesque*, but Gilpin's patrons who saw his Tours in manuscript form in the 1770s
were ahead of other improvers. Lord Warwick, who was a connoisseur of drawing and the
patron of John Warwick Smith, wrote to Gilpin in 1777 to say that he had decided to make
alterations following hints he had taken from his *Tour of the Lakes* (not published until 1789),
which he had been lent.[8] The next year they became acquainted when Lord Warwick and his
family took a house near Gilpin's New Forest parish.

Gilpin was delighted with the young nobleman and told William Mason that his taste is
'wholly of the sublime kind, formed upon the mountains and lakes of Switzerland, and
Cumberland' and that what he proposed to do at Warwick Castle 'will out-Brown anything
that is done there'.[9] Richard Warner, the traveller, who for three years was Gilpin's curate
and ally, confirmed the picturesque nature of the Warwick improvements. In his *Tour through
the northern counties*, 1802, he applauded the wooded serpentine path opening into occasional

170 (left). Warwick Castle is
one of the few mediaeval castles
which have survived destruction
and decay. 'Few places are more
gratifying to the sentimental
tourist', according to Henry
James.

171 (right). Robert Marnock's
restored formal rose garden
between the castle and the
lodge.

glades with the castle rising picturesquely above the groves giving a contrasting gloom to the open lawn leading down to the river. He awarded the 'palm of taste' to Lord Warwick and describes the scene in Gilpin terms:

> Nature and ancient art, indeed, had done much for him in furnishing this spot with a beautiful river, august woods, and a magnificent old castle; but that nice perception of the beautiful, that delicate discriminating taste, which constitutes the picturesque feeling; which sees when to conceal, and when to display; which knows how to associate, and how to detach; could alone produce the striking effect that now arises from their admirable and judicious combination.[10]

Miss Berry in 1807 enjoyed the picturesque vegetation growing on the banks along the river walks and her climb up the Mount to the outer walls of the castle.[11] The Victorians reintroduced formality to parts of the garden when Robert Marnock designed an hexagonal parterre in front of the Orangery. This has been maintained virtually unchanged since it was laid out in 1869. Recently Marnock's formal rose garden between the castle and Castle Lodge has been restored by Paul Edwards for Madame Tussaud's, who took over in 1978. With its ironwork arches for rambling roses, its arbours and covered walkway it evokes the sensual pleasures of Fulke Greville's 'second Eden', and the winding paths of the Mount, which had so impressed the seventeenth-century tourists, have also been restored, enabling the visitor to 'come to the top without payn'.

PETWORTH HOUSE
PETWORTH, WEST SUSSEX

Petworth is one of England's most palatial country houses, set in an idealized Sussex landscape with deer grazing in the park, as immortalized by Turner. As the visitor now enters it seems more like a fortress than a country house, but Petworth was originally a castle of the Percys, who were licensed to crenellate an existing manor house in 1309. The Elizabethan house was rebuilt to turn its back on the town and was 'prince-like' with 'brave Parkes' and 'commodious Fish-Ponds', according to Lieutenant Hammond who visited in 1634. Like all travellers until the early eighteenth century he entered Petworth through the courtyard of the stables, immediately to the west of the house, which Defoe said were 'the finest of their kind in all the south of England, and equal to some Noblemen's whole houses'.[1] Hammond's route, paced out in his usual military way, can be traced from the north of the courtyard to the terraces, wilderness, bowling green and gardens in the Treswell survey of 1610 and in the painting of the old house of *circa* 1680:

> From hence I march'd along towards the cheife Mansion upon one of those 2 Files of Walkes which are hewen and made out of the Rocke, of 600 foote in length

172. The old house at Petworth in a painting attributed to Jacob Knyff, *c.*1680. Hammond entered through the stables, which Defoe thought were 'equal to some Noblemen's whole houses'. The terraces Hammond described are on the left. (Syon House, courtesy His Grace the Duke of Northumberland)

(ascending each other in the middst, of the same Stone) to the Wildernes; wherein are 2 walkes both alike in length and being 400 of my Paces, which are overshadow'd with Sycamore Trees, and guarded with 100 Rankes and Files of pleasant, young, florishing growing Plants, and all planted in a comely and orderly decorum. Then went I into a neat and delightful Bowling Greene, which is 60 paces long and 40 broad . . . close to this are the pleasant, sweet and delightfull Gardens.[2]

The 6th Duke of Somerset, known as the 'Proud Duke', who married the Percy heiress and whose children always had to stand in his presence, pulled down the ancestral house, and, according to Defoe, who visited in 1722, 'on the same spot has built from the ground, one of the finest piles of building, and the best modelled houses then in Britain'.[3] The much-travelled Macky, who saw Petworth about the same time, was, as he was intended to be, much impressed by the duke's house and life-style. 'Few subjects abroad have such Palaces, those at Prague in Bohemia come to the nearest of this . . . but what is particular in the Duke of Somerset is, that all his palaces are completely Furnished, and he moves to them without removing anything from his other Seats'.[4] By Macky's time the 'Sumptuous Stables' had been pulled down and Tillington village removed to give a more impressive approach to the house than the route taken by Hammond.

George London had been called in to provide an avenue approach and a suitably formal garden setting for the magnificent new western entrance façade. Hammond's terraces were made grander and, as learned from the accounts, ornamented with 'flower potts upon peeres

goeing up the ramparts'.[5] Joining the 'Noble Terras' Macky found the Orangery, 'where is the
most curious Collection of Evergreens, and the largest sized Trees kept in Tubs that ever I
saw'. A painting of *circa* 1700 shows the new orangery and formal garden in front of it. Macky
also saw a 'fine old Grove of trees', the wilderness which Hammond had seen planted with
young trees in 'a comely and orderly decorum' and now made by London into a fashionable
bosquet in the French manner.

Jeremiah Milles, who visited Petworth in 1743, found that the duke had not mellowed
with age, nor had he changed his gardens. 'He treats all his country neighbours, and indeed
everybody else, with such uncommon pride, and distance, that none of them visit Him'. The
baroque relationship of the house and gardens and unintegrated park still existed and seemed
very old-fashioned to Milles, who had seen many of the new landscaped estates on his tours.
'The misfortune is that the house is situated in a bade place. . . . The Gardens do not seem to
be large, nor in a good taste, they ar laid out in terraces one over the other; and ye Park rises
behind them commanding a very good prospect'.[6] Milles was not the only visitor to comment
on the unfortunate situation of the house at Petworth. Defoe said it stood 'as it were with its
elbows to the town, its front has no visto answerable',[7] and Macky thought that the
opportunity had been lost by not building the new house on the knoll to the north-west where
it would have had 'an open Prospect of the Neighbouring Country'.[8]

Charles Wyndham, 2nd Earl of Egremont, who inherited in 1750, was largely responsible for the Petworth we see today. He was a member of the Society of Dilettanti and it is the
Old Masters and antique sculptures acquired by him on the Grand Tour that form the nucleus
of the Petworth collection. He shared fellow Dilettanti's interest in landscaping and took the
decisive step of opening up the western façade to the old deer park and downland landscape by
removing the 'Proud' Duke's avenue approach and reverting to the mediaeval entry from the
town. Capability Brown, who was still working at Stowe, was asked for advice and his plan of
1752 and contract in the Petworth archives show the extent and nature of his work in rare
detail.

The terraces made by George London were 'reduced to a Fine Undulated hill Adorned
with Groupes of Cedars, Pines etc' and a stream was dammed to form a large lake in the middle
distance view. The bones of the wilderness were left unaltered but the perimeter was reshaped
and a ha-ha linked it with the park. There were new serpentine walks 'according to the Idea
agreed on with his Lordship', one of which was planned to go 'through ye Laurels leading up to
the Seat where the Dutchess of Somerset used to drink her Coffee', and he added the two small
temples. The borders of these Pleasure Ground paths were planted with flowering shrubs
including 'Persian jasmin, spireas, Virginian shumachs, tamarisks, trumpet flowers, portugal
laurels, laburnuns, acacias, lilacs, candleberry trees and bird cherries'. In 1811 Louis Simond,
back from America, found the Pleasure Grounds unlike anything else he had seen; it was
'planted with the largest trees, close together, something like a heavily timbered American
forest of which they suggest the idea. . . . We found here our old acquaintances, the hemlock,
the black spruce, the tulip tree, the occidental plane, the acacia, and several kinds of oaks',
growing in a peer's grounds without 'the loss of American liberty'.[9]

173. Brown's idealized Sussex landscape has been immortalized by Turner's painting, *The Lake, Petworth: sunset a stag drinking,* c.1830, which hangs in the house overlooking the actual scene.

Brown clearly did not make a clean sweep either in the Pleasure Ground or the park, where a great deal of the old timber was left. In the 1760s Walpole found 'oaks two hundred years old' in the garden,[10] and the Duchess of Northumberland, visiting in 1770, not 20 years after Brown's plantings, spoke of 'Chestnuts, Oaks and Beeches of a stupendous size and surpass all that I have seen in my life'.[11] In the disastrous gale of 1987 Petworth was devastated. The ringcounts of the trees blown down showed that many of the trees were pre-Brown; some chestnuts were dated to 1705, and were replantings after the equally disastrous 1703 gale. Even some of the clumps pre-dated Brown and may have belonged to the London design. It appears from an engraving by Kip that London clumped trees to the south of nearby Stansted to allow the Earl of Scarbrough coastal views.

The third figure in the history of Petworth, as it affects the visitors' appreciation of the house and landscape today, is the 3rd Earl of Egremont, who inherited in 1763. A patron of the arts and an agricultural reformer he was a close friend of Turner, who painted several beautiful landscapes of Petworth Park, one of which is now placed looking out over the actual scene. He was also a friend of Arthur Young, of whom he had a marble bust made. The earl naturalized Brown's setting even further by removing the dominating orangery to allow uninterrupted greensward round the house. He also introduced the urns on pedestals throughout the park, which probably came from the parapet of the house and the former parterre garden. In the Stag Park out of sight across the lake he built a model farm, which was greatly admired by Arthur Young, who saw it in 1808 as 'the greatest improvement that I know undertaken in this country' by 'an animated and enlightened improver' who grew 'extraordinary fine crops' and bred fat Southdown sheep. This was true landscape improvement. 'The whole of it is a garden'.[12]

174 (left). The wrought-iron railings placed above the ha-ha in 1872 are a copy of those by Tijou at Hampton Court (see Plate 62).

175 (below). Brown's landscape. It is being replanted by the National Trust after extensive damage in the 1987 gale.

William Cobbett, always on the look-out for signs of exploitation on his Rural Rides in 1823, acknowledged that Petworth was not only 'a most magnificent seat' with a very fine park but that there was also 'an appearance of comfort about the dwellings of labourers . . . that is very pleasant to behold'.[13] Even at the height of the agricultural depression annual feasts for tenants and workers continued in the park. J. C. Loudon on tour in 1829 also thoroughly approved of the earl's benevolence. Noting the earl's piggery sited just to the north of the house, he commented: 'On remarking to the person who showed us the rooms on the quantity of pigs grazing in front of the windows, and on the number of townsmen playing at skittles beside them, she observed that the earl, her master, took delight in seeing every living thing enjoying its existence; an expression indicative of a character which greatly pleases us'.[14]

Walpole, who delighted in a seat that had both good pictures and a good landscape, had nothing but praise for Petworth, where he felt that everything that the eighteenth century was trying to achieve by 'modern gardening' would come to 'venerable maturity'.[15] For Nikolaus Pevsner, the most thorough and percipient of modern travellers, Walpole's prophecy came true and the impression left of the beauty created by the ideas of the Egremonts and Capability Brown was 'overwhelming and ennobling. Some parks are no more than the sum of the objects inside them: Petworth is so much more that it is possible to come out of a walk in the park feeling that it represents a quite different order of environment, an order that can transfer its values to the views like a physical essence. It may be an illusion, but it is far more real than much 20th century so-called reality'.[16]

BOWOOD
near CALNE, WILTSHIRE

Bowood, like Petworth, is one of the best surviving landscapes of Capability Brown. However, today's visitor does not see the house his landscape was designed to complement as he does at Petworth. In 1955 the so-called Big House was demolished and a new Bowood House was made consisting of an adapted Little House with the Adam wing and courts. The present Earl of Shelburne has said that his father's decision 'that it was the Park, Pleasure Grounds and the Estate which should be given a hope for the future' was criticized at the time, but it has enabled the family to stay at Bowood and maintain its unique heritage, and the present ensemble of eighteenth-century buildings is in scale and character with the landscape, which has such a long and interesting history.[1]

Bowood was originally part of an extensive forest which belonged to the Saxon kings and passed to William the Conqueror; even after disafforestation a part of it, 'King's Bowood', was preserved as a royal hunting ground. During the Commonwealth it was surveyed and timber sold and land let. A house was begun in the early eighteenth century but not completed until

bought by the 1st Earl of Shelburne in 1754, and enlarged by Henry Keene. Lancelot Brown
was in Wiltshire in 1757 and was asked to consider the capabilities of a landscape for the
house. He was apparently impressed by the well-timbered park and the fruit, but the earl did
not seem to think he had had value for his 30 guineas professional visit, as he wrote to his son:
'What wou'd you give to know the consequences of the visit of the famous Mr Brown and the
fruit of the 30 guineas which I gave him? He passed two days with me . . . and twenty times
assured me that he does not know a finer place in England than Bowood Park, and that he is
sure no Prince in Europe has so fine a fruit garden'.[2]

The earl died in 1761 and it was his son, the 2nd Earl, later 1st Marquess of Lansdowne,
who drew up Brown's contract the following year. Robert Adam made further alterations to
the house at this time, including the handsome greenhouse range linking the pavilions, and
he also built the Mausoleum in the park as a memorial to the 1st Earl. Brown's contract
showed that he had agreed to 'make the Great Plantations . . . each side of the Mausoleum
and all those plantations proposed to Verge the Park', to turf lawns, make sunk fences, new
drives to the house and a lake for which he was required to 'make a good sufficient head to
cause water to flow in shape as agreed with your Lordship . . . and a sham bridge'. The
contracted work was considerable and he found that additional time had been needed earth-
moving 'on forming the Island, and in lowering the hill between the wood and the house'.[3]

Bowood must have been one of the places Goldsmith, who was a friend of Lord
Shelburne, had in mind when he accused the landowner of destroying villages to make 'space
for his lake'.[4] The hamlet of Mannings Hill had to be submerged along with the Bath road in

176. Painting at Bowood by an
unknown artist of the early
Georgian house before
landscape improvements.
(Courtesy Trustees of the
Bowood Estate)

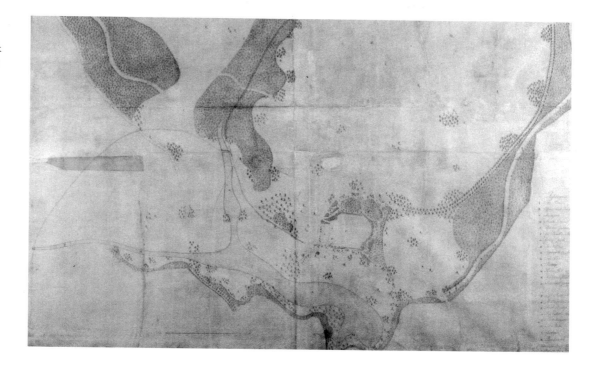

the making of Brown's lake. Due forms of law were observed, however, and the J.P. was brought along to give consent to blocking up the highway; this was given on condition that a new road was made and that the earl guaranteed to provide a ferry should anyone ask to cross the old road, day or night. The ferry cottage can still be seen on the other side of the lake. Lady Shelburne was delighted with the result and wrote in her journal on 16 June 1766: 'As soon as breakfast was over we took a walk and were vastly pleased with the effect of the water which flows into a magnificent river and only wants now to rise to its proper height, which it comes nearer to every day'. It took time to acquire all the land needed to attain views to the horizon, as Lady Shelburne discovered: 'This evening Lord S drove me to the downs by the new Road he is making, and shew'd me an alteration he designs in the approach to ye House. It is indeed very fine and if my Lord can purchase 3 fields from my Lord Bottetourt or from Mr Pitt, the whole extent of ye country between us and ye downs will be his and we shall have a magnificent drive to them'.[5]

Neither her friend Horace Walpole, nor Whately's observations had prepared Miss Berry for such a landscape with such a lake and in 1838 she remonstrated that, 'too little is said of the out-of-door beauties of Bowood; but the water is the very least artificial water I ever saw'.[6] A picturesque addition to Brown's landscaping had been made in 1785 on the advice of Charles Hamilton, the creator of Painshill, who had retired to Bath in 1773. This was a cascade and grotto at the head of the lake, which was enthusiastically described in *The beauties of Wiltshire* by John Britton. He said that the cascade was based on a picture by Poussin and

that Josiah Lane, from nearby Tisbury, who had worked for Hamilton at Painshill, was responsible for the rockwork. The water, he said, gushed out of:

> several excavations in the rock; and the principal sheet, after falling a few yards, dashes against some projecting masses of stone, and flies off in a cloud of white spray. The dashing and the roar of the waters, jumbled confusion of the rock, the wildness and seclusion of the place, and the various subterranean passages under the head of the river, conspire to render it a scene strikingly pleasing to every man of taste; but more peculiarly so to the painter and admirer of the picturesque; for here he may indulge himself in the reveries of fancy, and by a small effort of the imagination may think himself amongst the wild waterfalls of North Wales, or the thundering cataracts of Switzerland.[7]

Charles Hamilton, a notable conifer planter, may also have influenced the additional planting of 1775 when hundreds of cedars of Lebanon were planted. William Pitt, a skilful landscaper and frequent visitor, is also said to have advised at Bowood. Miss Berry noted that 'there are the finest evergreens, such as cedars, evergreen oaks and all the pine tribe, that one can see'.[8]

The next Lansdowne to make an impact on the Bowood landscape was the 3rd Marquess, with the assistance of his head gardener John Spencer, who in 1848 produced a plan for the new pinetum with plants laid out according to their country of origin. In 1867 a visitor by initials W.B.R.D. wrote for the *Wiltshire Archaeological Magazine* that:

> to persons scientifically inclined, the Arboretum at Bowood is full of interest for not

only are there specimens of almost every known tree, but they are placed geographically, the ground being laid out on the plan of a map, and the specimens planted, as far as is practicable, in the latitude and longitude of their natural habit.[9]
Many fine trees remain from the nineteenth century and there is an excellent catalogue of all Bowood's trees and shrubs, which is a helpful guide for experts and would-be expert visitors. Roy Lancaster writes in the preface: 'I have had the good fortune of seeing a number of our most prized ornamental trees growing in their natural environment and nothing pleases me more than seeing a familiar tree from the wild growing happily in cultivation'.[10]

Bowood experienced the Victorian reaction to great country houses springing up out of the turf in the eighteenth-century fashion. Robert Smirke had already constructed an upper terrace outside Adam's greenhouse range in 1817 and in 1851 George Kennedy made the lower parterre garden. This was featured in *The gardens of England* of 1857 by E. Adveno Brooke, who considered Bowood to 'form the beau-ideal of English garden scenery'. The

179. The cascade grotto at the head of the lake, on which Charles Hamilton of Painshill advised, was said to be based on a picture by Poussin.

American landscape architect, Charles Eliot, visiting in 1886, described this garden as 'very quaint with stone-edged parterres, much balustrading, walks on different levels, yews etc', but, whereas he appreciated the pinetum was new because of the size of the trees, he was completely taken in by the parterre garden, which he saw as 'ancient terrace gardens before the house . . . kept up in the old fashioned manner'.

Eliot knew where he was with Brown's landscape and felt compensated for having walked a hot four miles from the station and another mile through the drive when he explored the lakeside, which to his landscape architect's eye was 'very, very good . . . and the dam of the lake is well treated. There is a pretty region of wooded mounds, where no doubt earth from the lake excavation was dumped'. For a student of English landscape gardening Brown's work at Bowood was most rewarding, and he wrote to his father: 'Yesterday I saw splendid Bowood, which Mr Henry Winthrop Sargent pronounced the second best in all England'.[11] Winthrop Sargent's first choice was not recorded.

180. Watercolour by E. Adveno Brooke from *The gardens of England, c.*1857, showing the parterre terrace designed by George Kennedy in 1851, which was thought 'ancient' by Charles Eliot.

NUNEHAM PARK
NUNEHAM COURTENAY, OXFORDSHIRE

'Perhaps there is no other country house in England that has such beautiful and well chosen prospects as Nuneham', wrote Professor Hirschfeld in his authoritative five-volume *Theorie der Gartenkunst* in 1779.[1] Visiting in 1772, William Gilpin comments on the 1st Earl Harcourt's reasons for abandoning his ancestral home in 1755 for a new site with superior landscaping possibilities:

> The old family-seat of Stanton-Harcourt, where Pope, and Gay led the muses, is now a deserted ruin. Its situation was vile, compared with that of the present house; which commands, from a rising ground, an extensive prospect over all the intervening flat, as far as the towers of Oxford. In another direction it overlooks the windings of the Thames towards Abingdon. These grand views, terminated by the Berkshire hills, and other rising grounds, compose the distance; and are presented from different places around the house; particularly from a terrace, which extends at least a mile.[2]

The 1st Earl Harcourt had greatly admired the Palladian villas he had seen on his Grand Tour. For his new home he chose the ideal situation as advocated by Palladio himself: 'advantageous and delicious as can be desired, being seated on a hillock of most easy ascent, at the foot of

181. Joseph Farington's view of Nuneham from Boydell's *History of the river Thames*, 1794.

182. Portrait of Sir Brooke
Boothby by Joseph Wright of
Derby, 1781. Boothby is shown
as a noble savage lying in the
woods, Rousseau in hand. He
wrote the inscriptions to
Rousseau in the flower garden at
Nuneham. (Tate Gallery,
London)

which runs a navigable river and on the other side surrounded by several hills that seem to form an amphitheatre'. The view of the Oxford skyline was reminiscent of Rome from the surrounding hills, so beloved by landscape painters. By choosing this superb site for his villa, the 1st Earl, a president of the Society of Dilettanti, stole a march on owners of ancestral homes who were having to move earth and dam streams to make their scenic improvements.

The major obstacle to the earl's schemes for unlimited prospect had been the old riverside village of Newnham Courtenay. Its removal in 1761 was the inspiration for Goldsmith's *The Deserted Village*, with its condemnation of the 'man of wealth and pride' whose beautiful landscaped garden where 'vistas strike' was only achieved at the expense of the peasants:

> *While scourged by famine from the smiling land,*
> *The mournful peasant leads his humble band;*
> *And while he sinks without one arm to save,*
> *The country blooms—a garden and a grave.*[3]

Lord Harcourt had rehoused the mournful peasants in a model village on the turnpike, and although the Poet Laureate, William Whitehead, had written a retaliatory poem to prove that they had 'left their cots without a sigh',[4] the family was well aware that old Newnham Courtenay was Goldsmith's 'sweet Auburn' and Lord Harcourt the 'tyrant'. Bishop Porteus wrote in his diary:

> August 20 1800. Paid a visit to . . . Lord Harcourt at Nuneham. The village was
> originally in the Park at no great distance from the House and consisted of pretty
> white cottages, scattered round a small piece of water and shaded by a number of
> very fine trees. The late Lord Harcourt thinking the village too near the house, built
> a new one on the Oxford road, about a mile from the mansion house . . . and this
> was Goldsmith's Deserted village so Lord Harcourt told me. One poor old woman
> known by the name of Babs whose cottage was shaded by a tree of her own planting
> in a most beautiful situation begged she might be permitted to remain there during
> the remainder of her life. She was indulged in this request and died there.[5]

Goldsmith must have met Babs Wyatt as he features a 'widowed, solitary thing' living alone in the Deserted Village:

She only left of all the harmless train
The sad historian of the pensive plain.

Goldsmith had also pointedly said that the old village had a 'decent church that toppt the neighbouring hill', but Lord Harcourt had demolished this and with the help of 'Athenian' Stuart designed a garden temple to do duty as the parish church. The villagers were most distressed when the churchyard was levelled for the garden and the rector wrote in his diary in 1761: 'Lord Harcourt was much displeased . . . for my talking to Stewart . . . and for saying he had done everything to me except cutting my throat'.[6] The emphasis of the earl's northern landscape was on this classical building on rising ground and a Sandby painting shows the curving tree-lined terrace round the bowl of the hill with a formal clearing giving a surprise vista of the church, looking for all the world like a miniature Chiswick Villa. The family porch, resembling the Choragic Monument, is featured along a reciprocal vista from the house. The earl much admired Studley Royal and may well have taken his ideas for vistas from there.

When the 2nd Earl inherited in 1777 the poet-painter-gardener William Mason was called in to redesign the landscape on picturesque principles. He broke up the earl's unlimited prospects with foreground planting and when he removed the formal avenue leading up to the church porch and replanted the hill, Horace Walpole wrote approvingly that, 'by one touch

183. *The flower garden at Nuneham*, engraved by W. Watts, 1777, after Paul Sandby, who was Lord Nuneham's drawing master. Designed by William Mason, it was greatly admired by visitors and was very influential.

of Albano's pencil the church is become a temple and the principal feature in one of the most beautiful landscapes in the world'.[7] The earl was the patron of William Gilpin and wrote his own guidebook. This shows that his landscaped garden was to be seen and appreciated like a Gilpin picturesque tour with defined 'stations' for viewing the Thames Valley landscape. The same principles of 'poet's feeling and painter's eye',[8] followed by Mason on the northern terrace, were applied to the walks to the south of the house when Capability Brown was called in to landscape the park in 1778.

The earl describes in picturesque terms how 'the walk now returns towards the house through a closer part of the plantation; on the left there is a narrow opening, that admits a view over the underwood; and the trees on the foreground, apparently uniting with a clump in the garden below, lead the eye to other masses of wood, till it reaches Oxford, which is framed by the trees and shrubs through which it is seen. A little farther, the prospect in front is viewed beneath the branches of detached acacias, from a treillage seat covered with roses and honeysuckles'.[9] 'Brown's walk' and riverside landscape, in which, according to Walpole, are 'scenes worthy of the bold pencil of Rubens, or to be subjects for the tranquil sunshines of Claude de Lorrain',[10] are best seen looking upstream, where a bend in the river shows the house set back on a gentle slope above the hanging woods. The whole is so idyllic and seemingly uncontrived that in his 'The late improvements at Nuneham' Whitehead pointed out that it is difficult to see which is Brown and which Nature:

> Dame Nature, the Goddess, one very bright day
> In strolling through Nuneham met Brown in her way;
> And bless me, she said, with an insolent sneer,
> I wonder that fellow will dare to come here.

A ruined Courtenay castle was to have been built on Brown's hill, but in 1787 the earl was presented with the Carfax Conduit, which had stood in the middle of Oxford, and decided to make it his picturesque Gothic eye-catcher set in a background of ancient oaks.

Until the 2nd Earl's improvements Nuneham was not considered as one of the notable landscaped gardens to be visited by the garden tourists and it did not feature in either Whately's or Walpole's books on modern gardening of the 1770s, but it was soon to become, like Stowe, Blenheim and Painshill, a place 'to wonder at' and learn from. It appeared in every book of picturesque seats, and in Boydell's *History of the river Thames* of 1794, with the text by William Combe and illustrations by Farington, it is given more coverage than Windsor Castle. In his glowing tribute Combe says, 'Nature gave the outline and taste completed the picture . . . . Nuneham is a place of the first beauty; it may in varying opinion have an equal but its flower garden transcends all rivalry and is itself alone'.

The informal flower garden, as described by Mason in Book IV of his *The English garden*, was still something of a revolution even twenty years after it had been created. The 2nd Earl Harcourt was the patron of Rousseau, who is said to have stayed at Nuneham for a short while during his exile.[11] The flower garden, enclosed from the landscaped garden, with garden and wild flowers mingling, meandering paths and flowery thickets, was influenced by the description of Julie's garden in *La nouvelle Héloïse*, from which there is a quotation at the entrance to the garden: 'Si l'Auteur de la nature est grand dans les grandes choses, il est très grand dans les petites'. A statue of Rousseau was put in the shrubbery with a verse by Brooke Boothby, a Harcourt cousin, who, like Lord Nuneham, was an 'âme sensible' cultivating Nature and noble savagery, albeit in a flower garden:

Say is the heart to virtue warm?
Can genius animate the feeling breast?
'Tis ROUSSEAU, let thy Bosom speak the rest.

Rousseau, back in France, was apparently very touched to hear he had a place in Julie's Elysée. Frederick Montagu, visiting in 1782, wrote to Mrs Delany: 'Lord Harcourt has such a flower garden as excels every flower garden which ever existed either in history or romance. Bowers, statues, inscriptions, busts, temples—all planned by Mason'.[12] Reynolds found it all 'irresistible' and John Wesley wrote that it was 'filled with all the beauties that nature and art can give'.[13] The two views of the flower garden painted by Sandby were engraved in 1777 and made Nuneham even more popular. Queen Charlotte wanted a Mason garden for Frogmore and Walpole tried to lure the gardener to Strawberry Hill.

William Gilpin's nephew, William Sawrey Gilpin, in accordance with 1830s ideas, gave the villa terraced 'dress grounds'. Hitherto the house had sprung out of the turf and Fanny

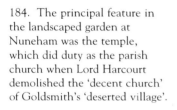

184. The principal feature in the landscaped garden at Nuneham was the temple, which did duty as the parish church when Lord Harcourt demolished the 'decent church' of Goldsmith's 'deserted village'.

Burney complained that she even got her feet wet getting out of the carriage. [14] The house was greatly extended for Archbishop Harcourt[15] and in Edwardian days more elaborate terraces were added. Picnic huts were provided in the landscaped woods for river trippers from Oxford. Alice Hargreaves recalled that, on one river trip when she was 'Alice' being told stories by Lewis Carroll, 'the hut might have been a Fairy King's palace and the picnic a banquet in our honour'. [16]

Some of the views of the Thames valley landscape from Nuneham, described by William Combe and the 2nd Earl, have been marred by development, particularly gravel workings and the ring of pylons obscuring the view of Oxford, but the general idea of the garden tour with its framed pictures can still be appreciated today. The view of the villa on rising ground, as seen from the river in its amphitheatre of trees, is much the same as described by the picturesque travellers and painted by Sandby, Samuel Ireland, William Cooke, John Hughes and Farington.

MOUNT EDGCUMBE
CREMYLL, CORNWALL

Mount Edgcumbe, on a Cornish headland overlooking Plymouth Sound to the east and the ocean to the south, has from its earliest days been celebrated for the magnificence of its situation. It has been repeatedly said that Admiral Medina Sidonia, commander of the Great Armada, had heard of its charms and resolved that he would make it his home when England was in the hands of the Spanish crown. It is not surprising that discerning eighteenth-century visitors used only superlatives in describing Mount Edgcumbe. However strongly they commended Stowe, Painshill, Stourhead or Studley Royal, their Genius of the Place looked meagre beside the bounty of a sea-girt landscaped garden. Even at Hagley, where Walpole 'wore out' his vocabulary in praise, he added, 'Indeed, I prefer nothing to Hagley but Mount Edgcumbe'. [1] Repton thought it was 'altogether the most magnificent, the most beautiful, the most romantic, and abounded in the greatest variety of pleasing and interesting objects'. [2] For J. C. Loudon, 'the effect on the mind is sublime in the highest degree, but yet blended with the beautiful. There was something to us quite unearthly in the feeling it created'. [3]

The Edgcumbes had intentionally taken advantage of the scenic position when siting their house in their deer park in 1547. It was exceptional for its time in that instead of looking inwards to a courtyard, as did the ancestral home at Cothele, ten miles up the Tamar, it looked outwards with 'a large and diversified prospect of land and sea'. The early maps show treeless heathland and it required considerable effort by generations of Edgcumbes to clothe the barren hills. By the time Celia Fiennes visited in 1698, she found 'a hill all bedeck'd with woods which are divided into several rows of trees in walks'. [4] A Badeslade perspective view of

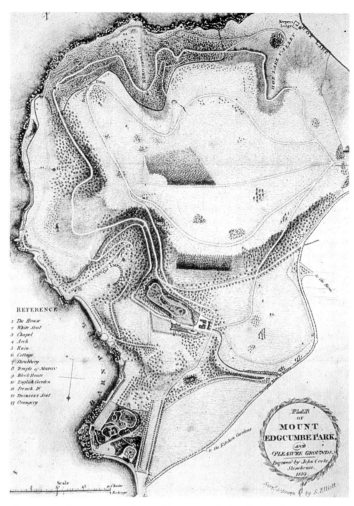

185 (above left). Wedgwood plate from Catherine the Great's dinner service now in the Hermitage, Leningrad. The image is taken from a Scott and Bampfylde drawing of 1755 showing the newly-made zigzags.

186 (above right). Plan of Mount Edgcumbe, 1819, by John Cooke. The universally admired sea-girt landscaped garden had evolved from a deer park where hunting was carried on from both sea and land.

the 1720s shows formal gardens, architectural groves and a wilderness. John Loveday, visiting in 1736, praises the 'fine wide Avenue taking in the whole front' and notes in his journal that 'the Wilderness and Gardens lie below the house; the Views through Walks in the Gardens are terminated, each very happily'.[5]

When, after years of faithful service as friend and ally of Sir Robert Walpole, Lord Edgcumbe's political career ended in 1742 he retired to his Cornish estate to make further improvements to his landscaped garden. A relative of Evelyn's, he had always been known as a 'great raiser of trees' and was a friend of Peter Collinson, who in 1768 wrote to the Duchess of Portland, herself a frequent visitor to Mount Edgcumbe: 'I have not the pleasure to be known to the present Lord but was favoured with a long acquaintance with his good father. Many of the Plantations and Improvements at Mount Edgcumb were by my recommendations near 30 years ago . . . for some of the Mount was much exposed, which are now grown up as I am told into one woods . . . the Sight of them would give a pleasure I can not express'.[6]

The views were not seen as controlled vistas as Loveday saw them when an anonymous poet in the *London Magazine* in 1750, in strains strongly reminiscent of Pope and Thomson, extolled the 'blest Elysium' where 'a thousand prospects open to the view'. Pococke, who also visited in 1750 and was shown round by Lord Edgcumbe and his two sons, had his appreciation of 'one of the most beautiful landscapes that can be conceived' heightened by the accompaniment of a 'moveable camera obscura, made in a sentry box, which shuts up'.[7] What Pococke found most remarkable was 'the side of the hill planted down not only to the East to the water, but also the South in the face of the very main ocean, where firs, pines, arbutus, laurustinus and cypress thrive exceedingly and there is a terrace on the side of the hill through this wood'. The long terrace following the natural contours overlooking the sea was Lord Edgcumbe's great achievement, and according to the Victorian Lady Ernestine Mount Edgcumbe it 'justly earned the gratitude of his descendants'.[8] One of the Scott and Bampfylde drawings in 1755, reproduced by Wedgwood for Catherine the Great's dinner service, shows the newly-scarred zigzag paths leading down from the terrace to the water's edge.

All visitors enjoyed the great diversity of scenes presented from the circuit walks, in particular, the contrast between the harbour and dockyard and the great emptiness of the sea. Fanny Burney, who was taken round by a 'gardener and a very commodious garden chair', was enthralled by the way 'the sea in some places, shows itself in its whole vast and unlimited expanse; at others, the jutting land renders it merely a beautiful basin or canal . . . a desert island one moment and a luxuriant country the next'.[9] The King of Saxony, who found Mount Edgcumbe 'a most delightful retreat' even in the rain, was also astonished by 'that contrast between the highest cultivation and entire wildness and barrenness'.[10] History and sublimity were all around, Drake's Island, the memory of the Armada, the forts, the ocean, rocks, and the naval dockyards. Thomson's seat bears an appropriate quotation from *The Seasons*:

> *Like a long wintry forest, groves of masts*
> *Shot up their spires . . . black and bold,*
> *The roaring vessel rush'd into the main.*

Foreigners gave a 'preference to Mount Edgcumbe for its great variety, to anything the Continent produces', according to James Forbes,[11] while Professor Hirschfeld of Kiel went so far as to say that for variety of prospect there was 'nothing like it in the world'.[12] For John Swete its appeal was that 'within the sweet recesses of this delicious spot one might retire from the world and yet be a Spectator to all its bustle . . . and in a fairy mirror behold an epitome of the World'.[13]

The arch-romantic William Beckford, visiting in 1781, revelled in the part of the garden that turned its back on the bustle when the Spectator enters a dark wood and emerges in sight of the ocean:

> Here I am breathing the soft air of Mount Edgcumbe standing upon the brink of a
> Cliff overlooking the Sea and singing Notturnos with Pacchierotti. Innumerable
> Insects are humming above the Myrtles and Arbutus which hang on the steeps and
> are covered with blossoms. I cannot help thinking myself in an isle of the Atlantic
> Ocean—to which if we believe Pindar and his poetic brethren the Souls of Heroes
> are transported . . . . Would that you could see me bounding along the Terrace
> which hangs bold and free above the Ocean. . . .Pacchierotti, as happy and
> enraptured as myself, does nothing but sing and thank Heaven that he has entered a
> Region so like his native Italy.[14]

187. A painting of 1903 by Thomas Hunn showing the Italian garden, one of the Reptonian 'special character' gardens laid out at Mount Edgcumbe in 1803 and now being restored. (Private Collection)

Richard Warner also describes the romantic experience where 'the Great Terrace now receives the traveller, wrapping him in gloom, with the fine accompaniment of the ocean roaring at a great depth beneath him'.[15] Likewise, James Forbes, who considered Mount Edgcumbe an 'earthly Paradise', records the powerful emotion when 'you hear the murmuring of the waves dashing against the rocks far below, without seeing anything of the sea'.[16]

All lovers of the picturesque, beginning with Gilpin, were delighted with the 'hide-and-discover' views presented from the terrace. Uvedale Price had high praise for 'that wonderful place' in his *Essays on the Picturesque* in 1798, where 'the vessels appeared . . . as if sailing over the tops, and gliding among the stems of the trees'.[17] If the fleet were in Plymouth Sound, Mount Edgcumbe's picturesqueness knew no bounds: 'I wish with all my soul you were here at this moment', wrote Lady Edgcumbe to her great friend Lady Harcourt of Nuneham in 1778, 'you have no idea what an amazing sight it is, thirty sail of the line now lying under a terrace of shrubs, as if only to ornament our park'.[18] Unfortunately that particular gathering of the fleet was a prelude to a second Armada scare which was to have a drastic effect on the Edgcumbes' park. Lord Edgcumbe, as Port Admiral, received notice to fell trees which might give cover to an enemy. 'The finest beeches, the loveliest old oaks, that Sir Francis Drake and Sir Walter Raleigh had seen perhaps', lamented Mrs Delany.[19]

However, visitors' comments in the next decade do not suggest that there had been total destruction of the park trees, and there were compensations. On a royal visit two years later

Lord Edgcumbe was made Viscount and later Earl Mount Edgcumbe for his patriotic gesture. Lady Mount Edgcumbe took advantage of the loss of trees in the wilderness, where Mrs Lybbe Powys had seen orange trees in the clipped walks,[20] to create a Nuneham-style flower garden with the advice of the Harcourts and William Mason. The Mount Edgcumbes chose inspirational lines from Cowper, rather than Rousseau, to inscribe on their garden seat to describe the 'snug enclosures' turned away from the overwhelming charms of their prospects: 'happy to renounce awhile, not senseless of its charms, what still we love, that such short absence may endear it more'.[21] The English garden house, as seen today, is on the site of the wilderness house shown in a painting by Badeslade of 1737.

A century later Lady Ernestine Mount Edgcumbe wrote that their 'English' garden with

188. Oil painting by W. Hannam, c.1775. Mount Edgcumbe was particularly picturesque in the days of sail. (Courtesy Mount Edgcumbe Country Park)

189. Stone pines above the ruin provide a Claudian foreground to a panoramic view of Plymouth and Drake's Island.

its magnolias, camellias and palms was 'scarcely well-named, as almost all the vegetation is foreign or even tropical',[22] and many guides and articles of the time expressed this view. It had apparently been forgotten that an 'English' garden was not conceived as a habitat for native plants but was one where the natural style of landscape planting prevailed. The 2nd Earl Mount Edgcumbe and his wife Sophia made French and Italian gardens, now being restored, adjacent to the English flower garden, all well insulated from each other with evergreen shrubberies providing shelter from the sea winds. Richard Warner saw this 'beautiful little specimen of ornamental gardening' just after Sophia had died in 1806 and an urn had been erected in the French garden in memory of 'the improvements her taste suggested and executed on the spot'.[23]

'This Mount all the Mounts of Great Britain surpasses', cried David Garrick.[24] The unique importance of Mount Edgcumbe in situation, diversity of prospect, garden history and literary and historical associations, make it outstanding. It has remained remarkably unspoiled and intact and by its designation as a Country Park, stretching from Cremyll Lodge to the Earl's Drive on Ramehead, together with the villages of Cawsand and Kingsand, it can be seen as the Mount Edgcumbe landscaped peninsula. The eighteenth-century provision of a dry coastal path with hide-and-discover views makes the Edgcumbe terraces and drives a unique asset for thousands of walkers today, and visitors have always commented on the profusion of exotic plants, 'all that earth's various regions know' in Lyttelton's words, which bloomed in the woods in the favoured climate. Following a full survey the park and gardens are now being restored. Lord Lyttelton's ode on the Genius of Mount Edgcumbe had ended prophetically: 'I made Mount Edgcumbe for you all'.[25]

6
NINETEENTH-CENTURY GARDENS

190. An illustration from Repton's *Designs for the Pavillon at Brighton*, 1808, his only Red Book to be published. To Repton's great disappointment the Prince Regent preferred Nash's proposals.

The Napoleonic Wars put an end to the Grand Tour but the Picturesque continued to preoccupy the sensitive-minded. Tours of the picturesque homeland became increasingly popular, especially with the new easily carried watercolour boxes for the amateur artist. Gilpin's Tours were intended as a guide to such travel, but after the publication of Uvedale Price's *Essay on the Picturesque* in 1794, picturesque theories also penetrated gardening and architecture. Gilpin's nephew, William Sawrey Gilpin, turned landscape architect and carried picturesque theory into practice as witnessed at Scotney Castle. The Picturesque coalesced with romantic currents at the turn of the century, when Taste was frowned upon as standardization, and Feeling, free and individual, was everything. The combination produced exotic and benevolent essays in architecture and gardening such as Sezincote and the Brighton Pavilion, and picturesque *cottages ornés* for estate workers.

Nineteenth-century picturesque ideas were taken back to the Continent as a new development of the English garden. 'The Picturesque came to us from England, un beau paysage is part of their religion', said Stendhal in his *Mémoires d'un touriste* after a visit in the 1820s, when Europeans were able to rediscover England. Prince Pückler-Muskau through his *Andeutungen über Landschaftsgärtnerei* in 1834 was largely responsible for the appearance of picturesque parks on the Continent. The prince, a most romantic and volatile character, who was said to be a 'susceptible admirer of beauty in every form, whether it be a building, a woman, a view, a horse, or a Constitution', also gives us valuable information about the Regency view of gardens.[1] He came to England to study ideas on landscape gardening and in search of a rich heiress, having already run through his abandoned wife's money in the planting of Muskau, where John Adey Repton had advised. Repton's other son, George Stanley, accompanied him on part of his English tour. He referred to their father as 'Amenity Repton', as, although Repton was himself the type of improver satirized by Jane Austen in *Mansfield Park*, he talked about the 'feasibilities' rather than the capabilities of an estate, concerning himself, he said, with the comforts of owners, many of whom were exposed to naked Brown parks. In spite of Repton's new ideas about 'dress grounds', the prince was much taken with John Nash's metropolitan improvements which carried on the eighteenth-century landscaping tradition into public parks.

Public parks were very much part of the new democratic age and advocated by Loudon in his *Encyclopaedia of gardening* of 1822. The first real public park in England was Birkenhead Park, Liverpool, designed in 1843 by Paxton. Peter Joseph Lenné called on Loudon in 1823 and was found to be 'one of the most intelligent of the various young German gardeners who have visited England since the Peace'.[2] He laid out many public pleasure-gardens including the Berlin Zoo, and was concerned with land use. He was particularly shocked by the 'arrogance, extravagance and egotism' of deer parks like Blenheim which seemed to exist for the 'nourishment of game instead of human beings' and thought they should be converted into the orchards or vineyards seen in German landscapes.[3]

The real passionate rediscovery of the nineteenth century was horticulture. It was a time of improved methods of cultivation and more extended use of hothouses and conservatories. The *Gardener's Magazine*, first published by Loudon in 1826, became the forum for discussion

191 (top). Plate from Nash: *Views of the Royal Pavilion*, 1826. Nash's layout is now being restored by the Brighton Pavilion in conjunction with the Sussex Historic Gardens Trust.

192 (bottom). The railway station at Alton Towers, opened in 1850, led to the new phenomenon of the family excursion. It is now available through the Landmark Trust as a holiday cottage.

193. E. Adveno Brooke: coloured lithograph of Shrubland from *The gardens of England*, c.1857.

on horticultural matters and was the first of many periodicals to be devoted specifically to gardening. When in 1832 William Sawrey Gilpin published his *Practical hints on landscape gardening* without mentioning horticulture, Loudon felt obliged to remonstrate in his *Gardener's Magazine* that 'mere picturesque improvement is not enough in these enlightened times, it is necessary to understand that there is such a character of art as the gardenesque as well as the picturesque'.[4] There was an increased interest in garden tours following the write-ups by the 'Conductor', as Loudon styled himself, and a new breed of curious garden visitor bent on seeing a night-flowering cactus in blossom came into being. Even the King of Saxony was insistent on his Journey of 1844 that he should pay a visit to Mrs Lawrence's 'splendid collection of orchidaceous plants' at Ealing, where he was charmingly received and regaled with 'ices and Champagne'.[5] Competitive shows were the order of the day and there was a vast new wealth of plants to be seen and enjoyed. The arboretum, such as that at Bowood with its new American conifer introductions, also became a popular place to visit.

Tourists, many specifically in search of gardens, were greatly on the increase, especially with the advent of the railways. Alton had its own splendid new station in 1849 (now a Landmark Trust holiday let) and the new phenomenon of the family excursion brought crowding to stately homes. Advanced technology made great changes in every aspect of the nation's life. Joseph Paxton, who built the Crystal Palace to house the Great Exhibition of 1851, is the key figure in the application of science and technology to Victorian gardens like Chatsworth. There was a new interest in painting Victorian gardens and the magnificent book *The gardens of England* by E. Adveno Brooke appeared in 1857, claimed by its promoters as the first of its kind. His paintings are of the architectural and highly ornate gardens of the Barry and Nesfield style and show terraces and bedding-out delights as seen at Shrubland Park.

Reginald Blomfield and Inigo Triggs as architects applauded the idea that, as in the Renaissance, the architect and not the gardener should be responsible for the main lines of the garden design.

William Robinson, the influential author of *The wild garden* of 1870 and *The English flower garden* of 1883 and champion of the gardener's garden, took up the cudgels in *Garden design and architects' gardens* in 1892 and thundered in Ruskinian prose that it was 'barbarous, needless and inartistic' to make gardens harmonize with architecture. Blomfield's *The formal garden in England*, in which he had set out his ideas, was the bible for revivalist gardeners, who equally deplored Victorian bedding-out schemes and Robinsonian wild gardening, and wanted to seek out seventeenth-century gardens like Melbourne for design ideas. G. S. Elgood's illustrations of such gardens admirably capture the new cult of old-fashioned gardencraft. Arts and Crafts gardeners, like Gertrude Jekyll, could see both sides of the argument: that there should be an artistic unity between the house and garden but that the garden designer should be a knowledgeable plantsman. Gertrude Jekyll and her partner Edwin Lutyens were particularly interested in the vernacular traditions that William Morris had promoted at Kelmscott. The Americans stimulated the cult of vernacular traditions by their sentimental discovery of their roots in rural England at the end of the century; deep in the souls of these passionate pilgrims 'a natural affection answered'. Led by Henry James, they nostalgically searched out 'the England that the American imagination, restricted to itself, constructs from the poets, the novelists, from all the delightful testimony it inherits';[6] and it was often in the old gardens with old-fashioned flowers and clipped hedges that they found what they were seeking.

STONELEIGH ABBEY
STONELEIGH, WARWICKSHIRE

Stoneleigh Abbey was one of the largest commissions that Humphry Repton received and has one of his best Red Books (impressive volumes bound in red leather in which he presented his proposals to his clients).[1] When he was called in the landscape was untouched by an improver's hand and much of his work is still discernible and awaiting restoration. Its great interest is that the Stoneleigh improvements were immortalized by Jane Austen as those of Mr Rushworth at Sotherton Court. Literature and garden history rarely come together so delightfully as they do in *Mansfield Park*, where Jane Austen comments on the moral issues of landscape improvement, discusses the work of Repton and calmly tells us that he can be hired for five guineas a day. Jane Austen only wrote about the things that were really familiar to her; if she introduces landscape gardening and mentions Repton by name we may be sure that it was a subject which interested her family and that Repton had somewhere crossed their paths.[2]

194. Humphry Repton: Red Book for Stoneleigh, 1806. The 'framed' scenes from the knoll suggested by Repton have always been known simply as The View.

Jane Austen's mother was born Cassandra Leigh and Stoneleigh was her ancestral home, although she had never visited it until her elderly cousin, the Reverend Thomas Leigh, Repton's patron, inherited it in 1806. Mrs Austen and her daughters were staying with him at Adlestrop when the unexpected news about his inheritance came through and they all went off to see what Jane Austen was later to describe in a letter as 'one of the finest estates in England'. They found an imposing Elizabethan house incorporating the remains of a Cistercian abbey, on to which Smith of Warwick had added a huge west wing in the early eighteenth century. It was the only really great house in which Jane Austen had stayed. She was more familiar with parsonages and the manor houses of the smaller gentry; even her brother's Godmersham was modest compared with Stoneleigh. Its old-fashioned gardens with a bowling green, terrace walk and riverside wilderness pleased Mrs Austen, who wrote to her daughter-in-law on a hot August afternoon:

> I had expected to find everything about the place very fine and all that, but I had no idea of it being so beautifull. I had figured to myself long Avenues dark Rookeries and Dismal Yew Trees, but there are no such melancholy things. The Avon near the house amidst green Meadows bounded by large and beautiful woods full of delightful walks. . . . We walk a great deal, for the Woods are impenetrable to the sun even in the middle of an August day. I do not fail to spend some time every day in the Kitchen Garden where quantities of small fruits exceed anything you can form an idea of.[3]

The Reverend Thomas Leigh, however, thought the grounds were in need of improvement

195. Repton's view of the house across the water. He saw this view as a painting by Claude.

and planned to contact Repton who had already won his approval for the way he had landscaped his grounds at Adlestrop, which Jane Austen had already seen. Repton was delighted by the new commission and wrote in his flattering introduction to Thomas Leigh in the Red Book, dated 1809:

> Stoneleigh Abbey presents circumstances very different from any other place in which I have ever been consulted. . . . I am addressing myself to you, who have displayed so much good taste in what has been done at Adlestrop under your immediate direction, and who have been pleased occasionally to consult me on that subject—I must therefore congratulate you on having this more ample field to display your taste and at the same time that I congratulate the County on this most ancient domain (so long preserved in the same family) having now a possessor who knows both how to value and how to improve its Natural Beauties—for the opportunity thus given of recording my opinion.

Miss Berry visited Stoneleigh the following year and actually saw Repton on site in the course of carrying out improvements to the Leighs' natural beauties. The lady next in line of succession, who had a vested interest in the proposals, also managed to be on hand. (The Austens had also been much amused by her presence with her mother Lady Saye and Sele at the takeover in 1806.)[4] It is interesting that a key was needed to get into the outer park where the improvements were to take place as this is made much of in the Sotherton episode in *Mansfield Park*:

> We passed the house or abbey . . . and drove on to the park. Before we entered we

196. Repton's view of the cascade: 'if more finished a Ruysdael'.

met our acquaintance Mrs Leigh (whose husband is to succeed to this place after the present incumbent), and the old incumbent himself, and Mr Repton, planning future improvements; very probably, like the Irishman's, for the worse. They gave us a key to the park, but we continued on foot, and were led by Greathead to the most beautiful parts of the most beautiful woodland scenery. . . . if this park shows some marks of neglect, it is, at least, unspoiled by improvement. . . . We met Mrs Leigh and her party on our road home. Mr Repton (whom I had never seen before) fired off an exceeding fine complimentary speech to Agnes and me from the window of the carriage.[5]

It was indeed unusual for Repton to find a completely unimproved park to work on. The grounds were in the same taste as the cedar parlours within the house, for the Leighs' resistance to fashionable Whig landscape gardening was a deliberate manifestation of their Tory and Jacobite loyalties. There could scarcely have been another noble family in the country with a walled bowling green attached to the house in 1806, and in the Red Book Repton demonstrated by means of his usual before-and-after flap how essential the removal of these walls was for the improvement of Stoneleigh. Jane Austen puts Repton's Red Book suggestions into the mouth of the cocksure Henry Crawford when a party from Mansfield Park set out on a hot summer afternoon to visit Mr Rushworth's newly inherited Sotherton Court with a view to giving him friendly advice on his improvements. Crawford led the party into the grounds to 'examine the capabilities', and began his 'fault-finding' when confronted by the bowling green by announcing in anticipation of Repton, 'I see walls of great promise'.[6]

197 (top right). The west front of Stoneleigh as Repton found it, complete with old-fashioned bowling green: 'Walls of great promise'.

198 (bottom right). The scene under the flap shows the walls removed and the views of the Avon that Repton would open up.

In the discussions that took place before the party took off from Mansfield Park it had been explained that although the house stood 'in one of the lowest parts of the park', its redeeming feature was the 'stream which might be made a great deal of'. The Avon at Stoneleigh was in fact to be widened and its course altered by Repton and a bridge built to carry the drive up to the new entrance front. Repton suggested a picturesque vista of Stoneleigh could be achieved by clearing a knoll of undergrowth to look back on the house from a clearing in the grove, and it has ever since been known as The View. Henry Crawford encouraged his party at Sotherton to follow him to 'a knoll not half a mile off which would give them exactly the requisite command of the house'.[7] The heroine, Fanny Price, found the day too exhausting and, like Jane Austen at Stoneleigh, preferred to stay in the shade of the wilderness, while Aunt Norris, like Mrs Austen, was too interested in the produce of the kitchen garden to join the improvers.

Mr Rushworth had already told the party before they set off that the grounds were much in need of an improver's hand. Having recently visited his friend's estate at Compton whose hundred acres had been improved beyond recognition by Repton, he was naturally eager to see what Repton could do for Sotherton whose acreage was 'a good seven hundred without reckoning the water meadows'. 'I never saw a place that wanted so much improvement in my life. . . . As he has done so well by Smith, I think I had better have him at once. His terms are 5gns a day'. These could only have been the Reverend Thomas's own sentiments when he contemplated his 700 acres of unimproved parkland at Stoneleigh and remembered Repton's skilful handling of his 100 acres at Adlestrop. What Jane Austen herself thought of the wisdom of calling in Repton on inheriting an unimproved estate is left an open question, as it was Maria Bertram, whose judgement in other matters was shown to be so faulty, who insisted that 'Your best friend on such an occasion would be Mr Repton, I imagine'.[8]

ST JAMES'S PARK
WESTMINSTER, LONDON

The royal parks make a very special contribution to London's green spaces and recreational facilities, and St James's Park is a particular favourite with tourists and neighbouring Whitehall civil servants. Samuel Pepys, in 1666, taking time off from Admiralty worries, walked in the park and 'it being mighty hot and I weary, lay down upon the grass by the canalle, and slept awhile'.[1]

St James's Park was once marshy fields surrounding the ancient leper hospital of St James which Henry VIII demolished in order to make himself a residence convenient for Westminster, his uncomfortable riverside palace. St James's Palace was brick built and at first scarcely more than a hunting lodge in the new deer park. Although Henry VIII deprived the

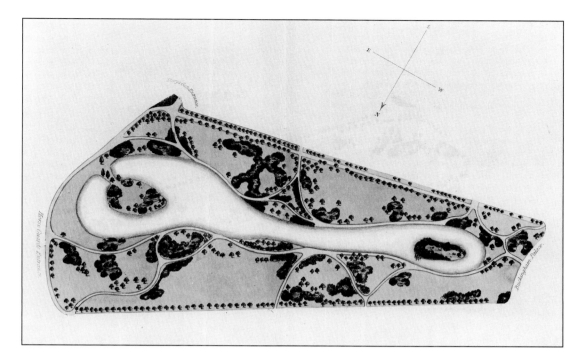

199. Nash's plan for improving the park in 1829. Prince Pückler-Muskau saw the picturesque shrubberies being planted and copied them on his own estate.

citizens of their former rights by fencing in large areas around London for his hunting and hawking, his action protected the countryside round London from development and in the seventeenth century his hunting parks became cherished public open spaces.

James I and Charles I made only minor improvements to St James's Park, but at the Restoration Charles II lost no time in having the area drained to make way for a formal park to unite his two principal London palaces of Whitehall and St James's. As at Greenwich the name of Le Nôtre is always associated with St James's, but according to Béat Louis de Muralt, a Swiss traveller visiting in 1694, Le Nôtre himself is said to have discouraged an excessively formal French layout and was of the opinion that the natural simplicity of this park, its rural and in some places wild character, brought 'the countryside into the city'.[2]

However, by later *rus in urbe* standards, there was clearly some regularity and art in the planting as seen in the Kip engraving. At Whitehall Palace a gallery had been built in the 1630s with an outside staircase, known as Park Stairs, leading into St James's Park, and on this a newly dug canal, 100 foot broad and 2,800 foot long, was aligned in 1660. A new semicircle of limes from which tree-lined walks radiated along the banks of the canal was seen and admired by Edmund Waller a year after the king's coronation. Commending Charles II's transformation of 'this fair Park, from what it was before', he wrote an ode 'On St James's Park as Lately Improved by His Majesty'.

The design was probably the work of André Mollet and his nephew Gabriel, as in June 1661 they were appointed the King's Gardeners at St James's Palace. Shortly afterwards they repeated the St James's Park layout on a larger scale at Hampton Court, with a semicircle of trees, a canal and flanking walks which earned Evelyn's praise. As at Hampton Court the middle toe of the three avenues of the *patte d'oie* took the form of a canal, enlivened by water fowl, which nested on the island. Charles II delighted in exotic birds and beasts and it was a common sight to see the king feed his ducks while out walking his spaniels in the park. The more exotic birds were kept in Birdcage Walk. Evelyn noted many 'curious kinds of poultry' in

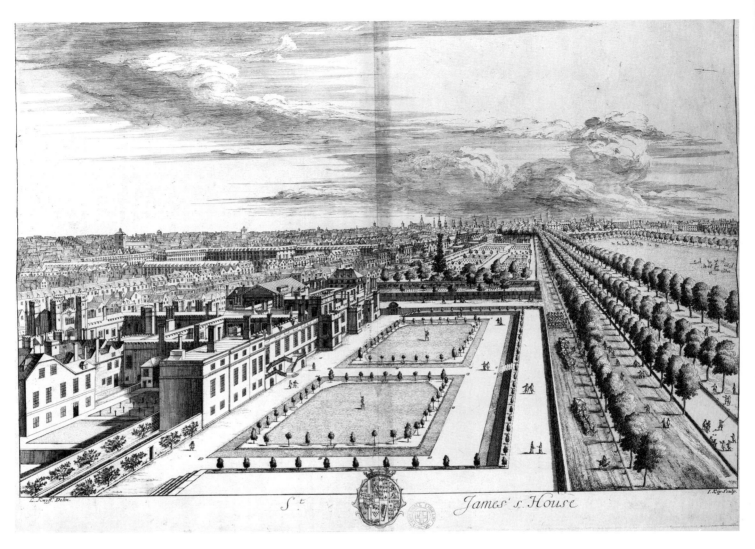

St James's House

the park 'breeding about the Decoy' and with true Royal Society scientific interest examined a pelican's throat, 'a fowle between a Stork and a Swan—a melancholy Water foule; brought from Astracan by the Russian ambassador'.[3]

The king enjoyed pall mall, a game something like croquet that had originated in Italy as *palla a maglio* and had become a fashionable craze in France. The pall mall alley was situated just inside the park wall and it was soon discovered that the clouds of dust raised by carriages going to and from the palace were irritating to players. The road was blocked and a new one, today's Pall Mall, was made in 1662. This was the year that Charles II married Catherine of Braganza and the street was to have been called Catherine Street in her honour, but Londoners preferred Pall Mall. Some changes were made in the park after the great storm of 1703, which terrified Queen Anne, who was living in St James's Palace. Many of the acacias from the original planting were blown down and new trees planted by the royal gardener Henry Wise. Queen Caroline, the German wife of George II, not appreciating the value of St James's Park to Londoners, asked Sir Robert Walpole what it would cost to restrict its use to members of the royal family. The prime minister's famous reply, 'Only three crowns, Madam', deterred any future action.

200. Kip's engraving, of St James's palace and park, with pall mall being played and cows grazing in the meadows.

The park continued to be a focal point for national activities in the heart of the city. Vast crowds assembled there in 1814 to celebrate the Hanoverian centenary and the end of the war with France. Over the canal John Nash built a bridge with a pagoda in the middle, from which there were lavish displays of fireworks. Little change was made to the actual layout of the park until Buckingham House at the western end of the canal was rebuilt as a royal palace for George IV, leaving St James's Palace, as at present, for court ceremonies. The much admired landscape we see today is the work of John Nash for the Prince Regent in 1829 and his elegant Carlton House Terrace is the backdrop to the Mall, which was reinstated as a ceremonial approach road for Buckingham Palace. Nash was responsible for the 'ornamental water, the forming of the ground for the plantations, the making and finishing of the gravel walks, making roads, draining the whole and everything else within the inclosure of the Park including the alteration of the Malls'.[4] The original plan had been on a grand scale with the park, Carlton House, Regent Street, Portland Place and Regent's Park as one visual unit.

Prince Pückler-Muskau, the confessed 'parkomane', greatly admired Nash's metropolitan improvements and inspected St James's Park daily as it was being laid out by his workmen. He was accompanied by his note-taking head gardener who had been brought over from Muskau. Regent's Park, which was then well advanced, he found 'faultless' and 'worthy of one of the capitals of the world', particularly admiring Nash's treatment of water. He paid several visits to Nash to whom he was indebted for 'much valuable instruction in my art'. He was particularly interested in the planting of picturesque shrubberies, which provided secluded walks in open public parks. In his published Tours he wrote of St James's Park that it was formerly:

> only a sort of meadow for cows, and now converted into beautiful gardens, according to a plan of Mr Nash's. The water is also much better distributed. I acquire a great deal of technical information here, and admire the judicious division and series of

201. The bridge and pagoda designed by Nash and erected in 1814 to celebrate the Hanoverian centenary and the end of the war in France. The pagoda was burned out by the firework display.

the work, the ingenious modes of transport, the movable iron railings. . . . The public are most respectfully requested during the operations which are designed for the increase of their own gratification, not to injure the carts and the tools of the workmen and to avoid as much as possible the part where the men are at work.[5]

202. The view from the bridge to the picturesque silhouette of the Whitehall buildings always delights visitors to London.

The German prince was amazed that the public had to be treated so gingerly and that in spite of the polite notice boys were wheeling each other about in carts and girls playing see-saw on the Office of Woods equipment.

Boating on the lake has always been prohibited in order to preserve the continuing tradition of Charles II's exotic wildfowl colonies. While Greenwich Park still remains basically a grand formal seventeenth-century layout, which, although now blurred, has not been radically changed by later landscaping, St James's Park is a superlative example of an early nineteenth-century landscape park, where the remaining formal element from Charles II's days, the Mall, adds dignity to ceremonial parades and state visits to the palace. The view from the bridge over the lake remains spectacular whether one looks east to the picturesque silhouette of the Whitehall buildings or west across the fountain and the imposing memorial to Queen Victoria to Buckingham Palace.

SEZINCOTE
near MORETON-IN-MARSH, GLOUCESTERSHIRE

Sezincote and the Brighton Pavilion are the two outstanding monuments to the short-lived cult of the Indian picturesque in England. Whereas the Prince Regent's 'stately pleasure dome' is seen as a seaside fantasy in keeping with the pier, Sezincote, even with its amber-coloured stone painted to look Indian and its copper green dome, has unbelievably settled into the Cotswolds, that stronghold of vernacular charm. J. P. Neale in his *Views of the seats of noblemen and gentlemen* in 1819 thought that Sezincote was laid out with 'very great taste and judgement'. John Betjeman, who, as an undergraduate at Oxford, used to go to Sunday lunch at Sezincote, always remembered the magical setting that today's visitor still sees as he approaches by a long drive to the bridge over the ravine above which appears the romantic house at the top of a gentle rise:

> *Down the drive,*
> *Under the early yellow leaves of oaks;*
> *One lodge is Tudor, one in Indian style.*
> *The bridge, the waterfall, the Temple Pool—*

203. Thomas Daniell: *Sezincote*, c.1805. Sezincote was the inspiration of the Brighton Pavilion. (Sezincote, courtesy Mrs David Peake)

204. Thomas Daniell: *The Indian bridge and dell at Sezincote*, *c.*1805. (Sezincote, courtesy Mrs David Peake)

205. Engraving by F.C. Lewis after John Martin of the Indian temple to the Hindu sun god Souriya above the lotus-shaped pool, *c.*1817.

206. The Indian garden scenery at Sezincote is both romantic and picturesque.

And there they burst on us, the onion domes,
Chajjahs and chattris made of amber stone:
'Home of the oaks', exotic Sezincote!
Stately and strange it stood, the Nabob's house,
Indian without and coolest Greek within,
Looking from Gloucestershire to Oxfordshire:
And, by supremest landscape-gardener's art,
The lake below the eastward slope of grass
Was made to seem a mighty river-reach
Curving along to Chipping Norton's hills. [1]

The Nabob in question was Charles Cockerell, who retired from the East India Company in 1805 and employed his younger brother Samuel Pepys Cockerell to design for him a retirement home to remind him of India. He married Lord Northwick's daughter from neighbouring Blockley, and she must have found her new Hindustan home, complete with purdah court and windows, quite a shock after a house in pure classic style built to Lord

Burlington's own designs. It was a lively trio who infused the magic into Betjeman's Sezincote: Samuel Pepys Cockerell, Thomas Daniell and Humphry Repton.

It was the Daniells, Thomas and his son William, who brought the vision of India to the Picturesque movement by their depiction of oriental scenery, Hindu temples and Mogul mosques, tombs and palaces in their *Select views in India*, published in 1788. Their work, showing the rich possibilities of Indian architecture, was as important for designers as the *Antiquities of Athens* had been for eighteenth-century landscaped gardens like Shugborough. The Daniells' aquatints had the advantage over Stuart's illustrations of classical buildings or Chambers's Chinese designs in that they could bring out the splendour of the minarets and domes shining out of the depths of woods. India was put before a Britain already infatuated with picturesque ideas which were merging with new romantic longings for exoticism and untrodden ways. Repton was one of the designers who was much impressed when he was shown the Daniell drawings at Sezincote:

> It happened that a little before my first visit to Brighton, I had been consulted by the proprietor of Sesincot, in Gloucestershire, where he wished to introduce the Gardening and Architecture which he had seen in India. I confess the subject was then entirely new to me; but from his long residence in the interior of that country, and from the good taste and accuracy with which he observed and pointed out to me the various forms of ancient Hindu architecture, a new field opened itself; and as I became more acquainted with them, through the accurate Sketches and Drawings made on the spot by my ingenious friend Mr. T. Daniell, I was pleased at having discovered new sources of beauty and variety.

This account of Repton's introduction to India at Sezincote was given in his Red Book of *Designs for the Pavillon at Brighton*, published in 1808. The Prince of Wales was one of the earliest visitors to Cockerell's Indian country house and asked for Repton to be sent down to Brighton to produce designs for an oriental seaside palace which would astonish his friends. The prince extravagantly praised Repton's designs, but after eleven years' delay commissioned John Nash to build a Moorish-Indian pavilion.[2] Repton never recovered from the disappointment, and, according to Loudon, 'never alluded to this subject without feelings of deep regret, yet untinged with anger'.[3] What Repton actually did at Sezincote is not documented, but in the Brighton Red Book he made it clear that Indian palaces should not spring up out of the landscape English fashion, but, as Daniell had shown in his *Oriental scenery*, should be surrounded by 'pleasure gardens . . . intersected by straight paved walks, bordered with flowers and shrubs'. Repton felt that 'we were on the eve of some great change in landscape gardening' as a result of this oriental influence, and henceforth ornamental flower gardens near the house became part of his recommended improvements.

We know Thomas Daniell designed the garden architecture at Sezincote—the Indian Temple to the Hindu sun god Souriya above the lotus-shaped pool, the fountains, the figures and the bridge—but Repton was probably responsible for the flower garden in front of the house as well as the planting of the cedars in the long view through from the bridge to the stream garden, which has now been beautifully replanted by Lady Kleinwort and Graham

207. The three-headed snake was a symbol of regeneration.

208. Sir Charles Cockerell was himself much preoccupied with the details of the lotus finials and the sacred bulls on the bridge at Sezincote.

Stuart Thomas. In 1817 John Martin was commissioned to make views of Sezincote, one of which shows the flower garden Repton advocated as the appropriate accompaniment to the south front of the house with its curving conservatory. This has now been replaced by a narrow rectangular canal and cypresses.

The owner himself was much preoccupied with the Indian details of the lotus finials and the sacred bulls. Daniell wrote expressing his concern about Sir Charles's ideas for positioning the bulls on the balustrade of the bridge. 'I am dreadfully alarmed about the Brahminy Bulls— because I am certain they cannot be better placed—could Viswakarma, the Artist of the Gods of the Hindoos, take a peep at Sezincote, he would say let the bulls remain where they are'.[4] Today they are where Viswakarma and Daniell recommended and are the first thing the visitor sees as he walks to the house.

Below the bridge is the Serpent Pool, so-called because the water circulates round a little island on which is a dead tree trunk with a three-headed snake coiling up it. It is in fact a water pipe conducting water to the snake's fangs where it spurts out in triplicate, a symbol of regeneration. The spirit of India complete with snakes, sacred bulls and lotus buds is all-pervasive as the visitor walks under the bridge on stepping stones to gaze at the serpent pool. Lanning Roper was not the only one to feel that the path under Daniell's bridge must be followed: 'This fanciful conception blends perfectly into the pattern of pools, streams and winding paths which thread their way down the slopes and through the trees, always leading where I most want to go'.[5]

SWISS GARDEN
OLD WARDEN, BEDFORDSHIRE

The Swiss Garden is an unique essay in the Picturesque, which was a movement well adapted to absorbing exotic influences like the Indian cult at Sezincote. The Swiss cult was also a romantic one but there were very few manifestations of it until after the end of the Napoleonic Wars. The exodus began when peace came to Europe in 1815 and two years later Jane Austen referred to an absent friend as having 'frisked off, like half England, into Switzerland'.[1] The best known memorial to the Swiss cult in England is London's Swiss Cottage, which was rebuilt some years ago and continues to give its name to a district and underground station. One of the earliest Swiss cottages is that at Endsleigh, Devonshire, of about 1809. It has now been restored and can be rented from the Landmark Trust as a holiday home. Swiss cottages were late arrivals as picturesque adjuncts in landscaped gardens and were usually found in remote romantic settings backed by dark fir trees.

Unlike eighteenth-century garden buildings—temples, pagodas and ruined abbeys—Swiss cottages were inhabited, thus bringing the peasant and the scenery into romantic juxtaposition while providing useful accommodation for an estate worker or retainer. The Swiss cottage near the cascade at Blenheim housed the keeper of the private garden, at Nuneham a gamekeeper could be visited in his Swiss cottage in the woods, and at Alton Towers a blind old Welsh harper who had been a family retainer was retired into a Swiss cottage on the heights overlooking the gardens. It was P. F. Robinson, a devotee of Uvedale Price and the architect of London's Swiss Cottage, who first realized that the intricacy and play of outline of Swiss rustic architecture, particularly chalets with projecting roofs, seemed to be in the best traditions of the *Essay on the Picturesque*. In 1827 he wrote that 'the style of architecture, purely Swiss, has rarely yet been attempted in this country'.[2]

209. Iron frames for trailing plants formed arches across the shrubbery glades.

Lord Ongley at Old Warden seems to have been the only landowner to lay out a Swiss garden with its central feature of a chalet and to have a *village orné* which included Swiss features. Deserted villages, like Nuneham Courtenay, were a thing of the past and a landowner was more likely to say, 'Come and see my cottages', to his guests after breakfast than escort them to his latest temple. Lord Ongley's cottages were in the mixed style, those with verandahs and overhanging eaves being identifiably Swiss. The village nestles in fir trees and the cottages are set at different angles, at different heights and perched on grassy banks. The village women were obliged to wear red cloaks to offset the red doors and tall hats to match the pointed dormers as their contribution to the picturesque scene.[3]

The Ongley estate was reminiscent of the soldier Prince de Ligne's Tyrolean fantasy at Beloeil, where the villagers lived in rustic shelters and played Alpine horns alongside sleek Swiss cows. Lord Ongley, who inherited in 1814 when he was eleven, came of a very military family with two soldier grandfathers, numerous cavalry officer uncles and four army officer brothers. He and his brothers all died unmarried. The Prince de Ligne's memoirs *Mélanges militaires, littéraires, sentimentaires* were published in 1814 and were probably essential reading in the Old Warden library. The soldier prince had a little melancholy walk in his garden where 'those with sad thoughts will be able to give themselves up entirely to the little miseries which often afford pleasure and to which one must yield without a struggle', and when the prince had had enough of such melancholy there was an 'Indian temple where I shall go and eat icecream'. Lord Ongley also had an Indian temple in his Swiss fantasy garden.

There was also a melancholy walk to a thatched tree shelter under which was inscribed on a marble slab a sentimental poem entitled 'The Forgotten One', in which, in strains reminiscent of Wordsworth's 'Lucy', Lord Ongley lamented the death of a childhood friend. It tells of sheltering under the tree in a shower of rain and how his eyes still filled with 'sweetest tears in thinking of those early years'. Later generations of villagers, ignorant of the principles of the Swiss picturesque, thought they had solved the mystery of Lord Ongley's strange behaviour. The Swiss garden had been made for his Swiss mistress whom he kept in the chalet on the little round hill and the poem on the marble slab was put there in contrition when she caught cold and died under the tree. This story found its way into guidebooks, but no attempt was made to explain why a bachelor with a large house should need to keep his mistress in a draughty Swiss garden chalet.

The garden must have been begun in the late 1820s or early 1830s and is referred to as the Swiss Garden on the 1834 Ordnance Survey. Mrs Catherine Young, a visitor in 1832, wrote in her diary: 'A heavenly day. Mrs Farr took me to see Lord Ongley's place at Warden. We were all enchanted with the Swiss cottage etc, which is quite fairyland'.[4] Cecilia Ridley, who liked nothing better than to go off with a shawl and a three-legged stool 'in search of the picturesque', was also enchanted by Lord Ongley's 'show place' with its coloured lamps lit, which was like fairyland indeed, but not particularly Swiss: 'a most extraordinary garden in the world made out of a bog, full of little old summer houses on little round hills, china vases, busts, coloured lamps—in short quite a fairyland but more of a Chinese fairy than a European one'.[5]

Lord Ongley's most likely source of inspiration was J. B. Papworth's *Hints on ornamental gardening*, published in 1823. Papworth lived nearby at Little Paxton and was employed at several houses in the vicinity in the 1820s and may have been consulted about the Swiss cottage. Although he did not specialize in Swiss architecture like P. F. Robinson, he advocated the use of unpeeled bark for rustic buildings resembling Swiss shelters, like that in the Swiss Garden with its remarkable interior decoration of bark and fircones, now restored. The chalet dominates the garden and is seen in a number of picturesquely contrived vistas; it sits on an unusually smooth round hill, bearing out Papworth's instruction that 'if the aim of the picturesque gardener was to imitate nature, then an undulating surface needs the curved mound or knoll'.[6] A charming feature, reminiscent of Papworth's work at Whiteknights, is the iron frames for trailing plants which form arches across the winding glades. Covered with creepers or roses contrasting with evergreens, they must have added to the feeling of 'fairyland' that delighted Catherine Young and Cecilia Ridley. The little iron bridges crossing the water, with rocks on the banks, were also enjoyed by visitors.

The garden became more romantic as the conifers and trailing plants increased in size. The *Gardener's Magazine* in 1902 called it a 'garden of surprises' with 'splendid conifers, secluded summer houses, shady bowers and walks, winding streams and the chalet on the hill'.[7] In 1913 the reporter for the *Journal of horticulture and home farmer* wrote: 'A noble feature at one point will be a superb tree, at another a group of magnificent flowering shrubs or again roses rambling a score or more feet over a hidden arch or tree or a clematis whose twining growths have risen dozens of feet up some giant trunk'.[8] In Lord Ongley's day there was a fine grotto which was later incorporated into a fernery and cruciform greenhouse. It has been restored by Bedfordshire County Council. The Swiss Garden is now preserved as a fascinating microcosm of the 1830s, combining romantic ornamental gardening with Swiss enthusiasms.

210 (below left). The Swiss chalet dominates the garden and is seen from a number of picturesquely contrived vistas.

211 (below right). The thatched tree shelter under which was inscribed on a marble slab a sentimental poem on 'The forgotten one'.

SCOTNEY CASTLE
near LAMBERHURST, KENT

Scotney Castle is the ultimate in the Picturesque. It is as romantically situated as Leeds Castle, but its ruined effect is totally contrived. Truly it is a moated mediaeval castle but, as Rose Macaulay, the great lover and visitor of ruins, found, its ruination was 'not in anger or arson, but in aesthetic enthusiasm . . . from the first it must have been beautiful; today, creeper-grown and the colour of lichen, standing with the grey and rust-coloured barbicaned castle tower against a steep wilderness of quarry flowers behind, and at its foot the lily moat reflecting sky, trees, tower and ruined mansion, today it makes an exquisite picture. If ever ruin-making has justified itself, this has'.[1]

It was Edward Hussey who in the 1830s decided to make a ruin of the old house and build a new one to look down on it. For his grandson, Christopher Hussey, Scotney was a source of aesthetic inspiration, not only in his writings but in his devoted work for the preservation of historic houses and gardens and the protection of the countryside. Both architectural and garden historian, he contributed articles to *Country Life* while still an undergraduate at Oxford, was its architectural adviser from 1930 until 1964 and its editor between 1933 and

212 (left). The Salvin house and quarry sketched by Edward Hussey, *c*.1845. (Scotney Castle)

213 (right). The moat at Scotney Castle: a romantic picture formed on the principles of W.S. Gilpin.

1940. His trilogy on *Georgian country houses* (1955–8) became a classic and his *English gardens and landscapes 1700–50*, published in 1967, was a major contribution to the history of the English landscape movement. To mark his seventieth birthday in 1969 *Country Life* invited him to write an article on the landscape of Scotney Castle in which he commented on visitors' reactions to his picturesque home:

> Discovering the place for the first time, some people accept it as an elysium magically conserved from a past golden age, which in a way it is; others as a product of fortuitous picturesque; and a few (I expect) as an ancient monument in need of the full treatment. It took me, I must say, some time to realise that the partial dismantling of the old house, the building of the existing one, and the creation of the landscape had been a single combined operation inspired by definite principles: those of Picturesque taste promulgated by Uvedale Price and Payne Knight about 1800.[2]

Christopher Hussey had described in more detail in his book *The Picturesque*, published in 1927, how he himself was at first taken in by the picturesque scene enjoyed from the library window at Scotney, until he turned to the shelves and studied the books that had obsessed his grandfather:

> The picturesque was the artistic tradition in which I was brought up, and I remember clearly the shock with which I suddenly became conscious that it was only one of many aspects of reality. It happened in the library of a country house built, in 1837, by my grandfather. Through the window of that room you see, in a valley below, a castle, partly ruined, on an island in a lake. A balustrade cresting a cliff forms the foreground, a group of Scots firs and limes the side-screens. Beyond, a meadow melts in the woods, rising to a high sky-line. I had often agreed that it formed a perfect picture, which has time and again been copied by my family, myself included, in water-colours, some of which are hung, with other examples of the family talent, on the staircase. . . . On this particular evening I was pondering on the happy chance, as it appeared to me, of my grandfather's desertion of the old castle, his building of the new house on this particular spot, and his digging of the stone for building it between the two—in the quarry that makes such a fine foreground to the prospect. It did not occur to me that he was guided by anything more than chance and natural good taste.[3]

In *The Picturesque*, which he described as an 'essay on a way of seeing', covering the appreciation of visual values in English literature, painting, architecture and gardening at the turn of the eighteenth and nineteenth centuries, he devotes considerable attention to the Reverend William Gilpin, the Picturesque traveller whose theories had fostered the picturesque taste of his grandfather's mentors, Price and Knight. He fails, however, to mention the Reverend William's nephew, William Sawrey Gilpin, whom Edward Hussey had turned to for practical advice on laying out his picturesque landscape. When Christopher Hussey inherited Scotney Castle in 1952 he set about a long-term restoration of the landscape and his researches into the family papers led him to realize that there had been a third party to the making of the Scotney landscape, and that had been the landscape architect and artist William Sawrey Gilpin. In the guidebook he wrote for visitors he gives due credit to William Sawrey Gilpin's advice on the choice of site and in his *Country Life* article describes the occasion when, then in his seventies, he arrived on the scene in the spring of 1836:

> My grandfather recalled that Gilpin arrived on a phenomenally stormy day but nevertheless, donning his overcoat, and umbrella, set out to reconnoitre. At that time the slope northwards of the moat was a barish field known as the Warren but carrying a few oak, beech and lime trees. Near the top of this, some 300 yards from the moat and 70 foot above it, Gilpin indicated a particular group of trees with approval, stuck his umbrella in the ground, and said 'here is the site of the house'.[4]

In the archives Christopher Hussey found Gilpin's on-the-spot pencil sketches of the principal views to be seen from the house and indications of lines of sight and where the sidescreen trees should be planted. No actual plan was found, but on studying Gilpin's *Practical hints upon landscape gardening*, published in 1832, Christopher Hussey began to realize that the setting of the new house and the treatment of the landscape were more determined by Gilpin's practical hints than by Price's theoretical *Essay on the Picturesque*. W. S. Gilpin was in fact Uvedale Price's practitioner, but in acknowledging his debt to the latter in his book he did not want it forgotten that it was his own relations, Uncle William and to a lesser extent his father Sawrey Gilpin, who had provided the basis for picturesque theory:

> If I add, that the name I bear is not unknown as connected with subjects of taste, it is merely to suggest the probability that an early and long-continued intimacy with the relations to whom I allude, would not leave me altogether uninformed of its true principles.[5]

214 (below left). View across the moated old castle to the new house above the quarry.

215 (below right). View down from the new house across the planted quarry to the old castle.

Scotney Castle was the culmination of W. S. Gilpin's aspirations, as castles, especially ruined

ones, were Gilpin predilections going back to their own Scaleby Castle in the Borders. Walter Scott had put life-blood into romantic castles when his Waverley novels appeared in the 1820s and W. S. Gilpin had given picturesque landscape settings for a number of Gothic castles that had gone up in their wake, but only at Scotney was there the authentic situation, where from a balustraded terrace could be seen the picturesquely ruined castle of the former barons of Bradwardine. The balustraded bastion terrace, overlooking the quarry at Scotney, is certainly a key feature and it seems that this was Gilpin's idea from a note in Edward Hussey's diary about his second visit in May 1838, when the new Salvin house was nearly completed. 'Gilpin came down for two days. Showed him all round, he approved of all, marked out terraces, piece of water and new plantation'. Salvin had by then excavated the stone for the new house, leaving the quarry, and the bold idea of planting it up, as at Belsay in Northumberland, must have formed in Edward Hussey's mind. Price had recommended that a quarry might be 'planted with kalmias, rhododendrons and azaleas', and on the acid Wealden soil at Scotney this was made a reality. Edward Hussey also took advantage of the newly-introduced American incense cedar, smoke bush and Wellingtonias.

The restoration of the landscape by an owner who so deeply appreciated its underlying picturesque principles gives Scotney a special interest. Christopher Hussey and his wife, also a keen gardener, opened their gardens to the public at an early stage, pointing out the singularly appropriate Hussey motto on the porch, '*Vix ea nostra voco*' (I scarcely call these things our own). Plants were never labelled as this would have detracted from the idea of a garden seen through the eyes of a painter. At Christopher Hussey's death in 1970 the gardens were given into the care of the National Trust and they are now enjoyed by over 35,000 visitors a year. Often and often visitors seeing Scotney Castle for the first time are heard to exclaim, 'but it's just like a picture', true proof of the success of the Hussey essay on the Picturesque.

ALTON TOWERS
near UTTOXETER, STAFFORDSHIRE

Alton Towers' latest tourist leaflet boasts, 'There's nowhere like it on earth' and that over two millions come every year to experience its 'unique blend of fantasy, magic and style'. Similar claims were made in early nineteenth-century guides to the Peak: 'Language indeed would fail to convey an adequate idea of the glory of such a scene as we now looked on, which is more like the baseless fabric of a vision than a reality, a mere creation of the mind that seems not of earth and yet is on it'.[1] Today the 'spine-tingling' Alton Beast and Alton Mouse rollercoasters and a skyride round the Earl of Shrewsbury's gardens may be added to this unearthly vision.

Alton had all the advantages of a spectacular situation, which, in Loudon's words, was 'peculiarly adapted for grand and picturesque effects'.[2] It was rather different from the flat

216. Alton Towers: The Chinese pagoda today, still holding its own in spite of competing thrills.

terrain of the Shrewsbury Oxfordshire seat at Heythrop, where the baroque house by Thomas Archer was finally abandoned in favour of the new-found delights of the Peak and the great Gothic pile with its chapter house, stained-glass windows and Pugin ecclesiastical decorations. They now make a splendid ruin. It was Charles, 15th Earl of Shrewsbury, who tamed the landscape from 1814 to 1823. With the help of hundreds of labourers, 'He made the desert smile'. This inscription under the bust of the earl in the Choragic Monument was the first thing that the nineteenth-century visitor saw as he entered the gardens: 'and true he did, for the whole of this magnificent spot was a rabbit warren only thirty years ago', wrote William Adam in his *Gem of the Peak*, first published in 1838.[3] Adam was a new type of garden visitor, interested in geology and natural and local history, reflecting the views of the new learned societies which would promote county transactions and field club studies, including visits to famous gardens. His description of the geological character of the terrain shows what effort went into making the desert smile:

> For miles around . . . the new red sandstone on which it stands assumes a far bolder character than is peculiar to it in most other parts. . . . the northside is craggy, the rocks overhanging considerably in places, evidently scooped out and undermined by the action of powerful streams. They consist of a fine micacious sandstone; some of the top-beds are full of rolled quartz pebbles . . . the other side of the valley at its commencement is not craggy, but amazingly steep, forming an angle of at least forty-five degrees with the horizon.[4]

Whatever difficulties this made in forming paths and terraces in the pleasure grounds, the earl could make good use of his geology as J. C. Loudon described:

> As the sandstone rock protrudes from the sides of the valley in immense masses, abundant use has been made of it to form caves, caverns, and covered seats; it has even been carved into figures, and we have Indian temples excavated in it, covered

217. Illustration from Loudon's *Encyclopaedia of gardening*. In the midst of all the astounding scenes was an 'octagon pagoda, which is said to be 100ft high and to spout water from the mouths of 100 dragons'.

218. E. Adveno Brooke: *The gardens at Alton Towers,* coloured lithograph from *The gardens of England, c.1857.*

with hieroglyphics, and in one place a projecting rock is formed into a huge serpent, with a spear-shaped iron tongue and glass eyes.[5]

Loudon was clearly fascinated and overwhelmed by Alton, but, as a Benthamite with utilitarian principles, it was a love-hate relationship. The fact that his advice had not been taken may also have tempered his judgement, and when re-visiting in 1836 he recalled the late earl's behaviour:

> This nobleman, abounding in wealth, always fond of architecture and gardening, but with much more fancy than sound judgement seems to have wished to produce something different from everybody else. Though he consulted almost every artist, ourselves among the rest, he seems only to have done so for the purpose of avoiding whatever an artist might recommend. His own ideas . . . were transferred to paper by an artist . . . and often, as we were informed by Mr Lunn, the gardener there in 1826, were marked out on the grounds by his own hands.[6]

The earl's achievements could not be overlooked and, even though it would be 'paying the author a compliment after his own heart', as Conductor of the *Gardener's Magazine* Loudon felt obliged to report on the 'labyrinth of terraces, curious architectural walls, trellis-work arbours, vases, statues, stairs, pavements, gravel and grass walks, ornamental buildings,

219. The view down from
Stonehenge to the seven gilt
glass-domed conservatories filled
Loudon and every other visitor
with astonishment and delight.
Illustration from Loudon's
Encyclopaedia.

bridges, porticoes, temples, pagodas, gates, iron railings, parterres, jets, ponds, streams, seats, fountains, caves, flower baskets, waterfalls, rocks, cottages, trees, shrubs, beds of flowers, ivied walls, rock-work, shell-work, root-work, moss houses, old trunks of trees, entire dead trees etc.' That his tongue was not entirely in his cheek is seen by his description of the view down from Stonehenge to the seven gilt glass-domed conservatories:

> In the centre of the picture, over the domes in the foreground, the valley loses itself into a winding bank of wood, in a style of great grandeur and seclusion. None of the details of the valley here obtrude themselves; and the stranger, coming from a wild country with no marks of refinement . . . fills him with astonishment and delight, to find so much of the magnificence of art amidst so much of the wildness and grandeur of nature.[7]

On his last visit to Alton Towers in 1840 Loudon even seemed to regret that the mature vegetation was obscuring the 'curious objects' he had found so tasteless on previous visits: 'the valley, in the time of the late Lord Shrewsbury, had a peculiar charm, from the great number of objects, all of an artificial and singular or grotesque character, in so romantic a situation, and from trees and shrubs being either small, or cut or clipped into artificial shapes'.[8] The three-storeyed Pagoda on the lake was now finished and its jets of water would doubtless have pleased his small daughter Agnes, who was with him this time. His wife Jane Loudon added a note to her *Ladies' companion to the flower-garden*: 'to know all the different scenes which may be introduced in a pleasure-ground in modern times, it is only necessary to visit such a place as Alton Towers, in Staffordshire'; one feels that, given the chance, she might even have taken young Agnes on a rollercoaster when J.C. was off his guard.

The 16th Earl called in W. A. Nesfield, the architect and landscape designer, to make further additions and the result was admired by Brooke in 1857. He particularly liked the way that some of Nesfield's parterre interstices were made of 'grog', local broken clay from the Potteries, 'quite novel, and we believe, peculiar to these gardens'.[9] Alton was at the top of the list for garden visiting, especially once the railway made it accessible to all and sundry. In the

1851 edition of the *Gem of the Peak*, Adam was able to announce that 'his Lordship has built a nice entrance from the Station into the grounds. The Valley is narrow but extremely beautiful, and as we saw it in a fine day this spring, in going for the first time per rail, it was most enchanting'.[10] Barbara Jones, the avid garden traveller in search of follies and grottoes, saw Alton after the wartime army occupation when the hillside and the paths were hopelessly overgrown and the follies hidden, but found it was still 'extraordinarily beautiful and hushed'.[11]

Twenty years later the hush had gone, but the gardens had been restored and Alton Towers made its name for a new type of garden visiting to which we are now growing accustomed, with its boating lakes, sealions, a fairground and recently the rollercoasters and monorail circulating above the gardens. The Swiss Cottage, where the old blind harper was once housed, has had a new lease of life. When William Adam visited 'the minstrel's only daughter in the absence of the Ancient Briton played merrily for us', but the harp was silent by 1857, when Adveno Brooke visited and lamented, 'how unspeakingly touching must have been the tones of his harp sweeping over the valley in the calm eve of a Summer's day! But the harp is hushed and the cottage hearth is desolate'.[12] Not so today, for the discerning visitor can now enjoy the 'gourmet delights of the à la carte Swiss Cottage Restaurant set high on the valley slopes overlooking the gardens below', no doubt with piped harp music. 'Conjuring up our historic past, you'll see costumed figures strolling elegantly along the pathways as part of our Edwardian Tableau'—not so very different from the Earl of Shrewsbury's weeder women in Swiss dress reported on by Loudon. The most enterprising change of use in Alton's famous pleasure grounds must surely be 'the former orangery, now the lavatories, with two end bays with glass domes and glazed four-centred, i.e. Gothic arches between', as recorded by Pevsner in his volume on the buildings of Staffordshire. It is only fair to say that the orangery has recently been restored and the lavatories sited elsewhere.

CHATSWORTH
near BAKEWELL, DERBYSHIRE

According to *Country Life* in 1900 the garden at Chatsworth was 'the best and largest example of the Paxtonian method displayed on the widest and most choiceworthy canvas'.[1] But when the young Joseph Paxton arrived in 1823 to take up the post of head gardener, which he held for the next 35 years, he took over a garden which had been one of the Wonders of the Peak even before Charles Cotton's poem of that name in 1681, and much remained of the work of his predecessors. This he repaired and preserved while adding his own inventions.

Of the garden of the Elizabethan house almost nothing remains. The most substantial survival is 'the Stand' on the brow of the hill, which was described in 1662 by Dr Edward Browne as 'a neat rotundo or Summer house', located 'upon a peake at the top of the Hill . . .

which seems as if it hangs over the other [i.e. the mansion] a quarter of a mile high in the Aire'.[2]

For Cotton the wonder of Chatsworth was its contrast to the surrounding landscape:

To view from hence the glittering Pile *above*
(Which must at once wonder create, and love)
Environ'd round with Natures *shames, and Ills,*
Black Heaths, wild Rocks, bleak Craggs, and naked Hills,
And the whole Prospect so informe, and rude;
Who is it, but must presently conclude?
That this is Paradice, *which seated stands*
In the midst of Desarts, *and of barren Sands.*[3]

Kip's view highlights this juxtaposition. It also depicts the immense formal garden created by London and Wise between 1687 and 1706 to complement Talman's rebuilding of the house. The first version of the cascade was built in 1694 and Thomas Archer's Cascade House was added in 1702. The Sea-Horse Fountain, the long canal, and the copper willow tree also date from this period. Talman designed a summer-house for the bowling green laid out to the south-west of the house, and this survives as the public entrance to the grounds at the end of

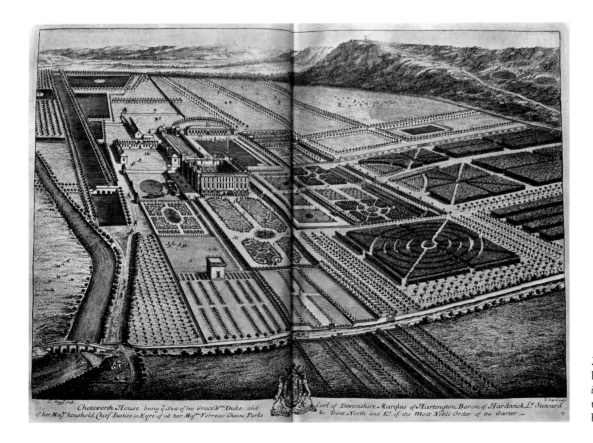

Chatsworth House being ÿ Seat of his Grace Wᵐ Duke and of her Maⱼˢ houshold, Chief Iustice in Eyre of all her Maⱼˢ Forrests Chaces Parks &c   *Earl of Devonshire, Marquis of Hartington, Baron of Hardwick, Lᵈ Stew_ard &c Trent North and Kᵗ of the Most Noble Order of the Garter —*

220. Chatsworth as depicted by Kip and Knyff in *Britannia illustrata*, 1707: 'Paradice . . . in the midst of *Desarts*, and of barren *Sands*'.

the Broad Walk. The 1st Duke of Devonshire also had a greenhouse built, again to Talman's design, and this too survives by the modern rose garden and makes an interesting comparison with Paxton's nineteenth-century conservative wall behind it.

Roger Gale, visiting in about 1694, enjoyed the walks along the 'noble canal . . . where as from heaven, one may survey the distant horrors of the kingdom of Erebus, in the dismal country round about us'.[4] Less pompously, a Cambridge undergraduate on a tour in 1725 recorded his pleasure in the waterworks, which, like Celia Fiennes, he greatly enjoyed: the jets in the Cascade House, 'which throw up several streams and wett people' (the spouts in the floor can still be seen), the Willow Tree Fountain, 'another merry conceit wetting the unwary' (again, the lead pipes which shot water up from the ground are still in place), and the rainbow made by the Sea-Horse Fountain.[5]

Part of the new design involved major earth-moving, described by an astounded Defoe in his Tour. He admired the 'exquisitely fine' gardens south of the house and then described how the duke, in order to create a vista beyond, 'perfectly carried away a great Mountain that stood in the way, and which interrupted the Prospect'. This, Defoe wrote, had been done since his previous visit, and left him 'perfectly confounded . . . for I had lost the Hill, and found a new Country in view, which *Chatsworth* it self had never seen before'.[6]

The richness and profusion of the London and Wise layout is conveyed by William Stukeley, who breathlessly described a visit in 1724 in his *Itinerarium curiosum*: 'The gardens abound with green-houses, summer-houses, walks, wildernesses, oranges, with all the furniture of statues, urns, greens etc. with canals, basons, and waterworks of various forms and contrivances, sea-horses, drakes, dolphins and other fountains'.[7]

In the early eighteenth century visitors like George Vertue, John Dodd and John Loveday heaped praise on the garden. Chatsworth, wrote Dodd, 'like a Diamond set in black, seems to take a Lustre from the wretched Country it is situated in. . . . The Gardens about this house are wonderfull Charming'.[8] But later visitors were beginning to grow tired of seeing 'what *Art* could, spite of *Nature*, do'. Mrs Lybbe Powys in 1757 found the waterworks 'more grand than pleasing', and criticized 'a kind of triflingness . . . in the copper willow-tree, and other contrivances beneath the dignity of the place'.[9]

When Walpole visited Chatsworth in 1760 he witnessed the sweeping changes being made by the 4th Duke, the son-in-law of Lord Burlington, who engaged Capability Brown to help him bring Chatsworth into the eighteenth century by landscaping broad sweeps in the park and redesigning areas of the garden. Walpole liked the 'great *jet d'eau*', on the grounds that 'whatever is magnificent of the kind in the time it was done, I would retain—else all gardens and houses wear a tiresome resemblance.' However he excepted 'that absurdity of a cascade tumbling down marble steps, which reduces the steps to be of no use at all'. He admired Chatsworth for its 'richness and variety of prospect'. Instead of seeing the garden as a gem in the midst of a desert, it now was seen to gain positive benefit from the surrounding countryside. But the countryside was no longer rural and unimproved: vast plantations had been laid out and the old village had been demolished to clear the views. In 1768, on a second visit, he wrote that Chatsworth was 'much improved by the late Duke [the 4th Duke died in

1764], many foolish waterworks being taken away, oaks & rocks taken into the garden, & a magnificent bridge built'.[10]

To a Romantic visitor like Louis Simond, Chatsworth remained a dinosaur of a garden, with its 'perhaps unique remains of the bad taste and magnificence of the beginning of the last century'. He scorned the absurd 'hydraulic curiosities': 'a metal tree', he snorts. He severely disapproved of conceits like showers on unsuspecting visitors, and reported with satisfaction that 'this practical joke is fallen into disuse, which our conductor seemed to regret'.[11]

It was the 6th Duke who brought Paxton, a twenty-three-year-old assistant gardener in the Horticultural Society nursery at Chiswick, to Chatsworth. The duke had inherited in 1811. He never married, but had a passion for building and gardening and he encouraged Paxton to work on a vast scale. The two men were drawn together over their projects. They toured the Continent viewing the gardens of France and Italy, and there is an engaging picture drawn by Lady Granville in a letter of 1835 to the duke of 'you and your Paxton sitting under a red rhododendron, under the shade of palms and pines in your magnificent conservatory'.[12] The duke included a warm tribute to Paxton's friendship in the *Handbook of Chatsworth and Hardwick* which he wrote in 1844.

Their approach to Chatsworth is an interesting mixture of innovation and conservation. Paxton repaired and relaid the cascade, and he even restored the copper willow tree. He constructed new reservoirs and the Piranesian aqueduct to power not only the existing baroque waterworks, but added his own, notably the spectacular Emperor Fountain in the seventeenth-century canal. (This was installed in 1844 and named in preparation for an aborted visit by the emperor of Russia.) Then, south of the baroque cascade, Paxton created his amazing rockworks, the 45-foot cascade over the Wellington Rock and the Strid—the latter designed as an imitation of the famous torrential stretch of the Wharfe near Bolton Abbey. 'The spirit of some Druid seems to animate Mr. Paxton in these bulky removals', wrote the duke in his guide.[13] This was a sort of mock-Sublime gardening; constructing crazy

221 (above). The 'French garden' on the occasion of a visit to Chatsworth by the Prince and Princess of Wales, 1872.

222 (right). The seventeenth-century cascade which Paxton restored. Horace Walpole objected to it on the grounds that its steps were 'of no use at all.'

tors out of rocks weighing anything up to fifty tons, yet somehow also maintaining the toy-like feeling of a 'rockery', with its little bridges and pools. Paxton's pastiche of the broken beauties of Nature was laid out within yards of the formal cascade, evidently with no sense of incongruity. If Brown had brought in oaks and rocks, now Paxton made one of Chatsworth's most impressive features out of the kind of scenery which the garden had once rigorously excluded.

Paxton and his duke also introduced a vast number of new plants. They created the arboretum and the pinetum, to which Paxton is said to have brought the seedling Douglas fir in his hat. He built the conservative wall in 1848. Originally it was not glazed, the tender climbers being protected from the cold by blue striped curtains pulled down at night during winter and spring. His most famous creation was the Great Stove, on the site of which the twentieth-century maze has been laid out. This vast conservatory was a *tour de force* by the young Paxton and served as the prototype for the Crystal Palace. William Adam in his popular guidebook, *Gem of the Peak*, described how this eighth wonder of the Peak was approached

through a rocky ravine and then 'appeared before us in all its grandeur. It seemed like a sea of glass when the waves are settling and smoothing down after a storm'.[14] The *Country Life* article of 1900 described it as 'the very temple of tropical gardening'. It had a central carriage drive, lined with bananas and palms, which took the visitor through the conservatory's treasures, past a pile of bold rockwork, covered with a luxuriant growth of creeping plants. For the adventurous, a spiral staircase behind the rocks led up to a gallery, which afforded a memorable view over the tops of the tropical plants and trees beneath their glass sky. It survived until 1920 when it was pulled down, although its walls remain to give some idea of its scale.

A vivid picture of Chatsworth is given in the *Gardener* in 1867:

The park and grounds were swarming with holiday-makers, for it was one of England's great holidays, Whit-Monday. Here were little pale-faced men and women from the cotton factories of Manchester, dark denizens of the Staffordshire potteries, and the sharp active-looking mechanics of Leeds, Bradford, and Halifax, all brought hither in special trains, and, in the full heyday of an English holiday, rushing through the gorgeously-fitted-up rooms of the ducal mansion—admiring the conservatories, rockeries and fountains, or, stretched at full length, discussing their commissariat under the cool shade of oak, elm, and beech trees.[15]

The American landscape architect Charles Eliot visited Chatsworth in 1886. 'The showing round through the great house was tedious', he remarked, 'but there are fine views from the windows'. He was impressed by the rock garden, 'where rocks are handled on a larger scale than I have ever seen', although on the whole he preferred the enchantment of neighbouring Haddon Hall with its romantic battlements and old yews. For lunch he went into Edensor, the village Paxton built after he had completed the process begun by Brown and demolished the

223 (above left). The 'Great Stove' built by Joseph Paxton and Decimus Burton, 1836–49. A carriage drive led directly through the Great Stove, 'the very temple of tropical gardening'.

224 (above right). 'Part of the Rock-work', engraving from a nineteenth-century guidebook to the gardens. Paxton's gigantic rockery was only yards from the formal cascade.

last of the old cottages. Eliot remarked on 'the most lovely outlooks in every direction', and in the true picturesque tradition he observed, 'There were cattle in the river as in all the photographs'.[16]

The present duke and duchess have continued to add to the gardens. Among their projects, they have planted the walks along the south lawn with rows of pleached lime trees, like those favoured in the seventeenth century, and they have also created the beech hedges around the late seventeenth-century Ring Pond (the terms in the topiary niches were brought from Chiswick House in the 1930s). The Great Stove they have replaced with the spiky new conservatory, where the visitor can see many of the exotics first brought to Chatsworth by Paxton.

CRYSTAL PALACE
SYDENHAM, LONDON

Thousands of south Londoners must share the childhood memory of the monsters in Crystal Palace. But the monsters are only one of several surviving fragments of the great public garden laid out by Joseph Paxton in the mid-nineteenth century. In many ways it epitomized the age, and its scale and grandeur can still be experienced:

> It was only two o'clock, and yet thousands of visitors had already arrived. The grass was dotted all about with them, and on the terraces, and in the open corridors facing the grand transept, there was a long, slowly moving line of bright dresses creeping about in the sunlight, with a thousand little dots of parasols, scarcely larger than wafers raised in the air. . . . The very flowers seemed to be slowly roasting in the hot rays; and indeed we noticed some scarlet geraniums in a marble vase close to us, that seemed to get redder and redder as if on the verge of bursting into a flame.[1]

So wrote the correspondent of the *Illustrated Times* in his account of the queen's visit to watch the display of the fountains at the Crystal Palace on 18 June 1856. The palace, moved to Sydenham from Hyde Park where it had housed the Great Exhibition, was the brainchild of Joseph Paxton, and at Sydenham, as Director of the Gardens, he was granted sole control over its setting. As had the building, so the gardens gave Paxton the chance to expand on features he had used at Chatsworth, especially the vast waterworks and the romantic wooded lake, with its islands and displays of artificial strata. In its heyday, with the 12,000 fountains in full operation, the acres of crimson and yellow flower beds, the Italianate terraces and walks, and above all the crowds, the garden must have been an amazing place.

It was intended that the resurrected palace should function as a national museum, 'formed', as Ruskin enthusiastically declared, 'on a scale which permits the exhibition of

225. A lithograph of 1854
showing Paxton's grand design
at Sydenham. The formal
'Italian' gardens, with their
enormous fountains, are behind
the informal lake.

monuments of art in unbroken symmetry, and of the productions of nature in unthwarted growth . . . placed in the neighbourhood of a metropolis overflowing with a population weary of labour, yet thirsting for knowledge'.[2] Edward Middleton Barry designed the suitably palatial station to receive the tourists for whom 'the Palace of the People' was built. The very Victorian concern for the public good was counterbalanced by aesthetic disdain for the building's vulgarity: 'a cucumber frame between two chimneys', the older and snootier Ruskin called it.[3] A similar split was evident in responses to the gardens. They were magnificent rivals to Versailles, and yet they were also crude. The *cognoscenti* of bedding-out scorned the displays, where nearly two-thirds of the plants were scarlet geraniums and yellow calceolaria, and even uneducated visitors noticed that for twenty-three hours in the day, or more, the waterworks consisted of cupids 'sucking little bits of lead pipe', and 'rusty iron pipes, thick as a nine-gallon cask, running like a huge serpent' along the floors of the basins.[4]

Paxton's design began with the massive terraces which are now being restored by English Heritage. These were originally planted with berberis and ornamented with statuary, vases and urns. The first terrace was flanked by the enormous red sphinxes which still survive, and then punctuated by statues representing the nations of most commercial importance to Britain. One or two of the statues survive precariously on the balustrade; the modern tourist, like some eighteenth-century visitor to Rome, may also find remains of other statues and urns, piled up behind scrub below the terrace.

The Italian gardens were laid out around an immense central walk. As it descended the terraces it was punctuated by terracotta tazzas and enormous marble urns, some of which remain in place, although the gardens they decorated have long vanished. Plane trees also lined the walk, and some of these have recently been replaced. The flower beds were simple in shape and content, and planted with the aim of dazzling the crowds. When Donald Beaton visited the gardens as correspondent for the *Cottage Gardener* in 1854, he complained at the lack of blue and white in the beds: left out because these colours would supposedly be supplied by the sky and the water.[5] Apart from the geraniums and calceolarias, verbenas and petunias were planted in large numbers, and all were kept to a strict height. In 1875 six beds were made in the shape of butterflies, with carpet-bedding designed to portray accurately the markings of actual species.

Water for the fountains came from an artesian well sunk at the bottom of the park, which was then pumped up to Brunel's great water-towers at the top; the jets thus supplied reached a height of 250 feet. The spectacle in June 1856 was described at length in the *Illustrated Times*.

> On every side were seen the foaming mounds spirting out from the countless jets.
> The air was filled with a roaring sound, and was cool as a grotto. At some of the fountains, the spray falling in the sunlight became dyed with bright rainbow tints, or else it formed a thin silvery cloud, which the wind carried away until it melted into the distance.
> Everybody was sorry when the turncocks made their appearance, and with their big iron keys began their circular walk of turning off the water.[6]

The waterworks were largely out of action by the beginning of the century and the grounds were left to decay after the fire of 1936 which destroyed the palace. In 1964 the National Recreation Centre was built on the site of the two Great Fountains, and the beds and basins of the lower terrace were buried under the spoil. The London Borough of Bromley has recently excavated some of this and plans to restore the two outermost fountains of the lower terrace with Victorian bedding around. The maze of 1872 is also being restored by the council, and new schemes for the site of the palace will result in gardens recreated on the ground above the terraces.

The best survivals are the landscaped areas to either side of the park—'pleasant sloping lawns, dotted here and there with trees, and thickly planted with shrubs'[7]—and around the lower lake. Here, in the words of one guidebook, the grounds were 'so constructed as to give a number of practical lessons in geology'.[8] There was a stalactite cave, and a facsimile of a

226 (left). An illustration by William Delamotte from one of the numerous guidebooks to the Crystal Palace, *c.*1860. A couple enjoying their 'practical lesson in geology'.

227 (below). Crystal Palace today: 'a very good expedition'.

Derbyshire lead-mine, and tons of different stone had been brought from different parts of the British Isles to form artificial displays of strata. In 1856 this was a new and bold concept. Lyell's *Principles of geology* had only appeared in 1838, and now at Sydenham the new science was presented for the people's consideration. In the lake the islands were formed, not on picturesque principles, although Paxton did design the scenes, but in a series, each representing a different prehistoric era, populated with models of that era's animal life. To viewers who thought the monsters must be creatures of nightmare, the guidebooks explained at length the principles of fossilization. Although the monsters' numbers have declined, those that survive are carefully preserved.

The finances of the Crystal Palace Company had always been rickety and in 1911 a sale was ordered by the Court of Chancery, at which a third of the land went for building. Despite a rescue bid by Lord Plymouth which resulted in the palace being reopened by the king and queen in 1918, the grounds continued to be cut up for sports arenas and sideshows. Throughout the middle years of this century the park was abused in what would have been a disastrous fashion by country house standards. And yet it remains a wonderfully popular place. Paxton had included sites for archery, cricket and quoits; velocipedes could be hired for cycling round the park and boats were for hire on the lake. By 1876 there was a rifle range, a gymnasium, swings and roundabouts, and, in winter, skating on the basins of the great fountains. And this tradition continues today, even if the activities themselves are now skateboarding, dry-slope skiing, and football. Barbara Jones caught the present mood exactly when she wrote that, while it may indeed be heartbreaking to look up *Crystal Palace* in a Baedecker of 1900 and read of its vanished wonders, 'at least the Geological Department remains':

> And there they all are, down at the bottom of the gardens, best reached from the Thicket Road entrance, the wild (and highly educational) animals, grouped round a lake, predator with victim, a peaceable kingdom for Penge. . . . There is a menagerie, boating lake, refreshments and the animals; a very good expedition.[9]

228. A late nineteenth-century photograph of the lake in the geological garden. 'Placed in the neighbourhood of a metropolis overflowing with a population weary of labour', the gardens of the Crystal Palace were always a genuinely popular place.

BIDDULPH GRANGE
BIDDULPH, STAFFORDSHIRE

Biddulph Grange is one of the most highly individual of the Victorian gardens, and one of the few of which it has been possible to attempt a restoration in the spirit and character of the original. Like all Victorian gardens it is eclectic in style, but it is of special interest because its creator, James Bateman, an early president of the Royal Horticultural Society and an authority on orchids, was both landscape gardener and plantsman. With the help of Edward Cooke in the 1850s he designed a number of picturesque settings which would provide the variety of conditions he needed to grow a wide range of plants. Edward Kemp, the landscape gardener, visited Biddulph in 1856 and wrote a series of articles on it for the *Gardeners' Chronicle*. Kemp was clearly impressed with the novelty of the concept of James Bateman's

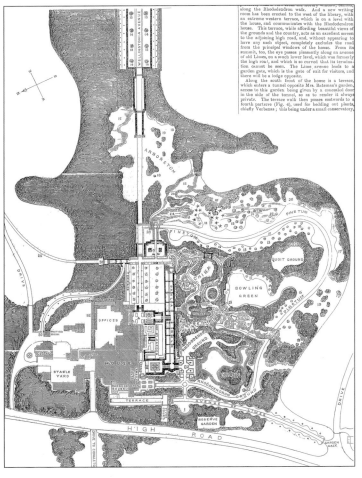

231. The Egyptian Court. The special gardens reflect the mood of the Great Exhibition, where the whole world was on show in different courts.

229 (far left). The region called China with its temples and picturesque rockwork scenes devised by Edward Cooke. The 1871 sale catalogue described it as having a 'willow-pattern plate' effect.

230 (left). Plan of Biddulph Grange from the *Gardeners' Chronicle*, 1862, showing the diversity of the grounds with separate enclosures for growing different kinds of plants.

garden, which he was later to assess as 'one of the most remarkable examples of artistic and practical gardening in the country':

> The leading idea which seems to have pervaded the mind of Mr Bateman in the production of such a marvellous diversity of surface throughout the place, has evidently been the preparation of a suitable and congenial home for nearly all the hardy members of the great plant family which the curiosity or taste of man has discovered and cultivated . . . the creation of a great deal of picturesqueness, and variety of outline, and the production of an unusual number of separate and independent areas, each of which has a character of its own.[1]

The diversity of these special gardens, which include the 'Egyptian Court' and 'China', reflects the mood of the Great Exhibition of 1851, where the whole world was on show in the Crystal Palace in different courts. In Biddulph's garden the various regions, as Kemp again describes, were segregated from each other by 'ornamental walls, or walls covered by ivy or other climbers, Yew, Holly and Beech hedges, covered ways or corridors of wood or stone, irregular or more formal archways, tunnels or cavern-like passages, mounds of earth, rockeries, masses of roots and trunks of trees, with larger or smaller groups of shrubs'. Barbara Jones, who found Biddulph most rewarding for a folly and grotto seeker, felt that China and Egypt, give or take the plants, were truly romantic concepts:

> So far as I know there are no written theories, no volumes of justification, no word at all, but Mr James Bateman must have been one of the greatest romantic gardeners, an artist able to use his site to the utmost in a composition all his own while

understanding with a clarity remarkable for his time the underlying principles of his two inspirations, both the sinuous and graceful surprises of the Chinoiserie with a touch or two of horror and a black grotto, and the sombre axial planning of Egypt, moving steadily into darkness.[2]

Bateman, a graduate of Magdalen College, Oxford, was much concerned with Dr Paley's natural theology which sought to reconcile geology with the biblical account of the creation, and built on to his house a geological gallery with an arrangement of fossils 'under the heading of "days", according to the Mosaic cosmogony, beginning with the granites and passing into the slates, the limestones, the old red sandstones, and coal formations, etc., with such animal and vegetable remains as occur in each'.[3] Students of geology and palaeontology as well as garden lovers were encouraged to visit Biddulph. A special entrance by the gardener's cottage was made for visitors with a 'commodious waiting room with all sorts of conveniences', or, if they preferred, they could sit in 'an ingenious seat placed beneath the shelter and shade of a handsome American thorn' while waiting for the guided tours to assemble. The *Journal of the North Staffs Field Club* reported that 'the first excursion of the North Staffordshire Naturalists Field Club was taken early in May 1865 to Biddulph, the seat of the President. There were 32 members in the party. After being shown through the beautifully arranged gardens, which are so well known to all in this neighbourhood, the Geological Gallery was visited'. They were then separated into botanical and geological sections to make detailed excursions under expert guidance.

After the full coverage of his gardens in the *Gardeners' Chronicle* giving him such credit, Bateman wrote in to put the record straight:

> Mr Kemp, having concluded his very clever and graphic, though far too favourable account of the grounds at this place, I feel that the time has come when I ought to tender my acknowledgements to another artist, my friend Mr Cooke to wit, to whose ever-ready pencil and inexhaustible invention my gardens, I am well aware, owe their chief attractions. With Mr Cooke's skill as a landscape painter the public is abundantly familiar, but it is not generally known that he occasionally forsakes his studio to practise the craft of a landscape gardener. In this capacity he has helped me through so many difficulties and enabled me to realize so many, but for him, impracticable conceptions that I feel naturally anxious at once to confess my own obligations to him and to point out the quarter from whence others may hope to derive the like assistance.[4]

Edward Cooke, the marine painter, first visited Biddulph in 1849 and was a regular visitor for the next twenty years. Like his friend James Bateman, he was a man of many parts. He was married to Jane Loddiges, daughter of the famous nurseryman, and his brother-in-law was Nathaniel Ward, who invented the Wardian case. He was an F.R.S., R.A., F.Z.S., F.L.S. and fellow of many other learned societies and his diaries reflect the incredible energies of the Victorians and their belief in progress on all fronts.[5] He was a friend of Ruskin, Huxley, Wyatt, Cockerell, Barry, Paxton, Landseer, Dickens, Eastlake and William Robinson. For a brief period he studied architecture under Pugin and he became a director of the Crystal

Palace Company. The two abiding passions from his early life were ships and plants. He made engravings for Loddiges' *Botanical cabinet* and of Turner's coastal scenes and loved anything to do with coasts—fishing, boats and particularly rocks. It was in rocks that his gardening and marine passions merged, for the study which was basic to his marine painting led to an interest in the placing of rocks in picturesque compositions for landscape gardening.

His taste for rock landscaping had first developed in gardens near Tunbridge Wells where he cleared overhangs of sand and humus deposits to contrive ledges and rock formations. Cooke's rockwork was based on his considerable knowledge of geology, which accorded with Bateman's own interests, and the prisms of stone like basaltic pillars in the Chinese water and the rockwork in the Glen show his undoubted skill. An entry in Cooke's diary on the making of 'China' speaks of team work: '19. ix. 49 Very busy with Mr B and 8 men building up stone work. Had great difficulty, got into quicksand but got through; at last succeeded in placing the stones for the water to run over without accidents.' The rocks in the Glen also had to be brought to the site and the skilful planting of ferns, marsh and bog plants along the stream in a rockwork hollow was much admired by Kemp:

232. Oriental gateway and Japanese maples at Biddulph Grange.

There is a high degree of naturalness, and therefore of artistic excellence, about the treatment of this interesting little glen . . . and what is a still greater merit than any yet recounted, the numberless stones are piled together on their natural bed, and there is nothing whatever to be seen of the usual rock-builder's trick of standing stones on their edges or their ends for the sake of giving prominence to any point, or producing a greater ruggedness of surface.

Robert Errington, the head-gardener-journalist, said after his visit to Cooke's picturesque rock scenes that 'the mantle of Price seems to have fallen on his shoulders', and William Robinson praised his handling of picturesque masses of artificial rock as a new landscape art.[6]

In 1928 Biddulph Grange became an orthopaedic hospital and, in spite of the unsuitability of Bateman's precarious rocky setting for invalids, the management board did everything in its power to keep up the gardens. Miles Hadfield, author of *A history of British gardening*, visited in 1959 and found much of the 1862 plan identifiable although there were giant tangles of old rhododendrons and azaleas. He saw it as a garden 'conceived with a singularly un-Victorian panache with a great deal of wit and learning',[7] and a revival of interest began which culminated in its acquisition in 1988 by the National Trust. A complete restoration is now being undertaken and today's visitors will soon be able to see all the features which delighted the thousands of nineteenth-century visitors, including the Chinese temple and bridge in its willow-pattern setting, the dragon parterre, the Great Wall and joss-house, the Glen, the stumpery and the Egyptian Court, not to mention the oriental plants, some of which were sent back from China by Robert Fortune.

SHRUBLAND PARK
near CODDENHAM, SUFFOLK

At Shrubland Park the modern garden tourist may see one of the most extravagant gardens of the Victorian period. Between 1849 and 1854 Charles Barry's theatrical Italianate design was laid out on the steep chalk scarp below the house and, apart from additions by William Robinson in the 1880s and the inevitable modifications to the ornate beds, it is largely unaltered.

Barry was called in to remodel the existing house and gardens in 1848. The house was a classical villa of the 1770s designed by James Paine, with additions in 1830–2 by J. P. Gandy Deering. It stood on the edge of the ridge overlooking farmland and the chestnut avenues of the old hall which had been abandoned in the eighteenth century. The old hall was built in 1637 for the Bacon family and the estate was sold to William Middleton, for whom in 1789 Humphry Repton had prepared a Red Book.[1]

Despite the rebuilding of the house, the park does not seem to have been extended during the eighteenth century. The prospect tower had been built by 1789, but the

233. Shrubland as depicted by E. Adveno Brooke, *c*.1857. Brooke especially admired the garden's 'particular tone of Italian scenery'.

seventeenth-century avenues of sweet chestnuts were evidently still in place, so little landscaping seems to have been carried out by the Bacons. Repton admired the topography and the 'Timber of prodigious size', but criticized the view from the house, 'teetering on the brink of a precipice'. He said it lacked foreground, a deficiency that Barry would supply in no uncertain way. Repton's advice was to plant up the slope and to break up the hedgerows on the flat below in order 'to give a parkish appearance to the scene'. The pleasure grounds, 'shrubbery & mowing lawn', would stretch from the house along the ridge to the old hall, and Repton made a plea that the chapel and part of the hall should be saved from demolition. A gravel walk 'along the natural Terrace under the spreading branches of the venerable Chestnut trees' to seats 'in or near these remnants of ancient Piety and hospitality' would be a delightful feature. His approach from the west would take advantage of the old formally planted trees: 'It is impossible to conceive anything more magnificent than the row of Chestnut trees under whose branches the view of the valley is seen'. These trees were also admired by the correspondent for the *Gardeners' Chronicle* on his visit in 1888: 'the grandest Sweet Chestnuts to be seen in the country—such boles! such a world of knots and cracks! such spiral furrows ploughed in their bark!'[2] Some of these prodigious chestnuts survive today: four or five along the natural terrace, and in the Warren, below Robinson's garden, where their old formal lines can still be perceived. To what extent Repton's proposals were executed is not recorded, but it seems likely that such modest ideas would have been carried out.

Middleton's son, another William, inherited in 1829, and called in Gandy Deering to make alterations to the house. There were two sloping terraces below the house, and Donald Beaton, who was head gardener here before Barry's arrival, had laid out elaborate flower beds, a rosery and the maze, which still exists on the slopes. Within a few years though, Charles Barry was employed to further remodel the house and to create gardens to match. According to E. Adveno Brooke, who wrote a lavish description with illustrations of Shrubland in 1857 just as the new works had been completed, Barry's brief was 'to make it a perfect Italian villa— and travellers say he has succeeded'.[3] The *Gardeners' Chronicle* begins a lengthy account of a

visit in 1867 with a view of the house: 'its beauty and grandeur are familiar to all travellers on
the Great Eastern Railway between Ipswich and Norwich and Bury St Edmund'.[4]

Barry's schemes involved immense earth-moving operations to level two great terraces.
The new scheme was reported at length in the *Cottage Gardener*, for whom Beaton had just
become a correspondent, and it was Beaton who visited Shrubland for the magazine. Garden
visits were a popular feature in the Victorian magazines. Led by the tireless Loudon in the
Gardener's Magazine, these tourists went out with horticultural advances as their chief
interest. Their notebooks were filled not with picturesque sketches or poems but with notes on
mulching, conservatory heating systems and the latest varieties from the nurseries. Beaton's
visit to Shrubland must have been a poignant one, but he surveyed the new work with
equanimity and approval: 'The ground had been cut down nearly ten feet deep on the highest
side, and wheeled in barrows over the steep side of the hill beyond, into a yawning gulf'. On
the lower side, the level was raised by as much as fifteen feet, and the excavated parts were
formed into 'dells, glens, and valleys, of all forms of outline, altogether making a most
picturesque and unique garden, for all sorts of wild, rock, and wilderness plants, shrubs, trees,
and all manner of things'. Of his own gardens on the lower slopes, 'laid out in various ways—
the Rosary among the rest', Beaton wrote, 'all this is now buried, no one knows where, or how
deep . . . the whole space, to a great extent, left and right, from the line of the steps, is now as
level as a die, and advanced far into the park'.[5]

On Barry's upper terrace, Beaton's principle of bedding-out was developed further, in
collaboration with Lady Middleton. Elaborate flower beds were planted in raised stone boxes:
the carved stone edging was raised about five inches from the gravel path, and was eight or

234 (left). Shrubland: the
great 'coup d'oeil from the
steps', photographed in 1901.

235 (right). The view up to the
house: 'a perfect Italian villa'.

236. The walk which, as suggested by Repton, leads 'along the natural Terrace under the spreading branches of the venerable Chestnut trees'.

nine inches wide. Within came, first, an eighteen-inch band of turf, then a six-inch band of silver sand, then one of box, and finally the soil and beds of flowers. The silver sand, dug on the estate, was one of the most unusual features in the designs. The *Gardeners' Chronicle* described how it 'illuminated' the gardens.[6] Mr Foggo, the head gardener, with a staff of forty under gardeners, informed Adveno Brooke that '80,000 plants of Geraniums, Verbenas, Petunias, Lobelias &c., &c., are annually required for turning out into the numerous beds, borders, vases &c.' One of William Robinson's criticisms of Shrubland was that, with all these, there were no flowers that could be cut for the house.

The terraces were linked by the great staircase and Brooke thought that 'the *coup d'oeil* from the steps . . . has few equals in any country'. A parterre, the 'panel garden', was laid out on the lower terrace, while the transverse walk led to further formal enclosures. As it was put in *Country Life* in 1901: 'You take your choice of anything you fancy, or can imagine yourself in Japan at one moment, or at Hampton Court the next'. The article lists the fountain garden, a Chinese garden, a box garden, a verbena garden, the maze, the poplar garden, a rose garden, a tent garden and the looking-glass garden.[7]

The walks were ornamented with busts, statues and geranium-filled vases: 'These', Brooke remarked, 'greatly assist in forming the particular tone of Italian scenery so characteristic of Shrubland'. In fact, he actually asserted that although Shrubland had to come second to Italy in climate and orange groves, 'when we consider the great superiority of English gardens, as regards floral embellishments and other advantages, Shrubland must far out-vie the best gardens of Italy'.

William Robinson was called in by the new owners when in 1882 the estate came by marriage to Lord and Lady Saumarez. The bedding-out system was hugely expensive, and Shrubland was, according to Alicia Amherst, among the first gardens where it was abandoned. Robinson admired Shrubland, and described his conversion of it to 'true flower-gardening' in later editions of *The English flower garden*. On the upper terrace he 'swept away' Barry's and Lady Middleton's 'scrolls and intricate beds', and introduced hardier permanent planting, chiefly roses, carnations, and lavender; and 'among them many of what are called common things', snapdragons, rockfoil, stonecrop, sweet pea and thrift.[8] He encouraged creepers on the stonework, where before they had been rigorously cut down. He also created a wild garden, which the *Gardeners' Chronicle* opined was one of the best modern developments. Robinson planted 'both sides of a ravine' with bamboo—a great novelty at the time—and other 'bold and graceful plants' to create an area which possessed 'that highest form of beauty—beauty of appropriateness'.[9] Robinson's beds on the upper terrace were grassed over in the late forties—the *Chronicle* thought they failed to match the house as well as the former designs—but their outlines can still be picked out.

The house is still owned by the Saumarez family and is now a health clinic. The planting has of course been much simplified and the parterres reduced; the fountain garden is now dry and the maze overgrown. But Barry's dramatic effects remain as powerful as ever, and if time and 'modern taste' have 'mitigated the severe classicisms of the Shrubland gardens', they remain, as *Country Life* put it in 1901, 'one of the finest examples of the Italian style as British architects understood it'.[10]

ATHELHAMPTON HALL
near DORCHESTER, DORSET

In the mid-nineteenth century the manor house at Athelhampton was in a state of romantic neglect. Lady Dorothy Nevill remembered it 'as a deserted and seemingly ruined building used as a farm', while the garden 'was a wilderness through which cattle roamed right up to the door'.[1] The young Thomas Hardy also knew the decaying house and its grounds, and later in his life its imagined past figured in a couple of poems. What we can see now is one of the best revivalist gardens of the 1890s—a formal layout designed, as J. D. Sedding put it, to 'curtsey' to the house.[2]

Athelhampton in the early nineteenth century was a small rustic manor house occupied by a tenant-farmer. In a short story, *The waiting supper*, Hardy portrayed him as a 'rough old buffer' hosting the parish feast in the hall and rubbing shoulders with the villagers in a dance on the lawn. The manor was originally owned by the Martin family who built the house in the late fifteenth century, and it had remained in the family until 1812, when it was acquired by the Earl of Mornington, a great-nephew of the Duke of Wellington. He let it as a farm-house, but in 1848 it was bought by George James Wood and his wife. This couple were strict Nonconformists and founded a school at which Tryphena Sparks, Hardy's cousin, was a pupil and student teacher. While the Woods did effect some much-needed repairs, they also demolished the gatehouse, the chapel, the walls of the front two quadrangles and a part of the house. Athelhampton's charms were not fully recognized until 1891, when the romantically inclined Alfred Cort de Lafontaine bought it and set about renovating it. Significantly, he steeped himself in the history of the manor and its owners, which he wrote up in the transactions of the Dorset Field Club. Lafontaine also describes the appearance of the manor when he arrived, 'neglected, ill-used, and, may I say, hardly known'; and the grounds, with their 'cowsheds and dilapidated buildings'.[3]

The work on the house and grounds was not restoration as it is now understood but a modern version of the old style: 'a wonderful combination of the old and new', as it was described in *Country Life*.[4] Lafontaine's starting point was his 'very deep regret' at the 'present mutilated condition' of Athelhampton: 'To me it seems to have been an act of terrible Vandalism to have destroyed so unique and beautiful a specimen of mediaeval domestic architecture as Athelhampton must have been'.[5] The Ruskinian moral outrage, the scholarly interest and the elegiac note were all a necessary prelude to the most vigorous and confident building programme.

Since William Morris had settled at Kelmscott, old manor houses had been reappraised and become the classic setting for the new ideal of Arts and Crafts. In 1907 it was possible to write that 'an old manor house is, as it were, a dewdrop from the past—pure, pellucid, peaceful'.[6] J. D. Sedding, a disciple of Morris and a founder member of the Art Workers' Guild, produced in 1891 *Garden-craft old and new* in which he propounded what he saw as the traditional relationship between house and garden. Reginald Blomfield had published *The*

237. A bird's-eye view of the house and garden at Athelhampton, drawn by Inigo Triggs himself, 1901.

238. A view of the garden taken for *Country Life* less than ten years after Thomas had completed his work. Thomas was one of the architects praised by Gertrude Jekyll as 'having again, as in the beginning, made themselves responsible for the main lines . . . of the garden'.

formal garden in England in 1892, and *Country Life* began promoting traditional vernacular methods for houses and gardens in 1897. This was the ethos in which Athelhampton was recreated.

For the grounds Lafontaine commissioned designs from Inigo Thomas, Reginald Blomfield's collaborator on *The formal garden in England*. Thomas had toured the country in search of survivals and information: the book was in part a history, but more, it was a passionate and partisan argument in favour of architectural gardens, old or new, and against landscape gardening. At Athelhampton, Thomas used motifs he had discovered on his travels to create a series of enclosures in yew and stone, linked by three axial vistas. These lines were intended to emphasize 'the garden in relation to the house', as Thomas termed it in his essay on Athelhampton for the *Gardener's Magazine*.[7]

Within eight years of being finished it featured in *Country Life*, and the author walked round the garden with Thomas for the article. *Country Life* was written for a readership wealthy enough to embark on restorations and to buy hand-crafted products. In 1916, in its thousandth issue, the editor defined the aim behind the journal's famous series 'Country homes and gardens old and new' as 'a single-hearted desire to study them for their merits and instructiveness'.[8] But in addition to the scholarly recording of materials and techniques, *Country Life* also celebrated the 'cause', as this article affirms in its first paragraph, of 'the beautiful in country life'. The author sets the scene at Athelhampton as if he were beginning a romantic tale and the combination is typical of *Country Life*'s approach to the past:

> Down in the water-meadows some miles out of Dorchester a cluster of gables and battlements nestles under the spreading boughs of a great cedar, and in the secluded courts can be heard the gentle coo of pigeons and the conversational patter of falling water.[9]

The 'thousand and one difficulties' of building and planting are recounted in a fashionably

239. The upper lawn or Great Court as it is today. While the massive yew pyramids dominate the scene, the eye is still led, as Thomas intended, from one enclosure to the next.

languid and mannered tone: the cisterns in the pavilion roofs deluging the ceilings, the problems with the water supply to the fountains and 'the usual difficulties interposed by the stupidity of the workmen'. Thomas, returning eight years after finishing his work, also grumbles about some details: his sundial in the Corona replaced by a fountain, the finials missing from the piers in the sunk garden, the owner's preference for glazed pots rather than 'good leaden vases with covers for winter'. But,

> on the whole the gardening seems to have followed the right direction. The paved court with its wicker chairs is the very place to bask through a cigarette after lunch.
> . . . In another eight years, or less, the hedges of yew should be as high and as dense as will ever be needed, and the stone has doubtless long since taken the soft lavender lichens that its surface affects and that painters delight in.[10]

In 1896 Alicia Amherst wrote *A history of gardening in England*, the first such history to use archival sources. In many ways her research supported the gardencraft movement and in 1938, towards the end of her life, she wrote *Historic gardens of England*, which, in a format suitable for use by tourists, identified surviving historic features. She included in the latter an entry on the gardens at Athelhampton, and pinpoints exactly the spirit in which they were designed:

> They are one of the most attractive examples of a revived formal garden strictly in keeping with the house. The terraces, lawns, small enclosed gardens, now well furnished with flowers, and above all the formal pool and the summer-house, are all excellent reproductions of a sixteenth-century garden suited to the size of the house.[11]

Athelhampton was much admired by devotees of gardencraft. These included Lady Ottoline Morrell, who visited in 1924, and Gertrude Jekyll who included photographs of the garden in her 1918 pattern book, *Garden ornament*. For Jekyll Athelhampton demonstrated the happy return of the architect to the garden and the 'having now a knowledge of former styles'.[12]

Lafontaine sold Athelhampton in 1916, after his son and heir was killed in the war. By the 1940s it was again in disrepair, but its fortunes revived when it was purchased by Robert Victor Cooke. He gave it to his son and daughter-in-law in 1966, and since then it has not only been preserved but has grown: the White Garden bounded by the river, and the Cloister Garden with its lime walk and central pool, have added sympathetically to Thomas's original series of formal garden enclosures. When English Heritage produced its *Register of parks and gardens of special historic interest* in 1985, Athelhampton was listed Grade I: the imitation historic garden had become historic in its own right.

240. One of the many statues in the garden at Athelhampton. This one, standing outside the Great Court, is the goddess Hygieia.

BIBLIOGRAPHY
OF GARDEN TOURISTS AND COMMENTATORS

ADAM William Adam, *Gem of the Peak* (5th ed. Derby and London, 1851).

ATKYNS John Tracy Atkyns, 'Iter Boreale, or the northern expedition. Commencing 10 July 1732, ending 18 Augt'. (By courtesy of the Yale Center for British Art, Paul Mellon Collection.) Transcript kindly supplied by Peter Goodchild.

AUBREY John Aubrey, *The natural history of Wiltshire*, ed. J. Britton (London, 1847).

BECKFORD *Life and letters of William Beckford*, ed. L. Melville (1910).

BERRY Maria Theresa Lewis, *Extracts from the journals and correspondence of Miss Berry from 1783–1852*, 3 vols (1865).

BIBLIOTHECA *Bibliotheca topographica Britannica*, ed. J. Nichols, 8 vols (London, 1780–90).

BIGLAND Ralph Bigland, *Historical, monumental, and genealogical collections relative to the county of Gloucester* (London, 1791).

BLOMFIELD Reginald Blomfield, *The formal garden in England* (1892).

BRAY William Bray, 'Tour in Derbyshire and Yorkshire performed in 1777', in MAVOR, vol. II.

BRITTON John Britton, *The beauties of Wiltshire*, 3 vols (London, 1801–25).

BROOKE E. Adveno Brooke, *The gardens of England* (London, c.1857).

BROWNE Edward Browne, 'Notes taken in a tour through the West of England 1662'. British Museum Sloane MS. 1900 fols 59–63.

BUDWORTH Joseph Budworth, *A fortnight's ramble to the lakes in Westmorland, Lancashire and Cumberland, by a rambler* (London, 1792).

BURNEY *Diaries and letters of Madame D'Arblay*, ed. Austin Dobson, 6 vols (1904).

BURRITT E. Burritt, *Walks in the Black Country and its green borderland* (1868).

CAMBRIDGE UNDERGRADUATE [A Cambridge undergraduate] 'A tour from Cambridge to Halifax and Wakefield, returning via Oxford, Bath and Bristol', 1725, Bath Reference Library MS. 914.238b. Acc. No. 38.43.

CAMPBELL Colen Campbell, *Vitruvius Britannicus*, 3 vols (London, 1725).

CATCOTT Alexander Catcott, 'Catcott's

Tour in England & Wales, 1748', 2 vols, Bristol Reference Library, MS. B 30100 BL 17F.

CHANDOS Julia Johnson, *Excellent Cassandra* (1981).

COBBETT William Cobbett, *Rural Rides*, 2 vols (London, 1853, repr. 1957).

COMBE [William Combe], *An history of the river Thames*, 2 vols (John and Josiah Boydell, London, 1794).

COOKE Edward Cooke's diaries, 1828–79, are deposited at the National Maritime Museum.

COSMO III Count Lorenzo Magalotti, *Travels of Cosmo III, Grand Duke of Tuscany, through England . . .[in] 1669* (London, 1821).

COTTAGE GARDENER *Cottage Gardener*, 1848–60 (continued as *Journal of Horticulture*).

COUNTRY LIFE *Country Life*, 1897–

CURWEN *Journal and letters of Samuel Curwen*, ed. G. A. Ward (London, 1842).

DEFOE 1724–7 Daniel Defoe, *A tour thro' the whole island of Great Britain*, 3 vols (London, 1724–7).

DEFOE 1738 Daniel Defoe, *A tour through the whole island of Great Britain*, 3 vols (London, 1738).

DEFOE 1742 Daniel Defoe, *A tour through the whole island of Great Britain*, 3 vols (London, 1742).

DELANY *The autobiography and correspondence of Mary Granville, Mrs Delany*, ed. Lady Llanover, 6 vols (London, 1861).

DE MURALT Béat Louis de Muralt, *Lettres sur les anglois* (1728), written c.1694.

DODD John Dodd, 'Journal of a Tour through England, 1735', British Museum Add. MS. 5957.

ELIOT [Charles Eliot's father], *Charles Eliot, landscape gardener* (New York, 1902).

EVELYN *The diary of John Evelyn*, ed. E. S. de Beer, 5 vols (Oxford, 1955).

EVELYN: ELYSIUM John Evelyn, 'Elysium Britannicum', Christ Church Library, Oxford, MS. Collection. (By courtesy of the trustees of the will of the late Major Peter George Evelyn.)

FIENNES *The journeys of Celia Fiennes*, ed. Christopher Morris (London, 1947).

FORBES James Forbes, 'Tour into Cornwall in 1794'. MS. deposited at Cornish Institution, Truro Museum.

GARDEN *The Garden*, 1871–1927.

GARDENER *The Gardener*, 1867–82.

GARDENERS' CHRONICLE *Gardeners' Chronicle*, 1841–

GILPIN: LAKES William Gilpin, *Observations . . . on several parts of England: particularly the mountains, and lakes of Cumberland and Westmorland*, 2 vols (London, 1786).

GILPIN: NOTEBOOK William Gilpin MS. Bodleian Library, Oxford, Eng. misc. e. 522.

GILPIN: WESTERN PARTS William Gilpin, *Observations on the western parts of England* (London, 1798).

GILPIN/MASON: LETTERS Bodleian Library, Oxford, MS. Eng. misc. d. 570.

GREY Joyce Godber, 'The Marchioness Grey of Wrest Park', *Publications of the Bedfordshire Historical Records Society*, vol. XLVII (1968).

HADFIELD Miles Hadfield: *A history of British gardening* (London, 1979). First published as *Gardening in Britain* (1960).

HAMMOND 1634 *A relation of a short survey of 26 counties observed in a seven weeks journey begun on August 11, 1634, by a captain, a lieutenant, and an ancient*, ed. L. G. Wickham Legg (London, 1904).

HAMMOND 1635 'A Relation of a Short Survey of the Western Counties made by a Lieutenant of the Military Company in Norwich in 1635', ed. L. G. Wickham Legg, *Camden Miscellany* vol. XVI (1936).

HANWAY Jonas Hanway, *A journal of eight days journey from Portsmouth to Kingston upon Thames*, 2 vols (London, 1757).

HARCOURT *The Harcourt Papers*, ed. E. W. Harcourt, 12 vols (Oxford, 1876–1905).

HAY Lady Margaret Hay, notes on travels, 1745, British Museum MS. Loan 29/234.

HENTZNER Paul Hentzner, *A journey into England . . . in the year MDXCVIII* (Strawberry Hill, 1757).

HIRSCHFELD C. C. L. Hirschfeld, *Theorie der Gartenkunst*, 5 vols (1779).

HUSSEY Christopher Hussey, *English gardens and landscapes 1700–1750* (London, 1967).

IRVING Washington Irving, *The Sketch Book* (1820).

JAMES Henry James, *English Hours* (London, 1905, 2nd ed., 1960).

JEFFERSON *Thomas Jefferson's garden book 1766–1824*, ed. E. M. Betts (Philadelphia, 1944).

JEKYLL/ELGOOD Gertrude Jekyll and George S. Elgood, *Some English gardens* (London, 1904).

JONES Barbara Jones, *Follies & Grottoes* (new ed., London, 1974).

KARAMZIN *Letters of a Russian traveller 1789–90*, ed. F. Jonas (1958).

KELSALL 'The diary of John Kelsall', Library of the Religious Society of Friends, London, MS. vol. S, 193/2.

KIELMANSEGGE Count Frederick Kielmansegge, *Diary of a journey to England in the years 1761–1762* (London, 1902).

LAUDER Sir John Lauder, 'Notes of journeys in London, Oxford and Scotland 1667–1670' in *Journals of Sir John Lauder*, ed. Donald Crawford (Edinburgh, 1900), pp. 167–205.

LELAND *The itinerary of John Leland in or about the years 1535–1543*, ed. Lucy Toulmin-Smith, 5 vols (London, 1907–10).

LENNÉ Peter Joseph Lenné's paper on an English tour was quoted by Loudon in the *Gardener's Magazine*, 1826, pp. 309–10.

LOUDON J. C. Loudon, *An encyclopaedia of gardening* (new ed., London, 1834).

LOUDON: G. M. *Gardener's Magazine*, 1826–43.

LOVEDAY Sarah Markham, *John Loveday of Caversham: the life and tours of an eighteenth-century onlooker* (Salisbury, 1984).

LYBBE POWYS *Passages from the diary of Mrs. Philip Lybbe Powys*, ed. Emily Climenson (London, 1899).

MACKY 1714 John Macky, *A journey through England. In familiar letters from a gentleman here to a friend abroad* (1st ed., London, 1714).

MACKY 1722 John Macky, *A journey through England . . .*, 2 vols (London, 1722–3).

MACKY 1724 John Macky, *A journey through England . . .*, 2 vols (London, 1724).

MASON George Mason, *An essay on design in gardening* (London, 1795).

MAVOR William Mavor, *The British tourists: or traveller's pocket companion*, 6 vols (London, 1798–1810).

MILLER Hugh Miller, *First impressions of England and its people* (London, 1847).

MILLES Jeremiah Milles, 'Summer tours to Wales and the Southern Counties, 1735–43', British Museum Add. MS. 15,776.

MONTAGU Emily Climenson, *Elizabeth Montagu: queen of the blue stockings*, 2 vols (London, 1906).

MORITZ C. P. Moritz of Berlin, 'Travels in 1782' in MAVOR, vol. IV.

MOULE Thomas Moule, *The English counties delineated* (London, 1837).

NICHOLS John Nichols, *The Progresses of Queen Elizabeth*, 3 vols (1823).

NORTHUMBERLAND Travel diaries of the 1st Duchess of Northumberland, Duke of Northumberland MSS., Alnwick Castle, MS. 121. (By courtesy of the Duke of Northumberland.)

OXFORD 'Travels of Edward Earl of Oxford', British Museum, MS. Loan 29/234.

PARNELL 1769 John Parnell, 'Journal of a tour through Wales and England', British Library of Political and Economic Science, London, MS. Coll. misc. 38 (4 vols).

PARNELL: PAINSHILL James Sambrook, 'Painshill Park in the 1760's', *Garden History*, vol. VIII, no. 1, pp. 91–106. Includes Parnell's notes on Painshill from his account of his 1763 tour, deposited in the Folger Shakespeare Library, Washington D.C.

PENNANT Thomas Pennant, *The journey from Chester to London* (London, 1782).

PEPYS *The diary of Samuel Pepys*, ed. Robert Latham and William Matthews, 11 vols (London, 1970–83).

PIPER Fredrik Magnus Piper, 'Beskrifning Öfwer Idéen och General-Plan till en Ängelsk Lustpark', transcribed and translated by John Phibbs and Eva Olofsson. (By courtesy of the Kungl. Akadamien för de Fria Konsterna, Stockholm.) Transcript kindly supplied by John Phibbs.

PLATTER Clare Williams, *Thomas Platter's travels in England, 1599* (1937).

POCOCKE 1750 *The travels through England of Dr. Richard Pococke . . . during 1750, 1751, and later years*, ed. J. J. Cartwright, 2 vols (London, Camden Society, 1888–9).

POCOCKE 1764 'Travels of Dr. Richard Pococke Bishop of Osary in 1764', 2 vols, British Museum Add. MS. 14, 260–1.

POPE *The correspondence of Alexander Pope*, ed. George Sherburn, 5 vols (Oxford, 1956).

PORTEUS The notebooks are deposited at Lambeth Palace.

PRICE Uvedale Price, *Essays on the Picturesque*, 2 vols (London, 1798).

PROSSER George F. Prosser, *Select illustrations of the county of Surrey* (London, 1828).

PÜCKLER-MUSKAU [Herman Ludwig Heinrich von Pückler-Muskau], *Tour in England, Ireland and France in the years 1828 and 1829*, 4 vols (London, 1832).

PYE Henrietta Pye, *A peep into the principal seats and gardens in and about Twickenham (the residence of the Muses)* (1775).

RASMUSSEN Steen Eiler Rasmussen, *London: the unique city* (1974).

RIDLEY *Life and Letters of Cecilia Ridley* (1958).

ROBERTSON 'William Robertson's Travel Diary, c. 1795', MS. collection, National Library of Ireland.

ROCKLEY Alicia Amherst, Lady Rockley, *Historic gardens of England* (London, 1938).

RUTLAND J. H. Manners, Duke of Rutland, *Journal of a tour to the northern parts of Great Britain* (London, 1813).

SALMON Thomas Salmon, *The foreigner's companion through the universities of Cambridge and Oxford* (1748).

SAXONY Carl Gustav Carus, *The King of Saxony's journey through England and Scotland in the year 1844* (London, 1846).

SHAW Stebbing Shaw, 'Tour to the west of England in 1788', in MAVOR, vol. IV.

SIMOND Louis Simond, *Journal of a tour and residence in Great Britain during the years 1810 and 1811*, 2 vols (Edinburgh, 1815).

SITWELL Sacheverell Sitwell, *British architects and craftsmen* (London, 1945).

SORBIÈRE Samuel de Sorbière, *A voyage to England* (London, 1709).

SPENCE Joseph Spence, *Anecdotes of men and manners*, ed. James M. Osborn, 2 vols (Oxford, 1966).

STUKELEY William Stukeley, *Itinerarium curiosum*, 2 vols (London, 1776).

SULIVAN 'Tour through different parts of England, Scotland and Wales by Richard Sulivan performed in 1778', in MAVOR, vol. III.

SWETE John Swete's MS. journals are deposited at the Devon County Record Office.

SWITZER: HYDROSTATICKS Stephen Switzer, *An introduction to a general system of hydrostaticks and hydraulicks*, 2 vols (London, 1729).

SWITZER: ICHNOGRAPHIA Stephen Switzer, *Ichnographia rustica*, 3 vols (London, 1718).

TAYLOR John Taylor, *A new discovery by sea* (London, 1623).

TORRINGTON *The Torrington diaries*, ed. C. Bruyn Andrews, 4 vols (London, 1935–8).

TRIGGS H. Inigo Triggs, *Formal gardens in England and Scotland*, 3 vols (London, 1902).

VAN SPAEN Heimerick Tromp, 'A Dutchman's visits to some English gardens in 1791', *Journal of Garden History*, vol. II, no. 1.

VERTUE George Vertue, 'Notebooks', *The Walpole Society*, 7 vols (1929–50).

VON UFFENBACH Zacharias von Uffenbach, *Reise*, 3 vols (1753).

VON UFFENBACH: OXFORD Zacharias von Uffenbach, *Oxford in 1710*, ed. W. H. Quarrell (1928).

WALDSTEIN *The diary of Baron Waldstein*, ed. G. W. Groos (1981).

WALPOLE Horace Walpole, 'The history of the modern taste in gardening', in *Anecdotes of painting*, 4 vols (Strawberry Hill, 1771), vol. IV.

WALPOLE: CORRESPONDENCE *Horace Walpole's correspondence*, ed. W. S. Lewis, 48 vols (Oxford and New Haven, 1937–83).

WALPOLE: JOURNALS 'Horace Walpole's journals of visits to country seats &c.', ed.

Paget Toynbee, *Walpole Society*, vol. XVI (1927–8).

WARNER Richard Warner, *A tour through the northern counties of England and the borders of Scotland*, 2 vols (Bath, 1802).

WARNER: BATH Richard Warner, *Excursions from Bath* (Bath, 1801).

WARNER: CORNWALL Richard Warner, *A tour through Cornwall in the autumn of 1808* (London, 1809).

WESLEY *The journal of the Reverend John Wesley*, ed. Nehemiah Curnock, 8 vols (London, 1909–16).

WHATELY Thomas Whately, *Observations on modern gardening* (3rd ed., London, 1771).

WHATELY 1801 Thomas Whately, *Observations on modern gardening*, with appendix and Horace Walpole's observations (London, 1801).

YORKE 'The travel journal of Philip Yorke, 1744–63' in Joyce Godber, 'The Marchioness Grey of Wrest Park', *Publications of the Bedfordshire Historical Records Society*, vol. XLVII (1968).

YOUNG, CATHERINE Diary of Mrs Catherine Young, later Mrs Maclear, deposited at the Bedfordshire County Record Office. Miss P. Bell kindly supplied this reference.

YOUNG: NORTH OF ENGLAND Arthur Young, *A six months tour through the north of England*, 4 vols (London, 1770).

YOUNG: SOUTHERN COUNTIES Arthur Young, *A six weeks tour through the southern counties of England and Wales* (2nd ed., London, 1769).

YOUNG: SUSSEX Reverend Arthur Young, *Agriculture of Sussex* (1808).

NOTES TO THE TEXT

For items given here in small capitals readers are referred to the Bibliography on page 300.

THE GARDEN TOURISTS

1 LELAND, vol. I, p.xli.
2 See particularly reports of Venetian ambassadors in Calendar of State Papers. Venetian.
3 EVELYN: ELYSIUM.
4 FIENNES, p.1.
5 T. L. Peacock, *Headlong Hall* (1816), chapter 4, The Grounds.
6 SAXONY, p.114.
7 R. A. Aubin, *Topographical poetry in eighteenth century England* (1936).
8 See p.171.
9 Jane Austen, *Northanger Abbey*, The Folio Society (1960), p.98.
10 William Combe, *The Tour of Doctor Syntax in search of the Picturesque* (1812), p.5.
11 Jane Austen, op. cit., p.154.
12 See R. G. C. Desmond, 'Victorian gardening magazines', *Garden History*, vol.5, no.3, pp.47–63.

MEDIAEVAL GARDENS

1 John Harvey, 'Queen Eleanor of Castile as a gardener', *Garden History Society Newsletter*, no.5, summer 1982, p.3.
2 John Harvey, *Mediaeval gardens* (1981), p.127.
3 ibid., p.84.
4 Etienne Robo, *Mediaeval Farnham* (1935), p.149.
5 John Harvey, 'Mediaeval plantsmanship in England: the culture of rosemary', *Garden History*, vol.I, no.I, pp.14–21.
6 Sylvia Landsberg, 'Queen Eleanor's garden, the Great Hall, Winchester', *Garden History Society Newsletter*, no.19, spring 1987, p.28.
7 Westminster Cellarers' and Gardeners' Account Rolls, Westminster Abbey Muniments Room. For infirmary gardens see Teresa McLean, *Medieval English gardens* (1981).
8 Brian Moffat, 'A progress report on the Soutra Hospital project, *Edinburgh Medicine*, no. 54 (1989), pp.16–19.
9 *Blenheim: Landscape for a Palace*, ed. J. Bond and K. Tiller (1987), p.28.

10 H. M. Colvin, *The History of the King's Works* (1963), vol.II, pp.1014–17.
11 William Shakespeare, *Henry VIII*, Act V, scene v.
12 HENTZNER, p.83.
13 John Dent, *The quest for Nonsuch* (1981, reprint of 2nd ed. 1970), p.113.
14 HENTZNER, pp.83–4.

TUDOR AND STUART GARDENS

1 PLATTER, p.200.
2 William Harrison, *The Description of England*, 1577 (in Holinshed's *Chronicles*).
3 Calendar of State papers. Venetian (1909), vol.XV, p.319.
4 Mavis Batey, 'Basing House Tudor Garden', *Garden History*, vol.15, no.2, p.101.

KENILWORTH CASTLE

1 John Harvey, *Mediaeval gardens* (1981), p.106.
2 NICHOLS, vol.1, p.473.

3 G. Turberville, *The noble art of venerie or hunting* (1575), p.94.
4 BURRITT, p.406.
5 Walter Scott, *Kenilworth*, chapter 34.
6 *Scott's Journal*, ed. W. E. K. Anderson (1972), p.453.
7 GILPIN: LAKES, vol.I, p.48.
8 TORRINGTON, vol.I, p.229.
9 W. Beattie, *Castles and Abbeys of England* (1842), vol.I, p.244.
10 JAMES (1960), p.125.
11 PÜCKLER-MUSKAU, vol.III, p.230.

THE TUDOR GARDEN

1 WALDSTEIN, p.59.
2 Ernest Law, *Shakespeare's garden* (1922).
3 Ernest Law, *Hampton Court Gardens old and new* (1926), p.65.

HATFIELD HOUSE

1 'The Building of Hatfield House' (Hatfield Archives), p.86.
2 ibid., pp.35; 86; 93; 236; 86.
3 Thomas Fuller, *The history of the worthies of England*, 3 vols (London, 1840), vol.II, p.38.
4 EVELYN, vol.II, p.80.
5 EVELYN: ELYSIUM, fol.129. Quotation kindly supplied by Robin Harcourt-Williams.
6 PEPYS, vol.II, pp.138–9.
7 SORBIÈRE, pp.64–5.
8 PARNELL 1769, vol.III, pp.9–10.
9 PENNANT, p.411.
10 PÜCKLER-MUSKAU, vol.III, pp.257–8.
11 LOUDON: G. M., vol.XII (1836), p.294.
12 *Gardeners' Chronicle*, 9 May 1874, Special Supplement.

CAMPDEN HOUSE

1 Paul Everson, 'The gardens of Campden House', *Garden History*, vol.17, no.2.
2 POCOCKE 1750, vol.II, p.279.
3 Ralph Bigland, *Historical, monumental, and genealogical collections relative to the county of Gloucester* (1791), vol.I, p.279.
4 S. E. Hicks Beach, *A Cotswold Family Hicks and Hicks Beach* (1909), p.100.
5 Alan G. R. Smith, *Servant to the Cecils* (1977).
6 HENTZNER, p.54.
7 EVELYN: ELYSIUM. See p.41.
8 WALDSTEIN, p.87.
9 Hugh Platt, *The Garden of Eden* (1659), p.43.

BOLSOVER CASTLE

1 Henry Hyde, Earl of Clarendon, *The history of the rebellion and civil wars in England . . .*, 6 vols (Oxford, 1705–6), vol.I, p.78.

2 Sir Philip Warwick, *Memoirs of the reign of King Charles I* (London, 1701), p.235.
3 Ben Jonson, ed. C. H. Herford, P. & E. Simpson, 8 vols (corrected ed., Oxford, 1963–7), vol.VII, pp.809–13.
4 Margaret Cavendish, Duchess of Newcastle, *The life of . . . William Cavendishe* (London, 1667), p.91.
5 PEPYS, vol.IX, p.123.
6 A. J. Foster, *Round about the crooked spire* (London, 1894), pp.115;122.
7 SITWELL, pp.25–6.

WILTON HOUSE

1 TRIGGS, vol.I, p.15.
2 *Aubrey's brief lives*, ed. Oliver Lawson Dick (Harmondsworth, 1972), p.297.
3 TAYLOR, p.38.
4 AUBREY, p.83.
5 HAMMOND 1635, pp.66–7.
6 FIENNES, p.9.
7 OXFORD, fols 59–60.
8 Reproduced in John Bold, *Wilton House and English Palladianism* (R.C.H.M.E., 1988), p.91.
9 ibid., quoted on p.78.
10 DEFOE 1738, vol.I, p.293.
11 VAN SPAEN, p.48.
12 YOUNG: SOUTHERN COUNTIES, pp.199–200.
13 GILPIN: WESTERN PARTS, pp.98–9.
14 LOUDON: G. M., vol.XII (1836), pp.509–12.

RESTORATION GARDENS

1 SORBIÈRE, p.64.
2 See *The gardens of William and Mary*, ed. David Jacques and A. van der Horst (1988).
3 PEPYS, vol.VII, p.213.
4 John Worlidge, *Systema Horticulturae* (1677).
5 CHANDOS, p.66.
6 1888 edition by Emily Griffiths. See also FIENNES.

GREENWICH PARK

1 MACKY 1714, p.45.
2 A. D. Webster, *Greenwich Park, its history and associations* (1902).
3 EVELYN, vol.III, p.370.
4 EVELYN, vol.II, p.563.
5 PEPYS, vol.III, p.126.
6 EVELYN, vol.III, p.85.
7 *The Wren Society, Proceedings*, VI (1929), p.17.
8 *Architectural Journal*, 27 June 1973, p.1540.
9 VON UFFENBACH, vol.III, p.445.

HAM HOUSE

1 DEFOE 1724–7, vol.I, p.118, letter 2.
2 EVELYN, vol.IV, pp.143–4.
3 Roger North, *Of building*, ed. H. Colvin (1981), p.144.
4 Batty Langley, *New principles of gardening* (1728), p.vi.
5 MACKY 1714, p.36.
6 WALPOLE: CORRESPONDENCE, vol.10, p.306.
7 BERRY, vol.II, p.423.
8 ibid., p.423, note.
9 FIENNES, p.175.
10 CHANDOS, p.67.
11 Graham Stuart Thomas, *Gardens of the National Trust* (1979), p.149.

OXFORD BOTANIC GARDEN

1 B. M. Lansdowne MSS., vol.107, no.92, fol.155. Quoted in *Cambridge Antiquarian Society Communications*, vol.IV (1876), p.7.
2 John Ayliffe, *Antient and present state of the University of Oxford* (1714).
3 Bodl. MS. Twyne 6, fol. 287.
4 Robert Plot, *The natural history of Oxfordshire*, edition 2 (1705), p.265.
5 *Transactions*. Medical Society London, vol.14 (1917).
6 LAUDER, p.173.
7 VON UFFENBACH: OXFORD, p.55.
8 COSMO III, p.262.
9 Mavis Batey, *Oxford Gardens* (1982), p.60.
10 CAMBRIDGE UNDERGRADUATE.
11 FIENNES, p.34.

KIRBY HALL

1 Holdenby Survey. Ralph Treswell Estate plan, Northamptonshire Record Office, Finch Hatton, MSS. 272.
2 John Norden, *Delineation of Northamptonshire*, 1610, p.50.
3 Kirby Survey, Northamptonshire Record Office, Finch Hatton MSS. 272. See J. M. Steane, 'The development of Tudor and Stuart garden design in Northamptonshire', *Northamptonshire past and present*, vol.V, no.5, p.400.
4 John Bridges, *History and antiquities of Northamptonshire* (1791), vol.II, p.315.
5 EVELYN, vol.III, p.134.
6 HADFIELD (1960), p.135.
7 John Morton, *The natural history of Northamptonshire* (1712), p.493.
8 Bridges, op. cit., vol.II, p.314.
9 'Correspondence of the Family of Hatton', ed. E. M. Thompson, *Camden Society* N.S., XXIII (1878), vol.II, p.87.
10 ibid., vol.II, p.82.
11 ibid., vol.II, p.147.
12 ibid., vol.II, p.205.

13 ibid., vol.II, p.86.
14 See Teresa Sladen, 'The garden at Kirby Hall 1570–1700', *Journal of Garden History*, vol.4, no.2 (1984) and John Harvey, 'The gardens of Kirby Hall, Northants, in the 17th century', *The conservation of historic gardens*, Garden History Society Symposium papers (1984).
15 See pp.100–3.
16 Staffordshire Record Office, Bradford papers, D1287 18/4, Winde letters uncatalogued (by courtesy of the Earl of Bradford).

HAMPTON COURT PALACE

1 Ernest Law, *History of Hampton Court Palace* (1885), vol.I, p.328.
2 EVELYN, vol.III, p.324.
3 Walter Harris, *A description of the king's royal palace and gardens at Loo* (1699).
4 EVELYN, vol.IV, p.645.
5 SITWELL, p.60.
6 FIENNES, p.60.
7 VON UFFENBACH, vol.III, p.203.
8 FIENNES, p.356.
9 DEFOE 1724, letter 3, p.8.
10 ibid., p.6.
11 Camden Series, 1878, vol.II, p.205.
12 KIELMANSEGGE, p.67.
13 BLOMFIELD, *passim*.
14 JEFFERSON, p.111.

LEVENS HALL

1 JEKYLL/ELGOOD, p.63.
2 Quoted in *Country Life*, vol.6 (1899), p.624.
3 ibid., p.656.
4 *The gardens of William and Mary*, ed. David Jacques and A. van der Horst (1988), p.64.
5 ROCKLEY, p.138.
6 Annette Bagot, 'Monsieur Beaumont and Col. Grahme. The making of a garden, 1689–1710', *Garden History*, vol.III, no.4.
7 *Cumberland and Westmorland antiquarian and archaeological Record Series*, vol.X (1988).
8 Nicholson's Diary, *Cumberland and Westmorland Transactions*, II (1902), p.207.
9 GILPIN: LAKES, vol.I, p.78.
10 BUDWORTH, p.25.
11 JEKYLL/ELGOOD, p.63.
12 *Country Life*, vol.6 (1899), p.656.
13 TRIGGS, vol.I, p.27.

WESTBURY COURT

1 Estate and personal accounts of Maynard Colchester (1664–1715), Gloucester Record Office, ref. D36 A4. Quoted in *Westbury Court Garden* (National Trust, 1980), pp.41–2.
2 Samuel Rudder, *A new history of Gloucestershire* (Cirencester, 1779), p.790.
3 *Country Life*, vol.XXIV (1908), pt.ii, pp.874–84.
4 *Garden History*, vol.II, no.2 (spring 1974), p.27.
5 TRIGGS, vol.I, p.32.
6 FIENNES, p.356.
7 DEFOE 1724–7, vol.I, p.123.
8 FIENNES, p.175.
9 ibid., p.346.
10 ibid., p.272.

CASTLE BROMWICH HALL

1 Staffordshire Record Office, Bradford papers, D 1287 18/4 Winde letters, 8 July 1690, uncatalogued (by courtesy of the Earl of Bradford).
2 ibid., Captain Hatton's letter, 8 March 1698/9.
3 Quoted in the *Pall Mall Magazine*, vol. 15 (1891), no. 63, p.301.
4 Richard Jago, *Edgehill* (London, 1767), Book III, ll. 484–8.
5 TORRINGTON, vol.III, p.220.
6 *Gardeners' Chronicle*, 22 June 1872, p.833.
7 *Pall Mall Magazine*, op. cit., pp.291–304.
8 *Country Life*, vol.VIII (4 August 1900), pp.144–51.

MELBOURNE HALL

1 ROCKLEY, p.140.
2 David Green, *Gardener to Queen Anne* (1956), p.41.
3 ibid., p.47.
4 ibid., p.41.
5 BLOMFIELD, p.220.
6 CHANDOS, p.67.
7 John Kerr, *Melbourne Hall* (1974).
8 BLOMFIELD, p.65.
9 JEKYLL/ELGOOD, pp.18–22.
10 David Green, op. cit., p.41.

WREST PARK

1 *Country Life*, vol.16 (1904), p.54.
2 CHANDOS, p.69.
3 GREY, p.41.
4 WALPOLE: JOURNALS, p.71.
5 PENNANT, p.383.
6 ROCKLEY, p.142.
7 GREY, p.62.
8 Lucas Papers, Bedfordshire County Record Office; quoted by kind permission of the Lady Lucas.
9 *Country Life*, vol.147 (1970), p.1252.
10 RIDLEY, p.33.

EIGHTEENTH-CENTURY GARDENS

1 HIRSCHFELD, vol.I, p.121.
2 MACKY 1722, vol.I, Preface ii.
3 WALPOLE, p.136.
4 Hist. MSS. Comm., vol. XLII (1897), 'The manuscrips of the Earl of Carlisle', p.144.
5 Alexander Pope, *Imitations of Horace*, First Book, Epistle I, 1.8.
6 *Spectator*, no.414.
7 F. Hardy, *Lord Charlemont* (1812), vol.I, p.63.
8 RASMUSSEN, p.164.
9 IRVING, quoted in A. F. Sieveking, *The praise of gardens* (1899), p.248 and given as 'Rural life in England'.
10 J. Wharton, *An essay on the genius and writings of Pope* (1782), vol.II, p.244.
11 Oliver Goldsmith: *The Traveller* (1764). See 'Oliver Goldsmith: An indictment of landscape gardening', *Furor Hortensis*, ed. P. Willis, 1974.
12 RUTLAND, p.89.
13 F. Kimball, 'The beginning of landscape gardening in America', *Landscape Architecture*, vol.VII (1917), p.183; quoted Isabel Chase, *Horace Walpole: Gardenist* (1943), p.257.
14 DELANY, vol.VI, p.100.
15 LYBBE POWYS, p.171.

BLENHEIM PALACE

1 DEFOE 1724–7, p.354.
2 H. T. Bobart, *A biographical sketch of Jacob Bobart together with an account of his two sons Jacob and Tilleman*, 1884, p.11.
3 STUKELEY, vol.1, p.46.
4 *Swift's poetical works*, ed. Herbert Davies (1967), p.60.
5 Joseph Addison, *Rosamond an Opera* (1707), Act III, scene 1. *Works*, ed. A. C. Guthkelch, vol.I, p.914.
6 John Vanbrugh, 'Reasons offer'd for preserving some part of the Old Manor at Blenheim' (1709).
7 David Green, 'Blenheim after Vanbrugh', *Blenheim: Landscape for a Palace*, ed. James Bond and Kate Tiller (1987), p.80. Papers given at a Conference organized by Oxford University Department for External Studies in association with the Garden History Society.
8 DODD.
9 KIELMANSEGGE, p.95.
10 PÜCKLER-MUSKAU, vol.III, p.253.
11 SALMON, p.6.
12 WHATELY, pp.78–81.
13 SHAW, p.229.

14 GILPIN: LAKES, vol.I, p.29.
15 Joshua Reynolds, *Discourses*, ed. Roger Fry (1905), 13th Discourse, 1896, p.368.
16 PRICE, vol.II, p.254.
17 PÜCKLER-MUSKAU, vol.III, p.253.
18 LOUDON: G. M. (1834), vol.10, p.99.
19 Ralph Cobham and Paul Hutton, 'Present management and future restoration', p.148 in *Blenheim* (see 7 above).
20 SITWELL, p.91.

CASTLE HOWARD

1 WALPOLE: CORRESPONDENCE, vol.XXX, p.257.
2 SWITZER: ICHNOGRAPHIA, vol.II, p.201.
3 RUTLAND, p.103.
4 ATKYNS, fol.24.
5 CAMBRIDGE UNDERGRADUATE, fol.44.
6 DEFOE 1738, vol.III, p.133.
7 HAY, fol. 74.
8 OXFORD, fols 87–9.
9 Quoted in Laurence Whistler, *The imagination of Vanbrugh . . .* (London, 1954), p.80.
10 YOUNG: NORTH OF NGLAND, vol.II, p.55.
11 PÜCKLER-MUSKAU, vol.IV, p.184.
12 SITWELL, pp.87;102.
13 HUSSEY, p.114.

CHISWICK HOUSE

1 POPE, vol.III, p.313.
2 DEFOE 1742, vol.3, p.287.
3 Pope, Epistle IV, *Moral Essays*, l.178.
4 *Blenheim*, p.82 (see note 7 in Blenheim above).
5 POPE, vol.I, p.338.
6 MACKY 1724, vol.I, p.87.
7 LOVEDAY, p.365.
8 DEFOE 1742, vol.3, p.288.
9 WHATELY 1801, p.153.
10 GILPIN: NOTEBOOK, fol.70.
11 KIELMANSEGGE, p.156.
12 JEFFERSON, p.111.
13 BERRY, vol.II, p.535.
14 Alice M. Coats, 'The Empress Josephine', *Garden History*, vol.5, no.3 (1977), p.40.
15 SIMOND, vol.2, p.119.

CLAREMONT

1 SWITZER: HYDROSTATICKS, vol.II, p.405.
2 POPE, vol.II, p.372.
3 CAMPBELL, vol.III, p.11.
4 *Historical Manuscripts Commission reports*, vol.XLII (1897), 'The manuscripts of the Earl of Carlisle', p.144.
5 WHATELY, pp.49–50.
6 PROSSER, no page numbers.
7 LOUDON: G. M., vol.X (1834), pp.329–30.

ADDISON'S WALK, OXFORD

1 Mavis Batey, *Oxford Gardens* (1982), p.13.
2 The manuscript essay was in the possession of J. Dykes Campbell who published a limited number of copies as *Some portions of essays contributed to the Spectator by Mr Joseph Addison* (Glasgow, 1864).
3 Addison, *Dialogues upon Ancient Medals* III. Misc. Works, A. C. Guthkelch (1914), vol.II, p.377.
4 *The memoirs of the life of Edward Gibbon by himself*, ed. G. Birbeck Hill (1900), p.49.
5 Magdalen Red Book dated 1 January 1801.
6 J. Buckler, *Observations on the original architecture of St Mary Magdalen college, Oxford* (1823), p.111.

RICHMOND AND THE VILLA LANDSCAPE

1 WALDSTEIN, p.167.
2 R. Halsband, *The life of Lady Mary Wortley Montagu* (1961), p.106.
3 PYE, p.52.
4 DEFOE 1724–7, p.124.
5 POPE, vol.IV, p.6.
6 G. de Beer and A. M. Rousseau, *Voltaire's British visitors*, Studies on Voltaire, xlix (1967), p.75.
7 Kimball, p.181; quoted I. Chase, p.257 (see note 13, Eighteenth-century gardens, above).
8 KARAMZIN, p.326.
9 P. Martin, *Pursuing innocent pleasures* (1984), p.147.
10 GILPIN: NOTEBOOK, fol.76.
11 PYE, p.16.
12 KIELMANSEGGE, pp.73–6.
13 COMBE, vol.II, p.1.
14 SIMOND, vol.II, p.117.
15 MORITZ, p.61.

CIRENCESTER PARK

1 POPE, Bathurst to Pope, 1732, vol.III, p.300.
2 TORRINGTON, vol.I, p.258.
3 SWITZER: ICHNOGRAPHIA, vol.I, p.xviii; III, 47; 45.
4 Stephen Switzer, *The practical kitchen gardiner* (London, 1727).
5 POPE, vol.I, p.515.
6 ibid., vol.II, p.82; III, 130; II, 82.
7 'Epistle to Burlington', ll. 187–9. All quotations from the one volume edition of *The poems of Alexander Pope*, ed. John Butt (London, 1968).
8 'Imitations of Horace', 'Epistle II, ii (1737), ll. 258–59; 'Epistle to Burlington', ll. 179–80.
9 Quoted in James Lees-Milne, *The Earls of*

creation (National Trust, 1986), pp.32–3.
10 POPE, vol.II, p.50.
11 ibid., vol.II, pp.115–16.
12 Samuel Rudder, *A new history of Gloucestershire* (Cirencester, 1779), p.355. All subsequent quotations from Rudder from the same page.
13 COMBE, vol.I, p.32.
14 MILLES, fols 127–8.
15 DELANY, 1st series, vol.I, p.421.
16 Lees-Milne, op. cit., p.26.
17 TORRINGTON, p.259.
18 JONES, p.33.

ROUSHAM HOUSE

1 HUSSEY, p.147.
2 WALPOLE, p.141.
3 Dmitri Shvidkovsky, *Garden History Society Newsletter*, no.21, p.6.
4 Robert Plot, *Natural history of Oxfordshire* (1705), p.266.
5 Bodleian Library, Oxford, MS. Gough Drawings a4.f.63.
6 POPE, vol.II, p.513.
7 *Suffolk Correspondence*, ed. J. W. Croker (1824), vol.II, p.76.
8 WHATELY 1801, p.153.
9 WALPOLE, p.141.
10 See *Victoria County Histories, Oxfordshire*, vol.XI, p.165.
11 Rousham archives.
12 See Kenneth Woodbridge, 'The Rousham Letters', *Apollo*, vol.100 (1974), pp.282–91.
13 See Mavis Batey, 'The way to view Rousham by Kent's gardener', *Garden History*, vol.11, no.2, pp.125–32.
14 WALPOLE: CORRESPONDENCE, vol.9, p.290.
15 DELANY, vol.II, p.221.
16 WALPOLE, p.141.
17 Joseph Warton, *An essay on the genius and writings of Pope* (1782), vol.II, p.244.
18 William Mason, *The English Garden* (1783), with a commentary and notes by W. Burgh, p.210.

STUDLEY ROYAL

1 Staffordshire Record Office D260/M/F/4/21. Hatherton Papers.
2 SULIVAN, p.116.
3 Levens Hall papers, County Record Office, Kendal.
4 YORKE, p.132.
5 HAY.
6 BRAY, p.348.
7 GILPIN: LAKES, vol.II, p.181.
8 SIMOND, vol.II, p.65.
9 RUTLAND, p.125.
10 WARNER, vol.I, pp.263–73.
11 TORRINGTON, vol.3, p.47.

12 PÜCKLER-MUSKAU, vol.IV, p.201.
13 HUSSEY, p.132.
14 *Yorkshire Post*, 3 June 1968; quoted in *Garden History Society Quarterly Newsletter*, 8, p.18.

STOWE

1 Quoted in Laurence Whistler, *The imagination of Vanbrugh . . .* (London, 1954), p.183.
2 MILLES, fols 3, 9.
3 Whistler, loc. cit.
4 *The Seasons*, 'Autumn', ll. 1072–4. See *The Seasons*, ed. James Sambrook (Oxford, 1981).
5 William Gilpin, *Dialogue upon the gardens . . . at Stow* (Buckingham, 1748), p.21.
6 SPENCE, No.1122.
7 MILLES, fol.9.
8 MILLES, fol.2.
9 PIPER, note 25.
10 Quoted in A. F. Sieveking, *The praise of gardens* (London, 1899), p.202.
11 LYBBE POWYS, p.155.
12 WESLEY, vol.VI, p.257.
13 VAN SPAEN, p.54.
14 PÜCKLER-MUSKAU, vol.III, p.275.
15 LOUDON: G. M., vol.VII (1831), p.389.

SHUGBOROUGH

1 PARNELL 1769, vol.I, fol.47. All subsequent quotations from same volume.
2 Frederick B. Stitt, 'Shugborough: the end of a village', *Essays in Staffordshire history*, 4th series, vol.VI (1970), pp.86–110.
3 PARNELL 1769, fol.51.
4 YORKE, p.137.
5 GREY, p.42.
6 PENNANT, p.69.
7 PARNELL 1769, fol.52.
8 *The letters of William Shenstone*, ed. Marjorie Williams (Oxford, 1939), pp.524–5.
9 Bedfordshire Record Office, L30/9/3/13. (By courtesy of the Right Honourable Lady Lucas.)
10 PARNELL 1769, fol.61.
11 ibid., fol.59.

THE LEASOWES

1 The phrase is Lord Lyttelton's, quoted in MONTAGU, vol.II, p.135.
2 See William Shenstone, *Works in verse and prose*, 2 vols (London, 1764), vol.II, 'Unconnected thoughts on gardening', p.125.
3 ibid., vol.I, pp.274–5.
4 LOUDON, p.321.
5 *James Thomson (1700–1748): letters and*

documents, ed. Alan D. McKillop (University of Kansas, 1958), pp.185–6.
6 Robert Dodsley, 'A description of the Leasowes', in Shenstone's *Works*, op. cit., vol.II, p.364.
7 Samuel Johnson, *Lives of the English poets*, ed. G. B. Hill, 3 vols (Oxford, 1945), vol.III, p.350.
8 Spence, 'The Round of Mr. Shenstone's Paradise' is in the Huntington Library, San Marino, California (HM 30312); Hull's 'Shenstone's Walks' is in the Osborn Collection at Yale.
9 MILLER, p.135.
10 Richard Graves, *Columella; or, the distressed anchoret*, 2 vols (London, 1779), vol.I, pp.116–17.
11 Shenstone, *Works*, op. cit., vol.I, p.339.
12 JEFFERSON, p.113.
13 LOUDON, loc. cit.
14 SIMOND, vol.II, pp.97–8.
15 GILPIN: LAKES, vol.I, pp.54–5.
16 'The history of a poet's garden', in *Collected works of Oliver Goldsmith*, ed. Arthur Friedman, 5 vols (Oxford, 1966), vol.III, pp.206–9.
17 PARNELL 1769, vol.III, p.85.

PAINSHILL

1 John Barrow, *Travels in China* (London, 1804), p.130.
2 WALPOLE: CORRESPONDENCE, vol.IX, p.71.
3 ROBERTSON, no page number.
4 WHATELY, p.187.
5 WALPOLE: JOURNALS, pp.36–7.
6 WALPOLE, p.145.
7 PARNELL: PAINSHILL, pp.93–4.
8 GILPIN, 'Mr. Hamilton's gardens at Painshill in Cobham in Surrey, May 20 1765', Bodleian Library, Oxford, Eng. misc. e. 522, fols 25–31.
9 YOUNG: SOUTHERN COUNTIES, pp.224–5.
10 PARNELL 1769, vol.I, pp.162–3.
11 Quotation kindly supplied by Mrs Mavis Collier, Painshill Park archivist.
12 MOULE, Surrey, p.105.

STOURHEAD

1 PARNELL 1769, vol.I, fol.79. All subsequent quotations from this volume.
2 POCOCKE 1750, vol.II, p.43.
3 PIPER, note 15.
4 PARNELL 1769, fol.107.
5 ibid., fols 95–6.
6 MS. at the Library of the Wiltshire Archaeological Society, Devizes (1834), quoted in *The conservation of the garden at Stourhead* (National Trust Report, Bath, 1978), p.53.

7 LYBBE POWYS, pp.169–70.
8 WARNER: BATH, p.105.
9 ibid.
10 WALPOLE: JOURNALS, p.43.
11 Quoted in *The conservation of the garden at Stourhead*, op.cit., p.52.
12 PARNELL 1769, fols 82–3.
13 WESLEY, vol.VI, p.128.
14 PARNELL 1769, fol.90.
15 PIPER, note 13.
16 PARNELL 1769, fol.91.
17 LYBBE POWYS, p.170.
18 WESLEY, vol.VI, p.128.
19 HANWAY, vol.II, p.138.
20 POCOCKE 1750, vol.II, p.43.
21 *The conservation of the garden at Stourhead*, op. cit., p.53.
22 WARNER: BATH, p.115.
23 PARNELL 1769, fols 111–13.
24 ibid., p.113.

GOLDNEY HALL

1 DELANY, vol.III, p.449.
2 Henry Jones, *Clifton* (Bristol, 1767), p.7.
3 KELSALL, fol.14.
4 NORTHUMBERLAND/177.
5 CATCOTT, vol.I, fol.130.
6 CURWEN, p.78.
7 DELANY, loc. cit.
8 YOUNG: SOUTHERN COUNTIES, pp.181–3.
9 NORTHUMBERLAND, loc. cit.
10 E. Shiercliff, *The Bristol and Hotwell guide* (Bristol, 1793), p.79.

STOKE PARK

1 POCOCKE 1764, vol.I, fols 137–9. All further quotations from Pococke are from this source.
2 J. Mathews, *The Bristol Guide* (Bristol, 1815), p.227.
3 O. A. Sherrard, *Lord Chatham and America* (London, 1958), p.286.
4 *The letters of William Shenstone*, ed. Marjorie Williams (Oxford, 1939), p.436.
5 *Gentleman's Magazine*, 1793, pp.8–12; 126–7.
6 Bedfordshire Record Office, L30/9/3/54. (By courtesy of the Right Honourable Lady Lucas.)
7 Henry Jones, *Clifton* (Bristol, 1767), p.17.
8 NORTHUMBERLAND/171.
9 MASON, p.127.
10 Gloucestershire County Record Office, D2700, 1020.3. (By courtesy of the Duke and Duchess of Beaufort.)
11 WESLEY, vol.V, p.93.
12 Gloucestershire County Record Office, D2700, Acc. 4629. (By courtesy of the Duke and Duchess of Beaufort.)

WROXTON ABBEY

1 FIENNES, p.26.
2 A. Jessopp, *Lives of the Norths* (1890), vol.I, p.348 and vol.III, p.291.
3 SALMON, p.11.
4 Bodleian Library, Oxford, MS. North b28 fol.26.
5 YORKE, p.139.
6 LOVEDAY, p.374.
7 Bodleian Library, Oxford, MS. North d.14 fol.209.
8 POCOCKE 1756, vol.II, p.240.
9 *Cake and Cockhorse*, vol.V (1974), p.153.
10 JONES, p.379.
11 WALPOLE: CORRESPONDENCE, vol.35, p.359.
12 WALPOLE: CORRESPONDENCE, vol.35, p.73.

CASTLE HILL

1 POCOCKE 1764, vol.I, fols 78–81. All further quotations from Pococke are from this source.
2 Contract between Morris and Hugh Fortescue, 22 February 1728. Quoted in Robin Fausset, 'The creation of the gardens at Castle Hill', *Garden History*, vol.XIII, no.2 (autumn 1985), p.103.
3 POCOCKE 1764.
4 James Fortescue, *Essays, and discourses, &c. in prose and verse*, 2 vols (Oxford, 1759), vol.I, p.127.
5 Robin Fausset, op. cit., p.122.
6 GILPIN: WESTERN PARTS, pp.174–5.
7 *Country Life*, vol.LXXV (1934), pt.i, p.272.

WARWICK CASTLE

1 PÜCKLER-MUSKAU, vol.III, p.210.
2 BURRITT, p.412.
3 *Sacheverell Sitwell's England*, ed. M. Raeburn (1986), p.212.
4 LELAND, vol.I, p.53.
5 'Iter Boreale', from edition of Richard Corbett's poems ed. J. A. W. Bennett and H. R. Trevor-Roper (1955), p.45.
6 HAMMOND 1634, p.73.
7 WALPOLE: CORRESPONDENCE, vol.9, p.121.
8 GILPIN/MASON: LETTERS, fol.66v.
9 ibid., fol.89v.
10 WARNER, p.259.
11 BERRY, vol.II, p.320.

PETWORTH HOUSE

1 DEFOE 1724–7, vol.II, p.67.
2 HAMMOND 1634, p.37.
3 DEFOE 1724–7, p.66.
4 MACKY 1714, p.66.
5 Petworth archives 6291. Accounts and memoranda 1724.
6 MILLES, fol.229.

7 DEFOE 1724–7, p.67.
8 MACKY 1714, p.66.
9 SIMOND, vol.II, pp.249–51.
10 WALPOLE, p.148.
11 Quoted in G. Jackson-Stops, *Petworth House*, p.34.
12 YOUNG: SUSSEX, p.188.
13 COBBETT, vol.I, p.178.
14 LOUDON: G. M. (1829), vol.5, p.576.
15 WALPOLE, p.148.
16 I. Nairn and N. Pevsner, *The buildings of England: Sussex* (1965), p.301.

BOWOOD

1 *Bowood* (1976).
2 Earl of Kerry, 'King's Bowood Park', *Wiltshire Archaeological and Natural History Magazine*, vol.XLII, p.19.
3 ibid., p.20.
4 Oliver Goldsmith: *The Deserted Village* (London, 1770), l. 277.
5 Earl of Kerry, op. cit., p.24.
6 BERRY, vol.III, p.461.
7 BRITTON, vol.2, pp.221–7.
8 BERRY, vol.III, p.461.
9 W.B.R.D., 'The forest trees of Wiltshire', *Wiltshire Archaeological Magazine*, vol.X (1867).
10 Allen J. Coombes, *A guide to Bowood trees and shrubs* (1893).
11 ELIOT, p.150.

NUNEHAM PARK

1 HIRSCHFELD, vol.V, p.274.
2 GILPIN: LAKES, vol.1, p.22.
3 Oliver Goldsmith: *The Deserted Village* (London, 1770), l.300. See M. Batey, 'Nuneham Courtenay: An Oxfordshire 18th-century Deserted Village', *Oxoniensia*, vol.33 (1968), pp.108–24.
4 William Whitehead, 'The removal of the village at Nuneham', unpublished poem in *Harcourt Papers*, ed. E. Harcourt (1876), vol.VII, p.375.
5 PORTEUS, vol.4, p.3.
6 James Newton's diary. Bodl. ms Eng. misc. e. 251. Extracts are published in H. Minn, 'The Diary of an Oxfordshire Rector', *Oxoniensia*, vol.X, p.274.
7 WALPOLE: CORRESPONDENCE, vol.29, p.85.
8 William Mason, *The English garden* (1783), Book I, l.21.
9 HARCOURT, vol.III, p.206.
10 HARCOURT, vol.III, p.196.
11 Thomas Mozley, *Reminiscences, chiefly of Oriel College and the Oxford Movement* (1882), vol.I, p.27.
12 DELANY, vol.VI, p.101.
13 WESLEY, vol.VII, p.26.

14 BURNEY, vol.II, p.447.
15 HARCOURT, vol.III, p.189.
16 Alice Hargreaves, 'Alice's recollections of Carrollian Days', *Cornhill Magazine*, vol.73 (July 1932).

MOUNT EDGCUMBE

1 WALPOLE: CORRESPONDENCE, vol.35, p.148.
2 Red Book for Mulgrave, 1793.
3 LOUDON: G.M., vol.18, p.547.
4 FIENNES, p. 254.
5 LOVEDAY, p.234.
6 Quotation from the Portland Papers by permission of the Marquess of Bath, Longleat House, Wiltshire.
7 POCOCKE, vol.I, p.107.
8 Lady E. Mount Edgcumbe, 'Mount Edgcumbe', *Pall Mall Magazine*, May 1897, p.15.
9 BURNEY, vol.IV, pp.319–22.
10 SAXONY, p.211.
11 FORBES, p.153.
12 HIRSCHFELD, vol.IV, p.117.
13 SWETE, fol.141.
14 BECKFORD, p.123.
15 WARNER: CORNWALL, p.74.
16 FORBES, p.154.
17 PRICE, vol.I, p.279.
18 HARCOURT, vol.VIII, p.277.
19 DELANY, vol.V, p.459.
20 LYBBE POWYS, p.71.
21 William Cowper, *The Task*, Book 1.
22 *Pall Mall Magazine*, see 8 above.
23 [Anon]: *A walk round Mount Edgcumbe* (1812), p.146.
24 ibid. (1821), Appendix Verses written at Mount Edgcumbe, p.41.
25 op. cit., p.45.

NINETEENTH-CENTURY GARDENS

1 *Westminster Review*, January 1832.
2 LOUDON, vol.1 (1826), p.309.
3 LENNÉ.
4 LOUDON, vol.8 (1832), p.700.
5 SAXONY, p.117.
6 H. James, 'Our Artists in Europe', *Harper's Magazine* (1889), p.58.

STONELEIGH ABBEY

1 Red Book dated 1809. Photocopy in Warwickshire County Record Office.
2 *Country Life*, vol.160 (1976), pp.1974–5.
3 Constance Hill, *Jane Austen: her homes and her friends* (1902), pp.163–4.
4 ibid., p.166.
5 BERRY, vol.II, p.433.

6 J. Austen, *Mansfield Park*, chapter 9.

7 ibid., chapter 10.

8 ibid., chapter 6.

ST JAMES'S PARK

1 PEPYS, vol. VII, p. 207.

2 DE MURALT, p. 156.

3 EVELYN, vol. III, p. 398.

4 Reports from Select Committees (Office of Works), vol. IV (446) (1828), p. 63.

5 PÜCKLER-MUSKAU, vol. IV, pp. 85 and 123.

SEZINCOTE

1 John Betjeman, 'Summoned by Bells', 1960.

2 J. C. Loudon, *The landscape gardening and landscape architecture of the late Humphry Repton* (1840), p. 19.

3 ibid.

4 E. Malins, 'Indian influences on English houses and gardens', *Garden History*, vol. 8, no. 1, p. 58.

5 *Country Life*, vol. 160 (1976), p. 602.

SWISS GARDEN

1 *Jane Austen's Letters*, ed. R. W. Chapman (1932), vol. II, p. 495.

2 P. F. Robinson, *Designs for ornamental villas* (1827). Design no. 1, p. 1.

3 *Bedfordshire Times*, 9 June 1899.

4 YOUNG, CATHERINE.

5 RIDLEY, p. 33.

6 J. B. Papworth, *Hints on ornamental gardening*, 1823, p. 50.

7 *Gardener's Magazine* (1902), pp. 547–50.

8 *Journal of horticulture and home farmer*, vol. 67 (Nov. 1913), pp. 502–5.

SCOTNEY CASTLE

1 Rose Macaulay, *Pleasure of ruins* (1953), p. 38.

2 *Country Life*, 16 October 1969, vol. 146, p. 958.

3 Christopher Hussey, *The Picturesque: Studies in a point of view* (1927), p. 2.

4 *Country Life*, ibid., p. 959.

5 W. S. Gilpin, *Practical hints on landscape gardening* (1832), p. 109.

ALTON TOWERS

1 ADAM, p. 230.

2 *Gardener's Magazine*, vol. 7, p. 390.

3 ADAM, p. 228.

4 ADAM, p. 240.

5 *Gardener's Magazine*, vol. 7, p. 392.

6 ibid., p. 390.

7 J. C. Loudon, *Encyclopaedia of gardening* (1834), p. 335.

8 *Gardener's Magazine*, vol. 16, p. 580.

9 BROOKE, no page numbers.

10 ADAM, p. 227.

11 JONES, p. 235.

12 BROOKE, no page numbers.

CHATSWORTH

1 *Country Life*, VII (1900), pt. 1, p. 832.

2 BROWNE, fols 59–63.

3 'The Wonders of the Peake', ll. 1313–20. See *Poems of Charles Cotton*, ed. John Buxton (London, 1958).

4 BIBLIOTHECA, vol. III, p. 76.

5 CAMBRIDGE UNDERGRADUATE, fols 73–5.

6 DEFOE 1724–7, vol. III, p. 69.

7 STUKELEY, vol. I, 55–6.

8 DODD, fol. 40.

9 LYBBE POWYS, p. 29.

10 1760 visit, WALPOLE: CORRESPONDENCE, vol. IX, p. 296; 1768 visit, WALPOLE: JOURNALS, p. 65.

11 SIMOND, vol. II, pp. 84–5.

12 Violet Markham, *Paxton and the bachelor Duke* (London, 1935), p. 52.

13 [W. G. S. Cavendish, 6th Duke of Devonshire], *Handbook of Chatsworth and Hardwick* (London, 1845), p. 174.

14 ADAM, p. 125.

15 *The Gardener*, September 1867, p. 347.

16 ELIOT, p. 157.

CRYSTAL PALACE

1 *Illustrated Times*, 28 June 1856, p. 466.

2 John Ruskin, 'The opening of the Crystal Palace' (1854), in *The Works of John Ruskin*, ed. E. T. Cook and A. Wedderburn, 39 vols (London, 1903–12), vol. XII, p. 418.

3 Ruskin, *Praeterita*, in *Works*, op. cit., vol. XXXV, p. 47.

4 *Illustrated Times*, loc. cit.

5 *Cottage Gardener*, vol. XIII (1854), p. 39.

6 *Illustrated Times*, loc. cit.

7 Samuel Phillips, *Guide to the Crystal Palace* (London, 1857).

8 *The grounds of the Crystal Palace* [12 views with descriptive letterpress] (London, 1860).

9 JONES, pp. 331–2.

BIDDULPH GRANGE

1 *Gardeners' Chronicle*, 1856, p. 679.

2 JONES, p. 119.

3 Sale Catalogue appendix to article by Peter Hayden, 'Edward Cooke at Biddulph Grange', *Garden History*, vol. VI, no. I, p. 36.

4 *Gardeners' Chronicle*, 1856, p. 821.

5 COOKE. For diary extracts see *Garden History*, vol. VI, no. 1, pp. 18–24.

6 *The Garden*, vol. I, p. 247.

7 HADFIELD, p. 355.

SHRUBLAND PARK

1 The Red Book is now deposited at the Suffolk County Record Office, ref. T4572/1–3. All further quotations of Repton are from this source. (Courtesy of the Lord de Saumarez.)

2 *Gardeners' Chronicle*, 1888, p. 329.

3 BROOKE. No page numbers; all further quotations of Brooke are from this source.

4 *Gardeners' Chronicle*, 1867, p. 1099.

5 *Cottage Gardener*, vol. X (1853), pp. 495–7.

6 *Gardeners' Chronicle*, 1867, p. 1170.

7 *Country Life*, vol. X (1901), pt. ii, pp. 560–7.

8 William Robinson, *The English flower garden* (8th ed., London, 1902), p. 52, and plan on p. 302.

9 *Gardeners' Chronicle*, 1888, pt. ii, p. 329.

10 *Country Life*, op. cit., p. 567.

ATHELHAMPTON HALL

1 Lady Dorothy Nevill, *Under five reigns* (London, 1900), p. 13.

2 J. D. Sedding, *Garden-craft old and new* (London, 1891), p. 153.

3 *Proceedings of the Dorset Natural History and Antiquarian Field Club*, vol. XX (1899), p. 127.

4 *Country Life*, vol. VI (1899) pt. ii, p. 272.

5 *Proceedings of the Dorset . . . Field Club*, op. cit., p. 124.

6 Foreword to Sidney Heath and W. de C. Prideaux, *Some Dorset manor houses* (London, 1907).

7 *Gardeners' Magazine* [continuation of *Gardeners' Weekly Magazine*], 15, 22, 29 February 1896.

8 *Country Life*, vol. XXXIX (1916), pt. i, p. 289.

9 *Country Life*, vol. VI, op. cit., p. 274.

10 ibid., p. 276.

11 ROCKLEY, p. 222.

12 Gertrude Jekyll, *Garden ornament* (1918, repr. Woodbridge, 1982), p. xi.

INDEX